D0065152

GLOBALIZATION
AND CROSS-BORDER LABOR SOLIDARITY
IN THE AMERICAS

GLOBALIZATION
AND CROSS-BORDER LABOR SOLIDARITY
IN THE AMERICAS

■

THE ANTI-SWEATSHOP MOVEMENT AND THE STRUGGLE FOR SOCIAL JUSTICE

RALPH ARMBRUSTER-SANDOVAL

Routledge
New York • London

Published in 2005 by
Routledge
270 Madison Avenue
New York, NY 10016
www.routledge-ny.com

Published in Great Britain by
Routledge
2 Park Square
Milton Park, Abingdon
Oxon OX14 4RN U.K.
www.routledge.co.uk

Printed in the United States of America on acid-free paper.

10 9 8 7 6 5 4 3 2 1

Library of Congress Cataloging-in-Publication Data
Armbruster-Sandoval, Ralph, 1968-
    Globalization and cross-border labor solidarity in the Americas : the anti-sweatshop
movement and the struggle for social justice / Ralph Armbruster-Sandoval.
        p. cm.
    Includes bibliographical references (p.   ) and index.
    ISBN 0-415-94956-4 (hc : alk. paper) — ISBN 0-415-94957-2 (pb : alk. paper)
    1. Offshore assembly industry—Employees—Labor unions—Central America.
    2. International labor activities—Central America. 3. Clothing workers—Labor
unions—Central America. 4. Sweatshops—Central America. 5. Globalization—
Economic aspects—Central America. I. Title.

HD6539.O33A76 2004
331.25--dc22
                                                                    2004009989

Dedication

To all the garment workers
and social justice activists
around the world.
¡Otro mundo es posible!
Another world is possible!

Contents

Acknowledgments

I started working on this book over ten years ago. Edna Bonacich and her colleagues (Lucie Cheng, Norma Chinchilla, Nora Hamilton, and Paul Ong) had just finished a study that examined the garment industry in the Pacific Rim region and were talking about embarking upon a new project. Someone suggested exploring the possibility and potential for cross-border (transnational) labor organizing between unions in the region. A division of labor was quickly established. One person would focus on Central America, another one the Caribbean, and so on. I chose China (ironically, looking back), but funding for this study never materialized.

Despite that fact, I continued reading books and articles on globalization, free trade, and cross-border labor organizing. With the passage and implementation of the North American Free Trade Agreement (NAFTA) in 1994, my geographical focus shifted to the U.S.-Mexico border. The Kathie Lee Gifford exposé and the El Monte Thai slavery case broke shortly thereafter. These two events, along with Edna Bonacich and Richard Appelbaum's work on the Los Angeles garment industry, made me realize that sweatshops were a local, national, and global phenomenon. Feeling outraged over the long hours and low wages that the world's garment workers faced, I began researching transnational campaigns targeting sweatshop labor practices in Central America. Central America was the key site where the contemporary anti-sweatshop movement took off in the middle and late 1990s.

This narrative explains how this project was born. It started out organically; from lunch time conversation topic to master's thesis to dissertation to book. Over that lengthy, but ultimately rewarding and enriching time period, I have incurred countless debts. The biggest ones go to the "sweatshop warriors," the Central American garment workers—including women like Monica Felipe Alvarez, Sara Aguillón, Gladys Manzanares, and many more just like them—

who organized and led these campaigns. Their courage, determination, humility, and passion inspired their co-workers as they worked together to create strong labor unions inside their respective work-places. Without on-the-ground actions in Guatemala, El Salvador, Honduras, and Nicaragua, these campaigns would not have been as successful as they were. I thank these women and all the garment workers who talked with me and spoke about their everyday lives and organizing experiences. Words cannot properly convey how deeply I appreciate what you shared with me.

I am also extremely grateful for all the organizers and social justice activists who worked on these campaigns and who took time from their busy schedules to talk with me. This list includes: Efraín Aguilar, Juan Francisco Alfaro, Otilio Candido, Teresa Casertano, Steven Coats, Rhett Doumitt, Bruce Fieldman, Homero Fuentes, Daniel García, Gilberto García, Roger Gutiérrez, Jeff Hermanson, Sharon Hostetler, Alan Howard, Charles Kernaghan, Marlene López, Hugo Maldonado, Marie Mejía, Norma Molina, Sergio Muñoz, Pedro Ortega, Bryon Padilla, Maritza Paredes, Bob Perillo, Carolina Quinteros, Rodolfo Robles, Marina Rodriguez, Flor de María Salguero, Isarel Salinas, Dennis Smith, Melinda St. Louis, and Alys Willman. I apologize profusely for leaving anyone out. Without these folks and many more like them who passed out leaflets outside department stores and shopping malls across the United States, wrote letters and e-mails, and attended rallies and demonstrations, these campaigns would not have achieved what they did. It took bold action from people all over the world to challenge transnational corporations for their sweatshop labor practices.

In addition to the garment workers and social justice activists who made these campaigns happen, I would also like to thank various people who read portions of this manuscript, made criticisms and suggestions, or provided encouragement: Paul Almeida, Richard Appelbaum, Carolina Bank, John Baranski, Edwina Barvosa-Carter, Edna Bonacich, Eileen Boris, Mark Brenner, Kate Bronfenbrenner, Dan Clawson, Ted Coe, Ed Collom, Jill Esbenshade, Oscar Fierros, Richard Flacks, John Foran, Mario García, Oscar Gil, Richard A. Greenwald, Henry Frundt, Glyn Hughes, Jonathan Inda, Rebecca Johns, Ted Levine, Nelson Lichtenstein, Edwin López, Stephanie Luce, William Robinson, Chela Sandoval, Jay Stemmle, Richard Sullivan, Dale Wimberley, and Tara Yosso. I also thank all my colleagues and the entire staff in the University of California Santa Barbara Chicana and Chicano Studies Department. I would be remiss if I did not mention Edna Bonacich's name one more time. She embodies what engaged scholarship, mentorship, and teaching are all about.

Much praise must be given to my students and friends here at UC Santa Barbara over these past few years too—Martha Alcantar, Maribel Amaya, Melissa Ardon, Manuel Becerra, Renee Bergan, Alfredo Carlos, Nicholas Centino, Sumi

Crimmel, Carmen Cuevas, Ozzie Espinoza, Melissa Kravetz, Chrystine Lawson, Emil Marmol, Soralla Marquez, Armida Montaño, Elizabeth Montaño, Rene Muñoz, Diahnna Núñez, Luis Pinedo, Carrie Pleschia, Angela Portillo, Emily Potts, Fernando Ramirez, Ana Rizo, Gloria Sanchez, Irene Sanchez, Marie Schiro, Rachelle Seglia, Saul Serrano, Rukshana Singh, and many more.

I would like to also extend deep appreciation to Karen Wolny, Rob Tempio, Angela Chnapko, and the entire Taylor & Francis team for publishing the manuscript. You have been extremely patient and kind—thank you for making this process humane and giving me the space to speak from my heart and soul.

Lastly, I thank my family—especially my mother, Rita Lorraine Sandoval, sister, Stephanie Armbruster, and my father, Ralph Armbruster, for all your love, support, and encouragement. I also thank my stepparents (Roberta Armbruster and Jim Willoughby) and entire extended family for everything that you have given me. My long-time friend, Mike Wilkins, and his wife Tremayne, and son, Riley, deserve a major "shout-out" here too. And finally, to the one who has waited far too long for this book to come out. Meg, I don't know what to say. You are simply amazing—thanks for all your love, *cariño*, passion, patience, faith, and understanding. With you and our new family, another world is truly possible. *Sí se puede*!

www.antisweatshopmovement.org

1

Globalization and Cross-Border Labor Solidarity in the Americas

The Struggle for Social Justice

The Dark, Satanic Mills of the Twenty-First Century

Every single day tens of thousands of people pour into clothing factories all over Central America. These workers—teenagers, sisters, brothers, mothers, fathers, grandparents, students, musicians, artists, and activists—often live in cramped, makeshift homes, with corrugated tin roofs, dirt floors, and little running water or electricity. They usually wake up before sunrise, get dressed quickly, and climb aboard old, overcrowded smoke-spewing yellow school buses. They know they must arrive on time; so many skip eating breakfast. Punctuality is crucial. Being one minute late can cost a worker one day's pay.

Most factories resemble large warehouses. They are typically well fortified. Steel gates, security cameras, and barbed wire are commonplace. Armed guards search all workers and inspect their plastic identification cards before they enter the factory. Once inside, the noise can be deafening and the heat intolerable. Dust and lint fill the air. Safety equipment (e.g., masks, earplugs, etc.) is rarely provided. Bathroom breaks are usually timed and regulated; overtime, mandatory; and the work pace, relentless. Some workers sew, for instance, one hundred zippers on trendy, brand name jeans every single hour. Work shifts often range between ten and twelve hours, but they can last as long as fourteen or sixteen hours. Wages hover, depending on the country, around fifty cents an hour. Health care, sick pay, vacation time, and other related benefits are virtually nonexistent.

The wages and working conditions in these factories—known as *maquiladoras* in Central America—resemble William Blake's nineteenth-century "dark, satanic mills."[1] The garment and textile factories or "mills" of that era were usually called "sweatshops." Contractors or "middlemen," who

1

received production orders from manufacturers, operated those shops. Their profits came from "sweating" their workers—mostly young women and children—through low wages, long hours, and poor working conditions.[2] The "sweating system" generated intense competition. Contractors and manufacturers constantly tried to keep production costs as low as possible, making everyday life intolerable inside and outside the factory.[3]

Garment workers did not meekly accept these conditions; they periodically resisted and demanded social change. In the United States, thousands of immigrant women shirtwaist workers organized a major strike, called the "Uprising of the 20,000," in 1909.[4] More strikes occurred over the next two years. In 1911, 146 garment workers died in the infamous Triangle Shirtwaist fire in New York City. Locked doors and faulty fire exits, combined with gross managerial and government negligence, left hundreds of workers trapped inside the ten-story building when the blaze first broke out. Firefighters reached the fast-moving inferno within minutes, but their ladders and water hoses were not long enough to reach the skyscraper's top floors. Faced very few options, many workers leaped to their deaths or perished in the flames.[5]

This tragic incident generated tremendous outrage. Garment workers and consumers—mostly working- and middle-class women—organized themselves. They strengthened nascent labor unions and consumer leagues and labor unions and called for better wages and working conditions through ethical buying practices, government regulation, and collective bargaining.[6] The historical "anti-sweatshop movement" of the early twentieth century struggled for years before garment workers and activists finally succeeded. The New Deal provided workers with basic labor standards (e.g., child labor, minimum wage, and overtime laws) and protected the right to organize. Through unionization and federal legislation, sweatshops essentially disappeared until the 1970s.[7]

The roll-back of the welfare state and the declining strength of the labor movement (among other factors) facilitated their resurgence.[8] The return of the sweatshop went relatively unnoticed within popular and academic circles until two high-profile cases made the issue "front-page" news.[9] In August 1995, federal and state labor investigators raided a barbed wire enclosed apartment building in El Monte, California, where they found seventy-two Thai workers. Armed security guards held them captive for as long as seven years, making them essentially "prisoners" or "slaves." They worked "sixteen-hour days, seven days-a-week," earning just about seventy cents an hour.[10] Supervisors and guards verbally and sometimes physically abused them. Workers slept in overcrowded, unsanitary rooms. They could not make phone calls without proper authorization and were forced to buy high-priced goods from the company. The workers inside this shop produced clothes for well-known retailers like Mervyn's, Miller's Outpost, Montgomery Ward, Nordstrom, Robinsons May, Sears, and Target.[11]

The Thai slavery case, like the Triangle Shirtwaist Fire eighty years before, created intense controversy. The public was shocked. Most people assumed that sweatshops had been permanently abolished. Less than a year later, celebrity talk-show host Kathie Lee Gifford broke down and cried on national television after labor rights activists discovered that her Wal-Mart clothing line was made with child and sweatshop labor in Central America and the United States. Gifford's tearful and angry outburst (she initially denied all charges of wrong-doing) sullied her clean-cut, All-American image, making her the symbolic "poster-child" of the anti-sweatshop movement.[12]

The extensive publicity surrounding these two events made the word "sweat-shop" a household item. Through comic strips (*Doonesbury*), films (*The Big One*), televisions programs (*60 Minutes, Hard Copy, Beverley Hills 90210, ER*), newspapers (the *New York Times*, the *Washington Post*, the *Los Angeles Times*) and other mass media and popular culture outlets, the public learned that not only had sweatshops "returned," but now they were a global reality.[13] Most cloth-ing and apparel products were produced in the United States before the 1970s. That is no longer the case today. The garment industry is the most globalized industry in the entire world. Shoes, shirts, socks, pants, and underwear are made in well over one hundred different countries.[14] Almost every single major label—Nike, Reebok, Liz Claiborne, Levi's, Bugle Boy, Tommy Hilfiger, Guess, Phillips Van-Heusen, Fruit of the Loom, Maidenform—is produced off-shore. Retailers like Wal-Mart, Kmart, J.C. Penney, Target, Kohl's, Sears, and the Gap also make their own "private labels" abroad.

Many politicians, corporate executives, and academics have praised this "global shift" for generating economic growth and creating sorely needed jobs within the developing world.[15] Social justice activists often acknowledge (albeit tepidly) these claims, but they also emphasize the low wages and poor working conditions within these "dark, satanic mills" of the twenty-first century have generated discontent, especially in Central America.[16] Garment workers there have slowed down production, organized strikes, and established community-based organizations and labor unions.[17] These strategies have prompted mass firings, death threats, beatings, arrests, and other forms of intimidation. Many factories have also simply closed down and moved someplace else when faced with union organizing drives.[18]

These repressive activities—combined with the El Monte and Kathie Lee Gifford cases—sparked the growth of the "contemporary" anti-sweatshop movement in the middle and late 1990s.[19] Like its historical predecessor, this social movement involves garment workers, labor unions, and consumer, faith-based, student, and women's groups, but it also includes a wide variety of "non-government organizations" (NGOs).[20] The Campaign for Labor Rights (CLR), the National Labor Committee (NLC), the United Students Against Sweatshops (USAS), the United States/Labor Education in the Americas Project (U.S./LEAP), the Union of Needletrades, Industrial, and Textile Employees (UNITE), and Witness for Peace (WFP) are some of the key NGOs leading the U.S. side of this movement.[21] All have worked extensively with Central American garment workers to confront sweatshop labor practices, passing out leaflets, writing letters, organizing rallies and teach-ins, holding press conferences, and providing resources (both financial and technical) for labor and community-based organizing campaigns.[22] These strategies are designed to persuade garment companies to take responsibility for improving wages and working conditions in overseas, as well as domestic, sweatshops.

Researchers have increasingly studied these "cross-border" or "transnational" labor solidarity campaigns over the past decade.[23] Some cases have produced positive results, but these gains have not been usually sustained over time. Garment factories that improved wages and working conditions later shut down or fired union leaders and workers, for example. What factors explain these disparate outcomes? Why do most cross-border labor solidarity campaigns typically "succeed" in the short-run, but "fail" in the long-run? How can garment workers and their transnational allies fight back more effectively and obtain better wages and working conditions today? Is "social change" or "agency" possible in a globalized, corporate-driven world? Can the world economy be organized in a manner where "people come before profit?"[24]

This book examines these key questions through four case studies that primarily involved Central American and U.S.-based labor unions and NGOs. These campaigns were selected because Central America (more specifically, Guatemala, El Salvador, Nicaragua, and Honduras) became a central site for garment production, labor organizing, and anti-sweatshop activity in the middle and late 1990s. In fact, one could argue that the contemporary anti-sweatshop movement "took off" in Central America.

After civil wars and human rights violations subsided in the late 1980s and early 1990s, regional apparel exports into the U.S. market soared.[25] As employment expanded, labor unrest grew. Garment workers and U.S. labor unions and NGOs eventually joined forces, creating "transnational activist networks" that challenged some of the most powerful companies in the world.[26] While similar campaigns took place elsewhere, these cases gained greater publicity and produced outcomes that paradoxically contradicted and confirmed popular assumptions about globalization and transnational social movements.[27] These campaigns, for instance, showed garment workers, acting independently, as well as collaboratively with their cross-border allies, could successfully target highly-mobile garment firms and enhance their wages and working conditions, but these gains were often ephemeral.[28] These striking, but sobering, results have far-reaching theoretical and political implications (which will be discussed in chapter 6) for academics, activists, and the broader public.

Despite the burgeoning literature on globalization, sweatshops, and cross-border labor solidarity, no one single volume has systematically and comparatively examined these four cases—Phillips Van-Heusen (Guatemala); Mandarin International (El Salvador); Kimi (Honduras); and Chentex (Nicaragua).[29] This book seeks to fill that missing gap. Based on ten years of extensive research, conducting scores of interviews with garment workers, social justice activists, and scholars, collecting primary and secondary sources (e.g., reports, flyers, contracts, etc.), and observing and participating in anti-sweatshop actions, I complied in-depth campaign chronologies, documenting each case's twists and turns. I also examined their overall trajectories and various outcomes.

During this lengthy, but ultimately rewarding process, I discovered that cross-border labor solidarity is no easy task. There are numerous barriers and obstacles that must be negotiated and addressed. The "borders" of race, class, gender, geography, and language, as well as the role of the state, can affect a campaign's direction and impact. No one single factor has more importance than the other. That being said, one of the most formidable challenges that garment workers, labor unions, and NGOs face today is the structure of the garment industry itself.

This chapter examines the relationship between the industry's dynamics, globalization, and cross-border labor solidarity. An analysis of cross-border labor solidarity strategies that have been used within the anti-sweatshop movement follows this section. The chapter concludes with a historical and theoretical discussion of cross-border labor solidarity, while making reference to a key campaign victory in Mexico.

The Pyramid of Power

The garment industry is organized like a pyramid (see Figure 1.1).[30] Retailers occupy the top slot. They sell clothing and apparel products to consumers. In the 1980s and 1990s, the retail industry became increasingly concentrated through mergers, buy-outs, and takeovers.[31] Discount and department store chains like Wal-Mart, Kmart, Sears, and Dayton-Hudson (owner of Target and Mervyn's) became the largest and most powerful firms within the industry. In 2002, Wal-Mart's total sales were $245 billion.[32] The combined total sales of the next three companies, Sears, Kmart, and Dayton-Hudson, topped $125 billion for that same year.[33] These figures indicate that Wal-Mart dominates the "inner circle" of the retail market.

Indeed, Wal-Mart has become so large that its presence can be felt all over the world. This one-time "small-town, five-and-dime store" has grown into a corporate behemoth over the past twenty years, sparking intense controversy based on its size, scale, and relentless drive for lower-priced goods. The Arkansas-based company, which built its reputation on economic nationalism and the "Made in the U.S.A." label, currently has ties with ten thousand suppliers all

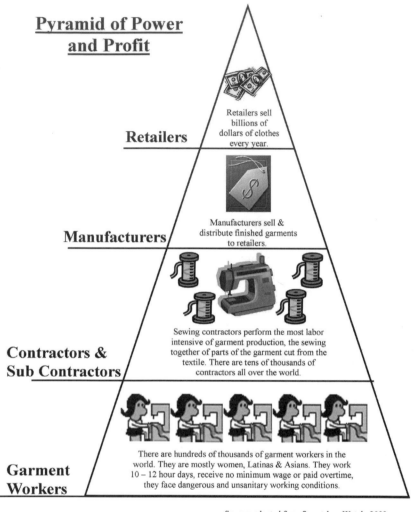

Source: adapted from Sweatshop Watch, 2003

Fig. 1.1 The Structure of the Garment Industry.

over the world. With this many contractors, Wal-Mart can literally pit "vendor against vendor, country against country." Persistent demand for lower prices and/or higher quality has left factory owners with few alternatives; many report that they cannot cut costs any lower—they have "reached their limits."[34]

Garment workers like Isabel Reyes understand this reality all too well. This thirty-seven year old Honduran woman sews sleeves onto 1,200 shirts every single day. She works ten-hour days and earns $35 a week. The polo shirts that she makes sell for $8.63 at Wal-Mart. Even though prices and wages are extremely low, company representatives state they would like to reduce production costs by 20 percent. To accomplish that goal, the retailer will more than likely expand its ever-increasing links with Chinese-based suppliers, leaving Isabel Reyes and thousands more unemployed.[35]

Manufacturers come next on the pyramid. These companies, despite their name, do not actually "manufacture" clothing. They design clothes that carry their labels (sometimes called "brands" or "logos"), buy the fabric and textiles, contract out production, and sell the finished products to retailers. Manufacturers had greater leverage (or power) before the retail market shifted. They set the price of the product because there were more buyers. Manufacturers lost this advantage after the retail industry became consolidated. Giant retailers now determine the prices that most manufacturers must accept.[36]

Over the past decade retailers and manufacturers have struggled for control of the garment industry. Some retailers have become "manufacturers," creating and producing their own "private labels." The Gap exemplifies this trend. This San Francisco-based company manufactures its own clothing line in over 1,200 factories around the world and sells them in 2,200 retail outlets.[37] Wal-Mart, Kmart, Sears, and Target also produce their own private labels. Manufacturers have not taken this trend lying down. Some of the biggest and most well-known companies—Nike, Guess, Liz Claiborne, Bebe, and Tommy Hilfiger—have gone into retailing, opening up stores all across the country. This is a financially risky strategy as some firms like Rampage (which was temporarily driven into bankruptcy) have found out.[38]

While the line between "retailers" and "manufacturers" has become more blurry, both share one common trait—they do not produce their own goods, contractors do. Contractors are independent companies that employ workers that sew clothing and apparel products within factories. There are literally tens of thousands of "contracting shops" located all over the world. Some factories employ more than a thousand workers while others have less than thirty. The entire industry includes hundreds of thousands of workers, most of whom are women who earn very low wages and work under extremely difficult conditions.

Who bears responsibility for these sweatshop labor practices? Manufacturers and retailers typically claim that their hands are "clean." Contractors, they contend, are the "guilty party." After all, they are the ones that directly employ workers. This statement is technically accurate, but it overlooks one key point—manufacturers and retailers tell the contractors the price at which clothing and apparel goods must be produced.[39] Given this situation, costs must be kept low. From the contractor's point of view, better wages and good working conditions are "luxuries" that they simply cannot afford. Contractors with higher costs risk losing production orders from manufacturers and retailers. These dynamics (which emerged over one hundred years ago) explain the pervasive nature of sweatshop labor within the garment industry.

Globalization, The Garment Industry, and The Race To The Bottom

The entire production system is a vise. Each layer of the pyramid squeezes the next, leaving workers very little. Retailers and manufacturers have tremendous power. They have established production facilities and factories all over the world. "Globalization" is a reality in the garment industry.[40] Several factors have facilitated this rise in global, off-shore production: the world-wide economic crisis of the 1970s; the search for cheaper labor; the growing weakness of labor unions; the passage of free trade policies and special tariff provisions (e.g., the North American Free Trade Agreement [NAFTA]); and the establishment of "export processing zones" (or "free trade zones"), complete with tax subsidies, incentives, and a non-unionized, low-wage labor force, in Asia and Latin America, have all been instrumental.[41] The widespread adoption of corporate-oriented, free-market principles (sometimes called "neo-liberalism"), combined with pressure from the International Monetary Fund (IMF), World Bank, and World Trade Organization (WTO), has also played a role.[42]

Transnational corporations within the garment industry can move almost at will. Because garment production is labor-intensive and requires low start-up costs, factories can be moved rather quickly.[43] Since there are so many developing countries competing for production orders, garment companies can scan the global economy, looking for the best "investment climate" possible. If wages and working conditions rise in one country, then they can simply move some-place else.

Jeremy Brecher and Tim Costello claim that globalization has helped unleash a seemingly never-ending "race to the bottom."[44] Figure 1.2 illustrates this process. In this hypothetical example, the Gap contracts out some of its production to an independent company in El Salvador (arrow one). Within this factory, wages and working conditions are sub-standard, sparking shop-floor discontent. Workers slow down production and organize spontaneous strikes and demonstrations. They eventually establish a union that is legally recognized. Demands for contract negotiations emerge.

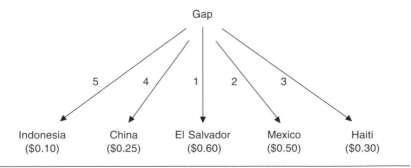

Fig. 1.2 The Race To The Bottom.

The Gap has two options based on this scenario—pressure the contractor to begin collective bargaining with the union or "cut and run," moving from El Salvador to Mexico or Haiti (arrows 2 and 3) where wages are lower and workers are tightly controlled.[45] China and Indonesia (arrows 4 and 5) also represent possible production sites, given their lower wage levels and more extensive restrictions on labor unions.[46] This situation suggests how capital mobility has exacerbated competition between developing countries and pitted workers against each other. These dynamics have generated downward pressure on wages and working conditions within the global apparel industry.[47]

Globalization and Cross-Border Labor Solidarity: Theoretical Perspectives

The "big picture" based on Figure 1.2 looks bleak for garment workers. Corporations can simply move wherever and whenever they wish. They have spatially organized the capitalist world-system in a manner that generates more and more profits for them. What can workers, NGOs, and social justice activists do given the reality of globalization and capital mobility in the garment industry?

Andrew Herod, following J. K. Gibson-Graham's innovative and trenchant analysis, contends that most geographers and social scientists, from various ideological perspectives (conservative, liberal, and radical), suggest that globalization is an inexorable process that workers cannot effectively challenge.[48] Transnational corporations (TNCs), the IMF, World Bank, and WTO are often portrayed as near-invincible institutions that have single-handedly re-organized the global economy. Because they have remarkable power and resources, workers and social justice activists have very little, if any, agency. Globalization and the geographical dispersion of production, have transformed them into hapless, powerless victims.[49]

This gloomy perspective is quite popular today. Corporations like Nike, the Gap, Guess, and Phillips Van-Heusen supposedly have the upper hand because they can "cut and run" whenever they are confronted with a labor organizing campaign in a developing country, leaving workers and communities impoverished and economically disenfranchised. Because this grim outcome has occurred many times, it cannot be easily dismissed as one possible result. However, framing it as a near-automatic certainty overlooks that there are, to borrow two book titles from David Harvey, "limits to capital" and that "spaces of hope" do exist.[50] Resistance is possible. Despite globalization and the power of capital, Herod argues, workers remain active agents that can reshape the spatial landscape of capitalism in ways that they believe will suit their interests.[51]

This is a simple, but profound argument. Capital is not omnipotent. Workers and labor unions have challenged corporations within and beyond the boundaries of the nation-state for over one hundred fifty years. The strategies and tactics adopted during these campaigns can be classified into two broad categories—"exclusionary" or "inclusionary."[52] The former refer to attempts to restrict workers (based on race, gender, nationality, skill level, etc.) from joining unions, while the latter favors including all workers.

Edna Bonacich's classic work on split-labor markets suggests that higher-paid U.S.-based workers typically favor exclusionary or "protectionist" approaches because they provide them with better wages and working conditions.[53] These benefits supposedly make cross-border labor solidarity, in the short-run, nearly impossible.[54] Inclusive approaches make more strategic sense in the long-run, however, because corporations will eventually seek out and probably obtain sources of cheaper labor.[55]

That is exactly what happened in the garment industry in the 1970s. As Dana Frank illustrates, when U.S.-based corporations began moving off-shore the International Ladies Garment Workers Union (ILGWU) embraced protectionist trade policies that were based on limiting apparel imports from developing countries. The ILGWU also encouraged U.S. consumers to "look for union label" and to buy "American-made" products.[56] These strategies did not work, however. Companies continued moving overseas. Through capital mobility, they divided higher-paid U.S. garment workers from lower-paid garment workers in the developing world, facilitating the "race to the bottom."

Garment companies did the same thing back in the 1920s and 1930s, moving factories from high-wage states in the North to low-wage states in the South. How did garment workers and unions respond back then? They organized across state lines, targeting low-wage labor.[57] This inclusive strategy produced limited results, but wages were eventually taken out of competition, giving garment workers greater power over corporations.

The task they face today is similar. Corporations have the upper hand because they can pit them against each other for their own advantage. The only way garment workers, as their counterparts learned long ago, can address and potentially overcome this endless cycle is if they join forces and work together across borders. This was Marx and Engels' logic when they made their famous call, "workers of the world, unite!"[58] Through "cross-border" or transnational labor solidarity, workers can minimize the race to the bottom, obtain leverage, and improve their wages and working conditions.

Cross-Border Labor Solidarity Strategies

Cross-border labor solidarity campaigns often involve multiple actors (e.g., workers, social justice activists, labor unions, NGOs) collaborating across geographical boundaries. They often challenge sweatshop practices and press for better wages and working conditions. Campaigns typically mobilize around specific "targets" (e.g., contractors, manufacturers, free trade zone owners, "company unions," nation-states, etc.) using a wide variety of strategies. They include:

codes of conduct, independent monitoring, comprehensive campaigns, worker rights petitions, community-based organizing, and cross-border union organizing.[59] Most campaigns involve some combination of these strategies.

Codes of Conduct

The widespread publicity surrounding the re-emergence and expansion of sweatshops led many manufacturers and retailers to adopt codes of conduct in the mid-1990s.[60] A code of conduct includes guidelines and procedures that state under what conditions a company's clothes will be produced. Most corporate codes of conduct, borrowing similar language from the United Nations and International Labor Organization (ILO), forbid child labor and require the provision of "decent" wages and working conditions. Some codes also protect the right to organize and collectively bargain.[61]

Companies that have established codes of conduct typically request that their overseas, as well as domestic, contractors sign and follow its policies. They usually hire private accounting firms like PricewaterhouseCoopers, Ernst and Young, or Cal Safety Compliance Corporation to conduct periodic inspections to determine whether or not the code has been properly implemented. These examinations often last one or two days. Supervisors are often warned beforehand. Investigators speak with workers inside the factory (making candid conversations nearly impossible). Based on this limited methodology, most companies, not surprisingly, receive a "clean bill of health" from their private monitors, telling them that no code violations exist.[62]

Anti-sweatshop activists claim this process is flawed. As Global Exchange Executive Director Medea Benjamin once said, private monitoring "leaves the fox guarding the hen house."[63] A fundamental conflict of interest exists when a manufacturer or retailer hires a private monitoring firm. The latter is much more likely to produce a report that favors the former, undermining the legitimacy of its findings. Without thorough, independent inspections, anti-sweatshop activists say, how do we really know what's going on inside garment factories? Until those factory doors are opened up for "independent" monitors, codes of conduct will appear as public relations tools for corporations to deflect public criticism and claim the mantle of "socially responsibility."[64]

The controversy surrounding codes of conduct and sweatshops became even more pronounced when the Clinton Administration established a presidential task force, known as the Apparel Industry Partnership (AIP), in September 1996.[65] The AIP included major garment manufacturers and retailers (the Gap, Liz Claiborne, Phillips Van-Heusen), the U.S. Department of Labor, UNITE, and human rights, religious, and consumer organizations.[66] The objectives of the task force were two-fold: to develop a code of conduct that would define what constitutes a "sweatshop" and to create a monitoring system based on those standards.[67] Companies that implemented and enforced the code's provisions could potentially advertise their products as "sweatshop-free," with a "no-sweat" label attached to them.[68]

After months of intense debate and deliberation, the AIP released its code of conduct in April 1997. It stipulated that garment workers in overseas factories should not work more than sixty hours a week and that they must be at least fifteen years old. Companies would also be required to pay the local minimum wage or "prevailing" industry wage (whichever is higher), recognize and respect the right to freedom of association and collective bargaining, and hire "private" or "external" monitors.[69] One labor rights newsletter critically interrogated these provisions, stating, "under the code's provisions, a company could employ a fifteen-year old worker for sixty hours per week, at the local prevailing minimum wage, which, in nearly all countries leaves workers far below the poverty level, and still not be considered a 'sweatshop.'"[70] This journal also noted under the AIP code company-financed monitors would be defined as "external" despite a clear financial conflict of interest.

UNITE and most other non-governmental organizations within the AIP opposed the code for those reasons, believing it would perpetuate, rather than eliminate, sweatshop labor. These groups thought that the AIP code should include a "living wage" provision and establish a "transparent" independent monitoring system that did not rely on company-financed monitors.[71] Based on these issues and concerns, UNITE and almost all other NGOs withdrew from the AIP.[72]

The AIP's remaining members—manufacturers and retailers, the U.S. government, and one labor rights-oriented NGO—created a non-profit organization called the Fair Labor Association (FLA) in November 1998. The FLA supports private ("external") monitoring and does not require a living wage or public disclosure of factories and labor rights violations.[73] In 1999, United Students Against Sweatshops (USAS) activists, along with other anti-sweatshop activists from all over the country, established the Workers Rights Consortium (WRC) as an alternative to the FLA. The WRC supports independent monitoring, a living wage, women's rights, and full public disclosure of factory locations and labor rights abuses.[74]

Independent Monitoring

Independent monitoring was developed to address the weaknesses associated with private monitoring. It proposes that NGOs within developing countries conduct regular inspections of garment factories to determine whether or not they are following corporate codes of conduct. These human rights, labor, and religious organizations generally have more experience working with labor rights issues than private monitors do. They also are more familiar with the country's social, cultural, economic, and political context, making them more sensitive about how certain nuances can affect the inspection process. These groups understand, for instance, that conversations with workers regarding labor rights violations or unionization must take place outside the earshot of supervisors. Workers will not usually speak freely until they feel that their jobs and lives are secure. These reasons, combined with the fact that corporations do not finance such NGOs, make independent monitoring a more open, transparent, and potentially effective strategy for combating sweatshops than private monitoring.

Independent monitoring has been, nevertheless, the source of considerable debate within the anti-sweatshop movement. U.S.-based NGOs like Global Exchange and the National Labor Committee have tended to support it more strongly than UNITE. Medea Benjamin explains this strategic difference:

> The U.S. unions [UNITE], while supporting the students [USAS] were skeptical of the whole notion of codes and monitoring, which they saw as PR [public relations] tools for companies or, even worse, efforts to replace the role of unions themselves. Instead of codes and monitors, the unions said, we should put our energies into helping workers form independent unions. The problem, however, is in some countries, like China, such activity will land you in jail or a mental institution and in other countries the government and businesses collude to keep unions weak or "company-friendly." When unions do get a real foothold, factory owners can just pick up stakes overnight and move to more business-friendly pastures. So while most activists and workers agree that strong, independent unions are the best way to enforce workers' rights, they also recognize that we are decades away from achieving that goal.[75]

These are excellent points. The labor movements of many developing countries are extremely weak because of years of repression and co-optation. Many workers fear that if they join a union they will be fired, arrested, or even killed. Others distrust unions for working too closely with management or the government. Given this situation, independent monitoring makes sense. It is a less risky and, therefore, more "practical" strategy for eliminating sweatshops.

Independent monitoring is not flawless, however. NGOs within developing countries are small and financially unstable. They can only monitor so many factories given their meager resources. Independent monitoring agreements are also not binding. When public outcry against labor rights violations declines, corporations can back out, leaving workers "high and dry." Thus, based on these two limitations, unions typically contend that collective bargaining is a more effective and long-lasting strategy than independent monitoring.

The debate between independent monitoring and collective bargaining is a healthy one. Those who have cast these strategies in rigid "either-or" terms, however, have created divisions within the anti-sweatshop movement. These two strategies are not mutually exclusive; they can complement one another. Gilberto García, Director of the Salvadoran-based Center for Labor Studies (CENTRA), expressed this point, "Independent monitoring can open up space for workers to form unions. There is no reason why these two strategies cannot be used together."[76] Many anti-sweatshop activists hold similar views, but often times the dialogue between them becomes polarized and undermines the effectiveness of cross-border labor solidarity campaigns.

Comprehensive Campaigns

Workers, labor unions, and NGOs have also used comprehensive campaigns as another cross-border labor solidarity strategy to improve wages and working conditions. These campaigns usually target one transnational corporation for specific reasons such as firing unionized workers, paying substandard wages, or hiring "permanent replacement" workers. Comprehensive campaigns often rely on militant rank-and-file activism, community-labor coalitions, global labor solidarity, and extensive "strategic" research.[77] This latter process focuses on mapping the intricate (and sometimes unsavory) ties between the targeted company and other corporations and government agencies. Through this creative methodology, unions can obtain damaging information that activists may disseminate through leaflets, rallies, demonstrations, teach-ins, videos, and Web sites. These tactics can undermine the target's public image or weaken its links with key customers, putting pressure on it to accept the campaign's demands.[78]

The Ravenswood Aluminum Corporation (RAC) campaign illustrates the effectiveness of this strategy. After carefully scrutinizing company records, the United Steel Workers of America (USWA) discovered that Marc Rich, a corporate "raider" indicted (later pardoned by President Clinton) on tax evasion and racketeering charges in the United States, indirectly controlled RAC. This finding was significant because RAC locked out 1,700 USWA Local 5668 members over a contract dispute in 1990. USWA highlighted the connections between Rich and RAC through "most-wanted" posters, flyers, press conferences, and other media outlets, undercutting the company's credibility. These tactics, combined with pressure from local union members and support from the AFL-CIO's Industrial Union Department, three international trade secretariats, and nearly thirty unions from all over the world, led RAC to rehire 1,500 Local 5668 members and negotiate a new contract.[79]

The Ravenswood case illustrates comprehensive campaigns can be quite useful. This model is not a panacea for labor's ills, however. Robert Hickey's research on the Paper, Allied-Industrial, and Chemical and Energy Workers' International Union's (PACE) five-year campaign against the Texas-based Crown Central Petroleum company showed, for instance, that even though this lengthy struggle produced a fairly positive settlement, "the strategy is reserved for where the existence of the union is at stake."[80] He argues that comprehensive campaigns are ultimately "defensive" and that unless they are combined with broader shifts, such as creating sustained cross-border labor linkages and developing a new ideological and cultural focus, labor union growth in the United States (and presumably elsewhere) will remain stagnant.[81]

Worker Rights Petitions

Unions and NGOs have also strategically linked trade with worker rights standards. Several U.S. trade policies, including the Generalized System of Preferences (GSP), the Overseas Private Investment Corporation (OPIC), and the Caribbean Basin Initiative (CBI), state that worker rights violations are an "unfair trade practice."[82] These laws also contain language stipulating that trading benefits depend on the protection of internationally recognized worker rights provisions like the freedom of association, the right to organize and collectively bargain, freedom from forced labor, restrictions on child labor, and "appropriate" wages and working conditions.[83]

Unions and NGOs like UNITE, the United States/Guatemala Labor Education Project (U.S./GLEP—now called the United States/Labor in the Americas Project, U.S./LEAP), and the International Labor Rights Fund (ILRF) have successfully used these provisions in Guatemala and the Dominican Republic.[84] In 1992, the ILGWU and ACTWU (which merged and created UNITE in 1995), U.S./GLEP, and several other NGOs filed a "worker rights petition" with the U.S. Trade Representative Office requesting that Guatemala's GSP benefits be placed "under review" for its failure to protect the right to organize. This petition provided these groups, along with Guatemalan *maquila* workers, with leverage, forcing the Guatemalan government, which feared losing $500 million in trading benefits, to recognize two *maquila* unions.[85] In 1993, the AFL-CIO filed a GSP petition, to cite another example, against the Dominican Republic for its inability to recognize unions in the country's export processing zones. Five unions achieved that status after this action was taken.[86]

These victories indicate that worker rights petitions have been useful. They have provided some *maquila* workers with the space to organize and form legally recognized unions. These outcomes are positive, but this strategy does have some problems. First, some unions and NGOs in developing countries have claimed that worker rights petitions are a thinly disguised form of "protectionism" designed to keep jobs in the United States.[87] U.S.-based unions and NGOs have worked carefully with their counterparts in developing countries to make sure that the petition process does not negatively affect *maquila* workers. Second, the petition review process has been heavily politicized in the past.[88] In the 1980s, U.S. allies like the Salvadoran right-wing government, for instance, received far less scrutiny than the Nicaraguan Sandinistas. Worker rights petitions can be made more effective through consistent review and enforcement procedures and the active, democratic involvement of workers, unions, and NGOs from the developing world.

Community-Based Organizing

Community-based organizing models usually recognize the multiple realities and identities of women *maquiladora* workers. Community-based organizations (CBOs) located along the U.S.-Mexico border like the *Comité Frontierzo de Obreras* (Border Women Workers Committee—CFO) and *La Mujer Obrera* (The Woman Worker) implicitly understand that women workers are concerned about safe drinking water, child care, housing, domestic violence, low wages, and poor working conditions. These groups stress women workers can address these issues through consciousness-raising techniques and popular education workshops that provide them with information about their legal and political rights.[89] These strategies are seen as crucial prerequisites for establishing democratic and participatory organizations that can develop campaigns around the diverse concerns of women workers.

The CFO and La Mujer Obrera have periodically obtained important concessions over the past decade. Some women workers have received protective equipment (e.g., masks and gloves), back wages, and profit-sharing bonuses, while others have declared that they have gained inner confidence and self-esteem through their organizing experiences.[90] Flor de María Salguero, an activist with *Mujeres en Solidaridad* (Women in Solidarity), a community-based women's organization based in Guatemala City, highlighted this point, stating, "organizing has made me a stronger person and strengthened my personal convictions about working for social justice."[91]

Despite these achievements, labor unions have sometimes criticized community-based organizations for focusing on "limited goals" rather than broader ones like negotiating collective bargaining agreements. CBOs, in contrast, have attacked some unions for ignoring and/or excluding women and bypassing their gendered and sometimes racialized networks. These patriarchal and racist practices have made some white women and women of color cautious, especially toward those white male organizers who have occasionally encouraged impulsive actions (e.g., strikes) without understanding local dynamics. Because community-based groups can grasp these nuances more clearly, their organizing campaigns tend to be more subtle and carefully planned. This methodology, ideally speaking, enables the workers, not the organizers, to decide when they will act. These tactics, women activists allege, have produced fewer firings than union organizing has.[92]

Notwithstanding this point and the positive results community-based organizations have obtained, this model does have two key limitations. One, the agreements that community groups have negotiated with corporations are usually non-binding and therefore, they can be retracted when popular pressure and media coverage dissipate. Two, CBOs often do not have the financial resources, size, and stability to expand their activities beyond the local level. The globalization of production requires not only local, but transnational strategies for improving wages and working conditions for garment workers all over the world. Community-based organizing thus represents a major step forward because it recognizes the multiple identities of women workers, but it still remains limited in scope. If this approach could be "globalized" to not only challenge class and gender inequality, but also the racial forms of oppression that most women garment workers confront all over the world, then it could have a much deeper impact.

Cross-Border Union Organizing

Cross-border union organizing campaigns focus on establishing *maquila* labor unions and negotiating collective bargaining agreements. The former objective has not been met that often because *maquila* workers usually organize spontaneously. They tend to lack a strategic plan for obtaining enough members to create a stable and long-lasting organization. The labor federations that these workers have ties with usually do not have sufficient resources to assist them either. These two factors—combined with the fact that most employers fire workers for joining unions—make *maquila* union organizing extremely difficult.[93]

Several U.S.-based unions have addressed these issues through directly funding local organizers and helping create strategic organizing plans that can facilitate unionization and collective bargaining. These cross-border union organizing campaigns usually involve *maquila* workers, labor unions within developing countries, U.S. local and international unions, international trade secretariats, and NGOs like the U.S./LEAP, Witness For Peace, and the National Labor Committee.

Cross-border union organizing between U.S. and Latin American labor unions has taken off since the early 1990s. In 1992, the U.S.-based United Electrical Workers (UE) and the Mexican-based Authentic Workers Front (FAT) formed a "strategic organizing alliance."[94] Through this coalition, the UE has funded organizers for the FAT and the FAT has reciprocated, sending the UE several organizers that helped it win an organizing campaign in Milwaukee, Wisconsin that involved mostly Mexican workers.[95] In the mid-1990s, UNITE, along with the now defunct American Institute for Free Labor Development (AIFLD), and the international garment workers secretariat, worked carefully with *maquila* workers in the Dominican Republic.[96] Based on this collaborative effort, five unions were recognized and negotiated collective bargaining agreements in that Caribbean-based country.[97] The Communication Workers of America (CWA), the United Steel Workers of America (USWA), and United Auto Workers (UAW) Local 879 and Region 1A have also funded organizers and worked directly with Mexican automobile workers over the past few years.[98]

Some cross-border union organizing campaigns, like the ones mentioned above, have generated successful results—higher wages, better working conditions, union recognition, and contract ratification. Nevertheless, this strategy has two crucial weaknesses. The first one is union organizing often involves great risk. Thousands of *maquila* workers, no matter how well organized or careful they have been, have been fired for joining unions. This situation has created tremendous fear, making organizing nearly impossible. The second problem with this strategy is that union organizing drives can be undermined through capital mobility. Companies have shut down and moved production elsewhere after workers organized and negotiated contracts.

Most cross-border union organizing campaigns have targeted specific factories so far. This approach, while useful, has not produced positive long-lasting outcomes. To be more effective, U.S. and Central American unions should expand long-talked about plans for organizing garment workers on a region-wide basis or all the workers working for the same transnational corporation.[99] If either one of these approaches was actually implemented, then companies, theoretically, would have nowhere to run or hide. They would have to deal with unionized workers wherever they went. U.S. and Central American unions lack the resources and political will to carry out both strategies, however. Until they do, capital mobility will remain a possibility that can torpedo any cross-border labor solidarity strategy or campaign.

Cross-Border Labor Solidarity: Past and Present

There are no simple answers. All the strategies mentioned above have some limitations. This does not mean that cross-border labor solidarity is impossible or that sweatshop labor practices cannot be eliminated. Workers have organized themselves across borders for years.[100] In the nineteenth century, they established the First and Second Internationals, along with more than a dozen international trade secretariats (ITSs). ITSs link together the unions of a specific industry or sector. The International Textile, Leather, and Garment Workers Federation (ITLGWF) is the ITS for garment industry unions.

The U.S. labor movement has been involved in international labor activities for well over one hundred years. The American Federation of Labor (AFL) and the Industrial Workers of the World (IWW) offered alternative visions of unionism and internationalism in the early twentieth century. The AFL mostly represented skilled white, working-class men and supported U.S. economic and foreign policy objectives in Latin America and Asia.[101] The IWW (also known as the "Wobblies"), on the other hand, organized all workers regardless of skill level, race, gender, or nationality and rejected imperialism, developing links with radical Latin American labor unions.[102]

After the federal government crushed the Wobblies during World War I, the AFL gained control of the U.S. labor movement until the Congress of Industrial Organizations (CIO) emerged in the 1930s. The CIO partially embraced the Wobblies philosophy of "one big union," incorporating women and workers of color and establishing ties with leftist Latin American unions and the Russian All-Union Central Council of Soviet Trade Unions (AUCCTU).[103] The CIO, AUCCTU, and the British Trade Union Congress (TUC) created the World Federation of Trade Unions (WFTU) in 1945, but the AFL refused to join because of its long anti-communist history.[104]

As the Cold War "heated up" and the Red Scare swept across the United States, the CIO purged eleven of its most radical affiliates and withdrew from the WFTU in 1949.[105] These two decisions helped splinter the international labor movement into two camps—the communist (Soviet-backed) WFTU and the anti-communist (U.S.-backed) International Confederation of Free Trade Unions (ICFTU).[106] The AFL and CIO, along with most Western European labor confederations, formed the ICFTU in 1949. The AFL and CIO, given the latter's ideological and political shift, eventually merged into one unified body (the AFL-CIO) in 1955.

The AFL-CIO became deeply involved in Latin American labor affairs over the next thirty-five years (1955–1990), establishing several affiliates, the most well-known one being the American Institute for Free Labor Development (AIFLD) in 1962.[107] AIFLD initially received funding from corporations, the U.S. State Department, and the Central Intelligence Agency (CIA).[108] AIFLD destabilized and helped overthrow "leftist" governments in Brazil, the Dominican Republic, Guyana, and Chile in the 1960s and 1970s.[109] AIFLD-trained operatives, spies, and agents also created pro-U.S. labor federations and split, through repression, intimidation, and bribes, leftist ones in Nicaragua, Guatemala, El Salvador, Costa Rica, and Honduras in the 1970s.[110] The institute also supported the Salvadoran government in the 1980s even though it brutally killed tens of thousands of people, many of whom were workers and trade unionists.[111]

AIFLD's policies sparked dissent in the mid-1960s from rank-and-file workers, journalists, and even union presidents like the UAW's Walter Reuther.[112] As more and more production moved overseas over the next fifteen years, demands for change grew. In 1981, ten of the federation's presidents, for instance, created the National Labor Committee in Support of Democracy and Human Rights in El Salvador (NLC).[113] The NLC criticized the AFL-CIO's foreign policy on humanitarian and practical grounds, claiming that the federation's support for authoritarian governments helped facilitate off-shore production because these regimes kept wages low and crushed labor unions. The NLC sponsored fact-finding delegations and released a series of reports based on those trips condemning the AFL-CIO's policies in El Salvador in the mid-1980s.[114]

Despite these criticisms, the AFL-CIO's Cold War leadership, under the direction of Lane Kirkland, did not change its direction. Corporations continued moving overseas throughout the 1980s. The federal government, under Presidents Reagan and Bush, attacked unions, cut-back social programs, and failed to enforce labor legislation. Consequently, U.S. union membership plummeted and the gap between the rich and poor widened.[115] The AFL-CIO finally began addressing those trends after the Soviet Union collapsed. The federation first loosened "informal" restrictions on its affiliates, allowing them to work with unions from all over the ideological spectrum. The AFL-CIO also joined the Coalition for Justice in the Maquiladoras (CJM) a tri-national organization of U.S., Canadian, and Mexican NGOs and unions that focuses on improving wages and working conditions along the U.S.-Mexican border.[116] In the early 1990s, the AFL-CIO became deeply involved in the fight against NAFTA and AIFLD assisted campaigns to organize *maquila* workers in Honduras and the Dominican Republic.[117]

Dissident voices within the AFL-CIO welcomed these changes, but they claimed that they came "too little, too late." In 1994, Lane Kirkland stepped down as AFL-CIO President. One year later, Service Employees International Union (SEIU) President John Sweeney narrowly defeated his hand-picked successor, Thomas Donahue, in the federation's first openly contested election.[118] Sweeney understood that the AFL-CIO's international labor activities were controversial and outdated. He, therefore, quickly closed down all the federation's foreign affiliates (including AIFLD) and opened up the American Center for International Labor Solidarity (ACILS) in their place.[119] ACILS representatives have played a key role in Central American *maquila* organizing campaigns over the past several years.[120]

Despite this shift, some distrust exists between the AFL-CIO, ACILS, and UNITE on the one hand and NGOs like the NLC and Global Exchange on the other. The conflict between these groups is a strategic one—the former support collective bargaining while the latter tend to back independent monitoring. On a rhetorical level, all these groups endorse both strategies, but in praxis, disagreements often arise. U.S.-based unions and NGOs have worked together on many cross-border labor solidarity campaigns, but strategic, tactical, and historical differences have sometimes undermined these efforts, as we shall see.[121]

Cross-Border Labor Solidarity Campaigns: The Kukdong Case

Cross-border labor solidarity campaigns are complex. They often involve numerous strategies, targets, and actors. Campaigns usually span several different countries and take years. Outcomes defy standard, neat categories—sometimes they can "succeed"—workers may obtain higher wages, health care, masks and gloves, and subsidies for food, transportation, and education, for instance, but they can also "fail"—workers may be fired or the factory shut down. The lines between "success" and "failure," I contend, should be broadly construed.[122] Campaigns often contain both elements—a "victory" can turn into a "defeat" and vice-versa. That is the nature of most social movements—they are fluid, not fixed. As Herod and Harvey suggest, corporations and workers will continually seek out "spatial fixes" or "geographical practices" that suit their interests.[123] Campaigns will, therefore, be "won" or "lost" based on the contingent, dialectical, and dynamic relationship between those between capital and labor.

There have been many cross-border labor solidarity campaigns over the last few years. One notable case took place in Puebla, Mexico. In January 2001, nearly the entire workforce at a Korean-owned factory named Kukdong, which produces collegiate apparel (mostly sweatshirts) for Nike and Reebok, held a three-day strike after five of their fellow co-workers were illegally fired for protesting poor working conditions (low pay, unsanitary food, physical and verbal abuse, inadequate union representation, and denial of maternity and sick leave) and trying to organize an independent labor union.[124] Riot police, along with officials from the company-backed union (called the Revolutionary Confederation of Workers and Peasants [CROC]), violently dispersed the striking workers, sending seventeen to local hospitals, with batons and shields.[125] After the strike, Kukdong and the CROC refused to reinstate many workers that participated in the strike and forced others to sign "loyalty oaths" to the CROC.[126]

These repressive activities galvanized anti-sweatshop and social justice activists in Canada, Europe, Korea, Mexico, and the United States. The USAS-backed Worker Rights Consortium (WRC), for example, sent a fact-finding team to the factory to conduct a preliminary investigation.[127] The International Labor Rights Fund (ILRF), a former FLA member, and Verité, a private, FLA-affiliated monitoring firm, also conducted their own inquires into the Kukdong conflict.[128] All three reports noted widespread national and international labor violations, as well as non-compliance with university codes of conduct. Based on this documentary evidence, students pressured universities from all over the country to reconsider their ties with Nike and Reebok.[129] These two companies eventually pushed Kukdong to rehire all the workers that took part in the work stoppage and to improve working conditions.[130]

Kukdong initially rejected these demands, prompting Nike to "cut and run" or stop sourcing with the factory.[131] Faced with no orders from its largest supplier, Kukdong began laying off workers and looking for ways to resolve the conflict.[132] Meanwhile, the independent union filed for official recognition, but state labor officials rejected its petition.[133] After activists visited Mexican consulate offices in Canada and the United States, the union was officially recognized in mid-September 2001. Several days later, Kukdong (renamed Mexmode) negotiated a contract with the independent union and the CROC left the factory.[134] In November 2001, Nike issued a statement claiming that it would resume placing orders with Kukdong by Spring 2002.[135] After receiving more pressure from student activists, Nike followed through on its pledge, sending the factory sizeable orders, although it still remains below full production capacity.[136]

The Kukdong case was successful. The Mexican *maquiladora* industry includes more than three thousand factories. Kukdong/Mexmode is the *only* one with a contract held by an independent union.[137] The factory has substantial orders coming from Nike and the union negotiated a 40 percent wage increase.[138] These outcomes illustrate that the campaign was a clear-cut victory.

Transnational Social Movements: The Boomerang Effect

How did the Kukdong workers and their transnational allies obtain these rather remarkable results? What theoretical frameworks help us understand why some cross-border labor solidarity campaigns "succeed" in the short-run, but "fail" in the long-run? The social movement literature on transnational social movements has rapidly expanded over the last several years.[139] Margaret Keck and Kathryn Sikkink offer one of the most innovative, although problematic, perspectives in their widely-cited book, *Activists Beyond Borders* (1998). I draw upon and modify their approach as a heuristic device for analyzing cross-border labor solidarity campaigns such as the Kukdong case.

Figure 1.3 illustrates Keck and Sikkink's model is based on a feedback loop-oriented process that they call the "boomerang effect." The boomerang effect occurs when powerful states restrict "domestic non-state actors" (unions, NGOs, etc.) from redressing their grievances (low wages, poor working conditions, lack of safety equipment, verbal abuse, etc.).[140] Nation-states can, for instance, block labor organizing campaigns by not properly administering legal procedures or arresting key organizers. Given these conditions, domestic NGOs can develop ties with NGOs beyond their borders, forming a "transnational advocacy network" of allies, whose members can, in turn, pressure their states to put direct or indirect pressure on the original recalcitrant state.[141]

Keck and Sikkink contend that the purpose of these transnational advocacy networks (TANs) is to persuade the state or some other powerful "target" (transnational corporation, free trade zone owner, contractor, government agency, etc.) to change or enforce its laws or policies or implement new reforms. TANs can achieve these sorts of goals by engaging in four types of politics—information, symbolic, leverage, and accountability.[142] Information politics publicize and disseminate "facts" (concerning global warming, human rights violations, sweatshops, etc.) through various methods of mass communication (films, reports, websites, etc.). Symbolic politics seek to "frame" complex

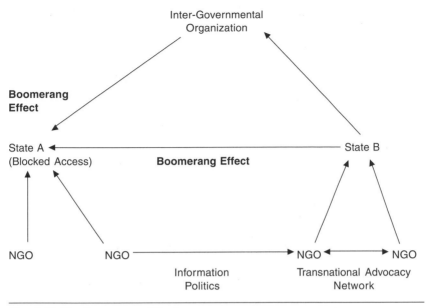

Fig. 1.3 The Boomerang Effect.

issues or events through various "signs"—alternative fashion shows, awards, costumes, murals, pictures, posters, puppets, or street theater. Leverage politics limit the strength of powerful targets through creative strategies and tactics. Accountability politics highlight the contradiction between the targeted actor's words and deeds through a careful analysis of its "mission statement" or code of conduct. These four types of politics are not mutually exclusive. They are often used in a combined and overlapping manner.

How can this model be applied in the context of analyzing cross-border labor solidarity campaigns? Despite Keck and Sikkink's puzzling comments about "transitory nature" of labor-oriented TANs,[143] I contend that their conceptual model is, for the most part, very useful. In the Kukdong case, the workers realized that they had very little, if any, leverage over their two immediate "targets"—Kukdong and the CROC. After the three-day strike was violently repressed, the workers contacted the WRC. Soon thereafter, the WRC conducted its initial investigation. The ILRF and Verité immediately followed suit with their own inquiries. The reports of all three organizations were released between January–March 2001.

These documents showed that the "facts" of the case strongly favored the Kukdong workers. Through the Campaign for Labor Rights, U.S./LEAP, and other NGO-based Web sites, activists, as well as the general public, became increasingly aware of the extensive labor violations that existed within the factory. Student anti-sweatshop activists used this information to put pressure on colleges and universities to hold Kukdong's two main suppliers, Nike and Reebok, accountable to their codes of conduct, which protect labor rights. Student activists also called on colleges and universities to reevaluate their contracts with Nike and Reebok.

The Kukdong workers obtained material and moral leverage based on these three strategies. Material leverage involves possible financial losses, such as the termination of a licensing agreement, whereas moral leverage often entails smearing the target's public image.[144] When anti-sweatshop activists disseminated the three investigative reports, highlighting the "gap" between university codes of conduct and Kukdong's labor practices, the public image of Nike and Reebok suffered as a result. Facing negative publicity for using sweatshop labor and the potential loss of lucrative agreements, Nike and Reebok buckled, putting pressure on Kukdong to resolve the conflict. Through information, accountability, and leverage politics, the transnational advocacy network, made up of anti-sweatshop, labor, student, and solidarity groups from five different countries, created a "boomerang" effect that targeted colleges and universities who pressured Nike and Reebok, who, in turn, leaned on Kukdong (see Figure 1.4).

Kukdong did not budge even though Nike was its largest supplier. The company stubbornly refused to rehire scores of workers and collaborated with the CROC to block the establishment of the independent union. The boomerang effect, based on this outcome, looks like it had a very limited impact. How do Keck and Sikkink explain this paradoxical dilemma?

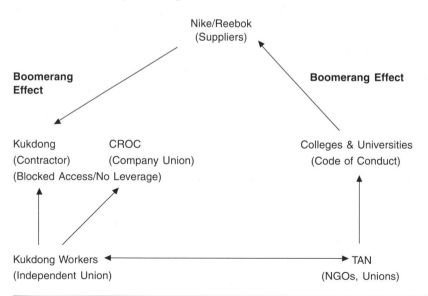

Fig. 1.4 The Kukdong Case and The Boomerang Effect.

They do not apparently consider the possibility, since their model primarily focuses on one single actor (the state), that some domestic non-state actors and TANs may face *multiple* targets. In the Kukdong case, the company's workers and transnational advocacy network confronted four targets—Kukdong, the CROC, colleges and universities, and the two suppliers (Nike and Reebok). The TAN had leverage over the latter two, but not over the former two. How was this situation addressed?

Keck and Sikkink implicitly suggest that since domestic non-state actors encounter resistance within the context of their own nation-state, the TAN is the "primary" agent of social change. They very clearly state this point, writing, "[when] State A blocks redress to organizations within it; they [the domestic non-state actor] activate the [transnational advocacy] network, whose members pressure their own states and (if relevant) a third-party organization, which in turn pressures State A." Based on this framework, domestic non-state actors have very little agency. They initiate the establishment of the TAN, but the network is *the* driving force.

The Kukdong case illustrates how this approach overemphasizes the role of the TAN. While it is undoubtedly true that NGOs like the Campaign for Labor Rights, U.S./LEAP, and USAS effectively challenged Nike, Reebok, and several major universities, they could not directly pressure Kukdong on the shop-floor nor could they negotiate and sign a contract for the factory's workers. Those tasks were the union's responsibility. Without a strong local union or domestic non-state actor, the results of this campaign probably would not have been as far-reaching.

The overall lesson here is transnational activist networks can only do so much. Keck and Sikkink unintentionally valorize the activists and organizations within these networks, making them the mythical "white knight in shining armor." Ethel Brooks has claimed that some first world anti-sweatshop activists have adopted this quasi-paternalist practice. She argues this process can lead them to view themselves as "saviors" and garment workers as "victims."[145]

Following this latter point, I contend that successful short-term cross-border labor solidarity campaigns depend on robust local *maquila* unions *and* fairly well-unified transnational activist networks. The former can be created through "organization-building" politics, expanding the group's membership base and strengthening its sustainability based on strategic, mostly clandestine, planning. Because they place nearly all the weight on the TAN, Keck and Sikkink tacitly ignore the power and agency that garment workers and the organizations that they have established possess. The perspective offered here counters this logic, acknowledging the role that "sweatshop warriors" and transnational networks can and often must play. Campaign outcomes usually depend on their presence or absence.

Beyond these two factors, one should also consider how vulnerable the targets are. Naomi Klein's *No Logo* (2000) contends well-known companies with high brand-name recognition that market themselves as "progressive" or "socially responsible" are especially susceptible to image-related attacks.[146] Nike and Reebok found this out all too well during the Kukdong campaign. The independent union and transnational network exploited the "disconnect" between these companies' rhetoric and their actual practices, prompting the improbable victory.

It should be emphasized here that even though this campaign was successful, the final, "ultimate" outcome is unclear. The Kukdong workers "won," but they still earn little more than the minimum wage despite a recent 40% wage increase. This result highlights this fundamental question—how can campaign victories be deepened and sustained over time? That dilemma will be fully addressed in the book's concluding chapter.

Book Overview

Challenging sweatshop labor practices across national borders is extremely difficult. The next four chapters illustrate that claim with intricate and sometimes heart-breaking detail. Chapter 2 examines the Phillips Van-Heusen workers' movement in Guatemala City. This campaign lasted eight years (1989–1997) before the workers negotiated and ratified the only contract that existed, at that time, in the entire Guatemalan *maquiladora* industry. That victory was short-lived, however. PVH eventually shut down its unionized factory and expanded ties with non-union subcontractors outside Guatemala City.

Chapter 3 analyzes the Gap/Mandarin International campaign in El Salvador. This case highlights, partially, the debate between unionization (collective bargaining) and independent monitoring. After the company fired hundreds of workers and effectively destroyed the union, U.S. and Salvadoran NGOs signed the first-ever independent monitoring agreement with the Gap in December 1995. The Salvadoran-based groups established a "watchdog" group that periodically inspected the factory and found working conditions improved dramatically, but wages did not.

Chapter 4 focuses on the Kimi campaign in Honduras. This case "heated up" when the conflict between collective bargaining and independent monitoring was at perhaps its highest point. This battle slowed down the campaign's progress, but the workers never backed down. They struggled for six years (1993–1999), fighting recalcitrant supervisors and overcoming police blows, tear gas, and a tragic hurricane, before they finally signed a two-year contract. Kimi closed down shortly thereafter, however, leaving these workers jobless.

Chapter 5 explores the Chentex campaign in Nicaragua. This case involved probably the strongest *maquila* union in Central America. The workers here, who were affiliated with a Sandinista labor federation, signed a contract that improved working conditions, but left wages intact. After hearing countless excuses from the company, the union called for a one-hour strike. The company responded harshly, firing seven hundred workers, along with all the union's leaders. The union then established ties with NGOs from Asia, Africa, the United States, Canada, and Europe. They held demonstrations outside the factory and chanted, "*ni un paso atrás* (not one step back)!" The workers were never rehired though and the most militant union in the region was destroyed.

Chapter 6 sifts through these mixed outcomes. Based on Keck and Sikkink's model and the work of other prominent social movement theorists, I comparatively analyze these four cases and explore what factors made each one momentarily successful. I also examine what forces undermined these efforts over time. I conclude with some suggestions and observations about the anti-sweatshop and global justice movements given the new political and economic climate after the September 11, 2001 terrorist attacks in the United States.

2

Globalization and Cross-Border Labor Solidarity in the Guatemalan Maquiladora Industry

The Phillips Van-Heusen Workers' Movement

Setting the Stage: Victory, Then Defeat

Cross-border labor solidarity campaigns often involve spontaneous and clandestine activity. I learned that fact first-hand while doing research on the Phillips Van-Heusen (PVH) campaign in Guatemala City. After organizing discreetly for more than a year, PVH workers handed Yvonne de Sevilla, the company's legal representative, a petition on September 2, 1996, stating that they had re-established a viable, functioning union and were now requesting the initiation of contract negotiations. This action surprised Sevilla. She, like most other company supervisors, assumed that the workers were relatively happy and that the "old" union had fallen apart. Upon re-gaining her composure, Sevilla grabbed the document and promptly ripped it up.

This incident sparked a three-week long deadlock. During that time period, the PVH workers' union and U.S.-based non-government organizations like the United States/Guatemala Labor Education Project (U.S./GLEP) maintained pressure on the company in Guatemala and the United States. Some workers, for instance, wore union t-shirts and chanted slogans ("What do we want? A contract. When do we want it? Now!") inside the factory, while U.S. activists distributed leaflets outside shopping malls condemning PVH's anti-union stance.

These activities were designed to bring the company to the negotiating table, but it stubbornly refused. In fact, PVH initially staked out a highly combative, even militaristic, position, hiring armed security guards to monitor the union's activities and to intimidate workers from joining it or participating in its events. This decision generated an impromptu meeting between representatives from the PVH workers' union, U.S./GLEP, and the International Textile, Garment, and Leather Workers (ITGLWF) (which was deeply involved with this campaign) in late September 1996.

I literally stumbled into that conversation. I was scheduled to interview Teresa Casertano, an organizer with the garment workers secretariat, about the PVH campaign, but when I arrived, I found out that she had gone down to the factory because the company had just hired the security guards. Things were moving quickly, I sensed, and so I jumped on an old, broken-down school bus near the National Palace and took off for the factory to see what was going on.

The bus' lethargic pace, along with its toxic fumes, made me sleepy and I dozed off for a little while. Upon waking up, I hopped out and looked around aimlessly for the factory. I thought, perhaps too optimistically, I would find it right away since I had the "exact" address. Several minutes passed before I finally spotted it. The large blue-and-white building was located across the street from a vacant lot filled with shoulder-high weeds, worn-out tires, and broken-down wooden pallets. I looked for Teresa, but did not see her. Feeling curious, I peeked inside the factory, but saw nothing but rows and rows of sewing machines. The workers behind them were busy producing men's dress shirts for export into the United States. Company supervisors noticed me glancing inside. Their menacing faces told me that I should move along and so I did.

I resumed my search, combing the vacant lot for clues. I noticed a deserted *tienda* (food stand) and walked behind it. There I saw Teresa Casertano, U.S./ GLEP Representative Rhett Doumitt, and two organizers from the PVH workers' union (their names are omitted here, per their request) sitting on soda pop (Coca-Cola) bottle crates. I apologized for interrupting their critical planning session and asked if I could speak to the union representatives afterwards. They graciously agreed.

This was a crucial moment in the campaign because the armed guards had scared many PVH workers, given Guatemala's long history of violence and repression against labor activists. This hastily-arranged, "covert" meeting was set up to discuss strategies to address these fears and to keep the heat on PVH. After about thirty minutes passed, the two PVH workers' union representatives sat down with me and talked about their main grievances—low wages, ever-higher production quotas, lack of dignity and respect, and company threats to close down the factory. One of the organizers then mentioned simply, "we want to be able to feed our children and to give them better opportunities than we have had."[1]

I finally asked her about the armed guards, "how will they affect the campaign—will the workers be too scared to continue their struggle to negotiate a contract?" She replied, "the company says the guards are here to 'protect' us, but that's a lie. We know that's not the truth. They have frightened many workers, but I think that most of them will stay in the union. We know what we are fighting for is right."[2]

The interview ended when the workers left the factory after finishing their nine to ten-hour shifts. Many warmly greeted their *compañeras y compañeros* (comrades/friends) across the street for a seemingly spur-of-the-moment demonstration, despite the presence of the armed security guards. I noted that this daring action illustrated the confidence and prescience of this organizer and quietly thought that continued local activism and transnational labor solidarity might just make this campaign successful.

Transnational corporations are not sitting targets, however. They cannot be easily defeated. PVH's activities during this campaign illustrate this point. After the spontaneous meeting and rally, for example, company supervisors mistakenly claimed that the union had not met all the necessary legal requirements to begin contract negotiations. The company also lowered the wages of some union supporters and pressured others to quit their jobs. The Guatemalan Labor Ministry was concerned, moreover, that unionization and the negotiation of a collective bargaining agreement could scare away foreign investors. It, therefore, took PVH's side.

These machinations, much to the company and government's chagrin, did not derail the campaign. The PVH workers continued to hold actions inside and outside the factory. Meanwhile, social justice activists from labor, student, solidarity, and faith-based organizations in Canada and the United States continued passing out leaflets. Activists also filed worker rights petitions (see chapter 1), using trade pressure as a strategy for obtaining leverage.

To help break the impasse, the company and union requested that Human Rights Watch (HRW) conduct an independent investigation into the dispute. HRW representatives discovered evidence documenting the company and government's anti-union activities. This report damaged PVH's "socially responsible" image, leading it to begin contract negotiations with the union in March 1997. Talks lasted several months. Finally, on August 14, 1997, after an eight-year struggle, union members ratified the only contract that existed, at that time, in the entire Guatemalan *maquiladora* industry. This was a remarkable victory for the PVH workers. The PVH campaign was widely hailed within the anti-sweatshop movement because it showed that garment workers and social justice activists could fight back and win. On a broader level, this case illustrated that social change was *possible*, in spite of the mobility of capital and tremendous power of transnational corporations.[3]

Fifteen months after the contract was signed, however, PVH closed down its unionized factory on December 11, 1998. This unexpected move left over five hundred workers unemployed just two weeks before Christmas. PVH claimed that this decision was not a "union-busting" measure. The loss of an "important client," the company said, left it no other choice. Most workers accepted their severance payments from PVH and sought out new jobs, but others held a round-the-clock, seven-month vigil outside the factory in a last-ditch effort to reopen it. Canadian and U.S.-based activists also put pressure on PVH to reverse its decision, but the factory remained shut down. The PVH campaign was over.

How did this happen? How did this stirring victory turn into a tragic defeat? That is the crucial question of this book—why do some cross-border labor solidarity campaigns "succeed" in the short run, but "fail" in the long run? The PVH campaign is an excellent case study for shedding light on this question because it was a success *and* a failure.

This chapter examines why these two outcomes occurred. Before doing this, however, I briefly examine the history of the Guatemalan labor movement and the emergence of the *maquiladora* industry. This overview is crucial for understanding the political and economic context of the PVH case. An in-depth chronology of the campaign follows this section. The final segment of the chapter analyzes the key factors that influenced its disparate results.

The Guatemalan Labor Movement, 1900–1985

The history of the Guatemalan labor movement is one of repression and resistance. In the early twentieth century, railroad, port, and banana workers organized strikes and established the country's first labor unions.[4] Military dictators, large landowners, and multinational corporations like the United Fruit Company opposed these incipient organizations, but could not completely eliminate them.[5] In the 1930s, President Jorge Ubico banned labor unions and political parties, arrested labor organizers and radical political activists, and even outlawed using certain words such as *strike* and *worker*.[6] These policies substantially weakened the labor movement, strengthening the power of the reigning oligarchy.

Ubico ruled for thirteen years before he was overthrown. In 1944, university students, teachers, workers, and a group of young, disgruntled military officers organized large demonstrations, forcing him to resign from office.[7] Over the next decade (1944–1954) (known as the "ten years of spring"), the Guatemalan labor movement reemerged, expanding rapidly.[8] Under the democratically elected Arévalo and Arbenz presidencies, labor laws (guaranteeing decent working conditions, minimum wages, and the right to strike and organize unions) and land reforms (expropriating nearly 400,000 acres of unused United Fruit Company land) were passed, improving the everyday lives of the poor, working-class majority.[9]

These progressive policies, combined with the relatively close ties between Arbenz and some members of the Guatemalan Communist Party, upset the United Fruit Company, the U.S. State Department, the Central Intelligence

Agency (CIA), and the American Federation of Labor (AFL).[10] These organizations "red-baited" Arbenz, calling him a "communist." They also developed ties with dissident Guatemalan military officials who overthrew Arbenz in 1954.[11] Guatemala's new president, Carlos Castillo Armas, overturned Arévalo and Arbenz's labor and land reform policies, cancelled the registration of over five hundred labor unions, and abolished all political parties. Castillo Armas' officers also killed nine thousand people and arrested another seven thousand.[12]

The Guatemalan military continued these brutal anti-labor policies over the next thirty years (1954–1984).[13] In the mid-1970s, popular unrest against the military dictatorship grew. Students, *campesinos*, urban workers, women, and indigenous people organized themselves. This broad-based "popular" movement took off quickly, attracting tens of thousands of people.[14] Unions affiliated with militant, left-leaning labor federations organized general strikes and huge demonstrations.[15] Some labor activists and organizations within the popular movement worked together and challenged the military using non-violent strategies and tactics, while others opted for "armed struggle," establishing ties with one of the country's four guerrilla organizations.[16]

These activities did not go unnoticed. The Guatemalan military made no distinction between popular and revolutionary movement organizations. It saw all social movements—especially the labor movement—as a threat to the existing social, economic, and political order. All social justice activists were defined as "subversives" or "communists." Based on this stark perspective, the military attacked, tortured, "disappeared," and killed tens of thousands of people, burned hundreds of villages, and terrorized the entire population between 1978 and 1984.[17] Indigenous people bore the brunt of this genocidal campaign.[18] The military's "scorched-earth" policies drove the labor and popular movements underground over the next several years.[19]

Despite tremendous odds, Coca-Cola workers in Guatemala City resisted state repression and formed the Coca-Cola Bottling Company Workers' Union in the mid-1970s.[20] Company and military officials responded with force, killing eight union activists between 1978 and 1980.[21] Coca-Cola workers and union members continued organizing, however. They received national and international solidarity from Guatemalan unions, the International Union of Food Workers (IUF), the United Food and Commercial Workers (UFCW), the Interfaith Center for Corporate Responsibility (ICCR), and Amnesty International.[22]

These organizations targeted Coca-Cola through a "comprehensive campaign" (see chapter 1). Campaign strategies included shareholder resolutions, production stoppages, and a consumer boycott in over fifty countries.[23] These activities, combined with a year-long occupation of the factory, were ultimately successful.[24] Coca-Cola workers eventually signed a contract with the company in 1985, ending a courageous nine-year campaign.[25] The Coca-Case campaign illustrated the persistence of the Guatemalan labor movement and it indicated, despite state repression, cross-border labor solidarity and social change were possible—even under the most difficult circumstances.[26]

Export-Led Development and
The Guatemalan Labor Movement, 1985–1996

The Coca-Cola campaign occurred in the midst of a severe economic and political crisis. For many years, Guatemala's economy depended on stable prices for several agricultural exports such as coffee, bananas, cotton, sugar, and meat. Price fluctuations and political repression, however, generated economic instability, rising unemployment, and widespread social unrest in the late 1970s and early 1980s.[27] Guatemalan military, economic, and political elites, along with officials from the U.S. Embassy and the Agency for International Development (AID), thought that these problems could be ameliorated through economic diversification and the cultivation of "non-traditional" agricultural and industrial exports (e.g., snow peas, tourism, and clothing production).[28] Tax incentives, subsidies, low-wage, non-unionized labor, and the establishment of "free trade zones" were the key elements of this new export-led development strategy. Guatemalan and U.S. government officials claimed that these policies would generate foreign investment and economic growth. Policy analysts believed that Guatemala would follow the footsteps of the four East Asian "Tigers" (e.g., South Korea, Singapore, Taiwan, and Hong Kong) and become the "Jaguar" of Latin America.[29]

One key obstacle limited this model from being implemented. The U.S.-sponsored Generalized System of Preferences (GSP) states that recipient nations can obtain trade preferences and export specific goods, duty-free, into the United States, on the condition that they protect internationally recognized worker rights standards such as the right to organize and collectively bargain.[30] Nations that fail to protect these standards can lose their GSP benefits or be placed under "review" until they take "appropriate steps" to do so. Given these stipulations, the Guatemalan military, realizing that foreign investment and export-led economic growth depended on some labor rights concessions, reluctantly recognized the establishment of a new labor federation, the Guatemalan Confederation of Trade Union Unity (*Confederación de Unidad Sindical de Guatemala*—CUSG) in 1983.[31]

This decision did not initially stimulate foreign investment. Although CUSG maintained close ties with the Guatemalan government, shunned direct organizing, and received substantial funding from the AFL-CIO's Latin American affiliate, the American Institute for Free Labor Development (AIFLD), political instability made investors wary.[32] As the economic crisis continued and the international outcry against its human rights violations grew louder, the Guatemalan military "stepped down" from power in the mid-1980s.[33]

Table 2.1 The Guatemalan Labor Movement, 1982–Present

Labor Organization (Confederation)	Ideological Perspective	Year Established
CUSG	Centrist	1982
CGTG	Centrist	1983
UNSITRAGUA	Left	1983

The country's "transition towards democracy" opened up space for labor and popular movements to organize. Two new labor federations, the Union-Unity of Guatemalan Workers (*Union Sindical de Trabajadores de Guatemala*— UNSITRAGUA) and the General Confederation of Guatemalan Workers (*Confederación de Trabajadores de Guatemala*—CGTG) were established in the early 1980s.[34] Both organizations initially shunned overt activities, but after the military relinquished power, UNSITRAGUA worked directly with the popular movement, organizing several major demonstrations calling for price controls, wage increases, and union recognition in late 1980s.[35] The CGTG did not join these protests, but CUSG did. CUSG also worked briefly with the popular movement for several years.[36] Based on these positions, CUSG and the CGTG are usually classified, ideologically speaking, as "moderate" or "centrist," while UNSITRAGUA is seen as "leftist" (see Table 2.1).[37]

In the early 1990s, human rights violations declined and peace negotiations between the Guatemalan government and the revolutionary movement accelerated.[38] The violent forty-year civil war, which took more than two hundred thousand lives, finally ended in 1996. All three labor confederations—CUSG, UNSITRAGUA, and CGTG—hailed the signing of the peace agreements, but by that time they were extremely weak and divided, representing less than 3 percent of the entire labor force.[39]

The Maquiladora Industry

Greater political stability, the new export-led development model, and the feeble nature of the Guatemalan labor movement helped spark the growth of the *maquiladora* industry in the early 1990s.[40] *Maquiladora* factories are off-shore, assembly-line plants that produce clothes such as shirts, pants, blouses, socks, and underwear for the U.S. consumer market. Some of the most well-known labels that are produced in Guatemala include Sears, J.C. Penney, Philips Van-Heusen, Fruit of the Loom, Target, Wal-Mart, and Liz Claiborne.[41]

Widespread violence limited the emergence of the *maquiladora* industry in the early 1980s. In 1984, there were only six *maquila* factories in the entire country.[42] Over the next few years, as political conditions shifted, the industry exploded. In 1992, there were 250 *maquila* factories. Recent estimates indicate that there are more than 700 factories, employing over eighty thousand workers.[43] In 1986, Guatemala was the *forty-first* largest exporter, among countries within the Caribbean Basin Initiative (CBI), of apparel products to the U.S. market, supplying it with just 0.2 percent of the region's clothing exports.[44] In 1998, Guatemala jumped to the *fifth* largest apparel exporter among CBI countries, providing the U.S. market with 8.3 percent of the region's apparel exports.[45] Among Central American countries specifically, Guatemala ranks fourth, supplying 13.4 percent of the region's production. In 1990, *maquila* exports totaled $67.5 million, but skyrocketed towards just over $1 billion in 1998.[46] Despite the industry's rapid expansion, its growth has slowed down over the past few years because the North American Free Trade Agreement (NAFTA) has made Mexico a more "attractive location" for garment producers.[47]

Nearly 50 percent of the factories within the country's *maquiladora* industry are Korean-owned, 40 percent are Guatemalan-owned, and less than 10 percent are U.S.-owned.[48] The vast majority of these factories are located in Guatemala City, San Pedro Sacatepéquez, Mixco, and Chimaltenango. Young women between the ages of sixteen and twenty-five make up approximately 80 percent of the *maquila* labor force.[49] Fifty percent of these women are single mothers.[50] *Maquila* workers typically work more than fifty hours a week. Wages vary widely, ranging from fifty to ninety cents an hour. Benefits (health care, sick pay, vacation time, etc.) are not usually provided, even though they are legally mandated.[51]

Armed security guards search all workers before they enter the factory. Most plants are hot and poorly ventilated, creating respiratory illnesses and other health-related problems. Bathroom breaks are timed and regulated. Supervisors often verbally (and sometimes physically and sexually) harass workers.[52] As one former worker said, "they always yell—faster, faster—and call us bad names."[53] A labor activist stated some factories also give *maquila* workers amphetamines to work longer shifts and meet production goals.[54]

Flor de María Salguero, an energetic organizer with *Mujeres en Solidaridad* (Women in Solidarity), a community-based women's organization, openly discussed these issues and the grim reality that *maquila* workers face on a daily basis:

> Many workers work twelve to sixteen hours a day and they are often forced to work overtime. Many workers are women and they are very young—they're girls really. The labor code says that if you are under eighteen years old, you cannot work more than seven hours a day. But, there are some fourteen-year old workers that work over ten hours a day. . . . There have been many accidents and injuries in the factories too—they use toxic chemicals that have burned some workers and are responsible for health problems and illnesses like cancer. The companies also do not hire pregnant women and they fire you when you become pregnant because they do not want to pay the benefits.[55]

Maquiladora workers have periodically resisted these conditions. They have slowed down production, organized strikes, and established community-based organizations and labor unions. The Guatemalan labor code (introduced during the "ten years of spring" in 1947) stipulates that unions must have at least twenty members to obtain legal recognition. The code also states that if a union represents more than 25 percent of all workers within a particular factory or workplace, then the employer, after it has been properly notified, must begin contract negotiations. These "low-threshold" provisions indirectly facilitated the establishment of nearly twenty labor unions in the *maquiladora* industry in the 1980s and 1990s. These organizations were very small. None of them negotiated a contract, but most were legally recognized and demanded better wages and working conditions.[56]

The situation facing *maquila* workers today is extremely bleak. There are *no* unions and *no* contracts in the *entire* industry.[57] Previously established unions were eliminated through fear, firing, and intimidation. These repressive strategies have made labor organizing and social change nearly impossible within the Guatemalan *maquiladora* industry.

One of the few unions that briefly overcame these obstacles was the Camisas Modernas Workers' Union (*Sindicato de Trabajadores de Camisas Modernas*—STECAMOSA). STECAMOSA members worked for Phillips Van-Heusen (PVH). They struggled for eight years before they negotiated the only contract that existed, at that time, in the *maquiladora* industry in 1997. One year later, PVH shut down its unionized factory, however. How did these two different outcomes occur? That question, along with the history of the PVH workers' movement, is explored below.

Phillips Van-Heusen

PVH is one of the largest makers of men's shirts in the entire world. In 1988, this U.S.-based company opened up two new factories, known as *Camisas Modernas* I and *Camisas Modernas* II (or *Camosa* I and *Camosa* II),[58] in Guatemala City. These plants produced over three hundred thousand shirts a year while they were still operating. More than 70 percent of *Camisas Modernas* workers were women, mostly single mothers in their twenties and thirties. Most workers earned more than the minimum wage, but far less than a "living wage." The average wage for both factories hovered around seventy-five cents an hour, which is only half of what is needed to a raise a family above the poverty line.[59]

One former *Camisas Modernas* worker, with three young children, discussed the difference between the minimum wage and a living wage, as well as her reasons for joining STECAMOSA:

> Our supervisors tell us we make more than the minimum wage. That's true, but most us earn only five or six *queztales* (between seventy-five

and ninety cents) an hour. That's not sufficient—how can we live and feed our children like that? I feel sad and angry because I want to give my children more . . . it makes me upset when our supervisors say that we are paid enough and that we don't deserve higher wages. I don't believe that. We work hard. We make the company rich, but we often run out of money and have to borrow from others. I didn't know what to do for a long time. I wanted to do something, but I wasn't sure until my *compañera* told me about the union. She said that it was struggling so our families could be treated fairly and live with dignity and respect. That was all I needed to know and so I decided to join [the union].[60]

Another *Camisas Modernas* worker with two children talked about her personal and financial struggles:

I am happy that I have this job, but I don't have enough money for food, rent, and other necessities. I always run out of money before the end of the month. I think that we need a contract because our wages are too low and the company treats us like machines. I don't want to be treated like that anymore.[61]

These two statements contradict PVH's "socially responsible" image. Like most transnational corporations, PVH sees itself in a rather benevolent manner. PVH Chief Executive Officer (CEO) Bruce Klatsky, for instance, sits on the board of directors of Human Rights Watch and Business for Social Responsibility. He also played a key role in the Apparel Industry Partnership (AIP) in the mid-1990s.[62] These activities—combined with the notion that *Camisas Modernas* I and *Camisas Modernas* II were considered the "crown jewels" of the Guatemalan *maquiladora* industry (based on their relatively good wages and working conditions)—underscore the company's "progressive" orientation.[63]

The Battle for Recognition, 1989–1992

The *Camisas Modernas* workers knew that this rhetoric did not match the reality of their everyday lives, however. They began organizing in 1989, just one year after the two PVH-owned factories opened up.[64] The workers started this campaign because the company arbitrarily lowered the piece-rate, making them work faster and produce more for the same or even less pay.[65] Low wages, restricted bathroom access, verbal harassment, and an overall feeling of disrespect infuriated the workers, leading some to contact CUSG and UNSITRAGUA for assistance.[66] Company supervisors responded with the "carrot"—a company store and relaxed loan policy—and the "stick"—firing union supporters.[67] Both strategies led the campaign to fall apart.

In 1991, the PVH workers' union, with technical, legal, and financial assistance from CUSG, UNSITRAGUA, AIFLD, and U.S./GLEP, reemerged and filed an application with the Guatemalan Labor Ministry's office, asking for legal recognition.[68] The company replied this time with the full arsenal of co-optive and repressive tactics—offering union members severance payments and bribes of more than a year's salary, providing union staff with different jobs (thereby lowering their wages), creating a company union, and warning to shut down the factory if the union was recognized.[69] One manager also called the union a "guerrilla front" and made death threats against union members.[70] Later that year, an "unknown assailant" shot and wounded Aura Marina Rodríguez, one of the union's key leaders.[71] She luckily survived this attack, but later went into hiding. These events prompted nearly the entire union executive committee and twenty-eight other union members to resign from the factory in late 1991 and early 1992.[72]

PVH's maneuvers nearly destroyed the union. In February 1992, one of the union's remaining executive committee members withdrew its application for legal recognition after she received a bribe from the company.[73] The PVH workers' union survived this setback, electing a new executive committee in March 1992.[74] Several days later, the committee filed a new application for legal recognition. U.S./GLEP, the International Labor Rights Fund (ILRF), the International Ladies Garment Workers Union (ILGWU), the Amalgamated Clothing and Textile Workers Union (ACTWU), and several other unions and solidarity organizations, followed up on the union's action, filing a labor rights petition, after receiving backing of the Guatemalan labor movement, with the Office of the United States Trade Representative (USTR) asking for a formal review of Guatemala's trading privileges under the worker rights provisions of the Generalized System of Preferences (GSP).[75] The threat of losing over $500 million in trade benefits provided the PVH workers' union and its transnational allies with "leverage" and pressured the Guatemalan government into recognizing the first *maquila* union—STECAMOSA—in over six years.[76]

This was a major victory. How was it achieved? Using Keck and Sikkink's model (see chapter one), we can see that STECAMOSA faced two "targets"—the Guatemalan government and PVH (Figure 2.1). It initially had very little leverage over either one. The union, therefore, cultivated ties with labor and solidarity organizations in the United States, establishing a "transnational advocacy network." This network then pressured the U.S. government to review (with the option of suspending) Guatemala's trading benefits and to hold it accountable under the labor rights provisions of the GSP. This strategic decision gave the PVH workers *leverage* and hence, a *relative degree of power*, placing pressure on the Guatemalan government, which feared losing its trading benefits, to recognize STECAMOSA. This was a major feat, illustrating how

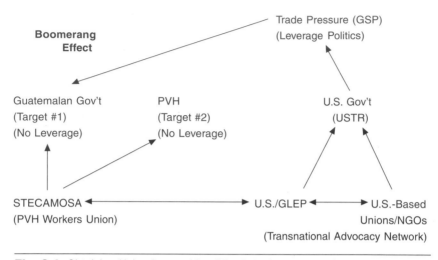

Fig. 2.1 Obtaining Union Recognition (The PVH Campaign, 1989–1992).

transnational advocacy networks, through the use of leverage politics, can create "boomerang effects" and generate social change.

This breakthrough did not mean the campaign was over—far from it. As any labor organizer knows, whether she or he is in Guatemala or the United States, obtaining legal recognition is only half the fight. The other half involves negotiating and ratifying a contract with the employer. This is no easy task—strength and solidarity are the necessary ingredients for achieving this goal.

STECAMOSA lacked both elements after obtaining recognition in September 1992. Intimidation, fear, firings, bribes, and the company's threats to close down the factory weakened the union, making it virtually impossible to organize and sign up new members. To make matters worse, the union's "parent" organization—CUSG—did not have a "strategic organizing" plan for strengthening it and it offered STECAMOSA very little assistance.[77] These two factors—PVH's union-busting tactics and CUSG's minimal level of support—explain why union membership remained low, falling far below the required 25 percent level.[78] Since STECAMOSA did not meet this legal threshold, PVH could not be compelled to begin contract negotiations and so it refused to do so. The company's decision left the union without a contract and over the next three years, it nearly disappeared.[79]

The Fight for the Contract, 1995–1997

In June 1995, however, one of the union's two remaining executive committee members, Mónica Felipe Alvarez, contacted Teresa Casertano, an organizer with

Fig. 2.2 PVH workers' homes–living conditions (September 1996). Photo credit–U.S./LEAP.

the International Textile, Garment, and Leather Workers Federation (ITGLWF), through STECAMOSA's parent organization, the Guatemalan Textile Workers Federation, which is affiliated with CUSG.[80] The ITGLWF is an international trade secretariat that includes garment worker unions from all over the world. It has a regional office in Latin America called the Inter-American Textile and Garment Workers Federation (FITTIVCC/ORI or FITTIV for short). Casertano and FITTIV had just started an organizing project, targeting *maquila* workers, with financial and technical support from the Union of Needletrades, Industrial and Textile Employees (UNITE—the U.S. garment workers union), when Alvarez made her request for assistance.[81]

At this point, STECAMOSA was extremely weak. It was inactive and lacked members. FITTIV, UNITE, U.S./GLEP, and STECAMOSA addressed these issues through a new organizing model that had never been used before in the Guatemalan *maquiladora* industry. Previously most *maquila* workers organized themselves right on the shop-floor—within the factory—and formed unions with very few members. Company supervisors often uncovered these efforts, through *orejas* (spies) and informants, and defeated them by firing union supporters or closing down production and moving someplace else.[82]

FITTIV, UNITE, U.S./GLEP, and STECAMOSA believed that these earlier campaigns failed because they occurred in the "open," "tipping off" company

Fig. 2.3 PVH workers' homes—living conditions (September 1996). Photo credit–U.S./LEAP.

supervisors.[83] To deal with this problem, STECAMOSA organized clandestinely and began slowly recruiting new members in secret—away from the *jefes* (bosses) and *orejas*. Casertano and Alvarez worked tirelessly alongside these new members, teaching them about organizing, negotiating contracts, and obtaining information about the company's production system.[84] They also developed new leaders and carefully planned with them for months before launching a lightening-quick attack, known as an "organizing blitz," to reach the 25 percent level in August 1996.

The blitz lasted three days. During that time period, union members, after ingeniously gathering their fellow workers' addresses, drove around using

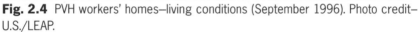

Fig. 2.4 PVH workers' homes—living conditions (September 1996). Photo credit—U.S./LEAP.

borrowed cars and knocked on their doors, conducting "house-visits." During these *casitas* (as they are called), union members asked their "sisters and brothers" about their work experiences, grievances, and fears. They also spoke positively about the union and encouraged them to join it within the privacy and security of their own homes. Nearly every *Camisas Modernas* worker was canvassed using this strategy. Over one hundred signed up as union members during the organizing drive.[85]

On the evening of September 1, 1996, the union held a general assembly meeting and declared that it had passed the 25 percent level.[86] The next day, STECAMOSA members, wearing blue-and-white union T-shirts, carrying balloons, and blowing whistles, entered the factory and handed Yvonne de Sevilla, the company's legal representative, a petition that spelled out their grievances and request to begin contract negotiations with PVH. One STECAMOSA member described Sevilla's response:

> She [Sevilla] and the other supervisors got very angry. They were totally surprised because they had no idea what we were doing. They didn't know about the *casitas* [house visits] and thought the union had disappeared. When we came into the factory that day, we were so happy. We wore our shirts and handed her [Sevilla] the petition. She read it and tore it up. She then said that the company would never negotiate with the union.[87]

Fig. 2.5 PVH workers demonstrate outside the factory gates shortly after passing the legal requirements for official recognition (September 1996). Photo credit— Hannah Frisch.

This statement clearly illustrates the clandestine organizing model caught the company momentarily off-guard. PVH quickly recovered, however. Company supervisors hired armed security guards and lowered the pay of some workers by giving them less work and assigning them to broken machines, indirectly forcing twenty union members to quit. PVH also transferred some production to its sub-contractors in nearby San Pedro Sacatepéquez. The company, moreover, claimed that the union had not reached the 25 percent level and so it refused to begin contract negotiations.[88]

The campaign had turned into a stalemate. The Guatemalan Labor Ministry tried to resolve the impasse by conducting an investigation of the 25 percent issue. Labor Ministry officials examined STECAMOSA's membership list (filed *before* the organizing blitz took place) and the minutes from the union's September 1 general assembly meeting. It concluded that it had only had 135 members.[89] Since the factory employed 664 workers, 166 were needed to reach the 25 percent level. The union actually had 177 members *after* the September 1 meeting, but it did not file, nor was it legally required to, its updated membership list with the Labor Ministry because it feared that PVH would obtain it and begin firing union members.[90] Despite these concerns, STECAMOSA submitted its official membership list on October 18, 1996, but Labor Minister Arnoldo Ortíz Moscoso did not accept it, mistakenly stating that it should have been filed earlier, along with the union's petition to begin contract negotiations.[91]

Before making this decision, Moscoso instructed his officials to conduct a "physical count" of the union's membership. The union and company accepted the basic premise behind this procedure, given certain parameters, as a strategy for resolving the 25 percent issue once and for all. The Labor Ministry suggested that each worker be called, one by one, into the *company's personnel office*, and asked whether or not they were union members. Company supervisors, labor inspectors, and union officials would be present during these proceedings. STECAMOSA rejected this latter stipulation, fearing possible retribution and firing of union members. It favored holding the count in a more "neutral" location and recommended that no one from the company or union be present for the process. The Labor Ministry declined the union's offer, mistakenly declaring that it "opposed a count of its membership." Human Rights Watch tersely stated this was a "misrepresentation of the facts" of the case.[92]

The Labor Ministry was not worried about the "facts," however. On November 11, 1996, it closed the case, claiming that it was "unable to determine the union's membership level," even though STECAMOSA's records clearly showed that over 25 percent of the *Camisas Modernas* workers were, in fact, union members. Human Rights Watch sharply criticized this decision and astutely observed its broader consequences:

> The Labor Ministry did not encourage and facilitate negotiation in its handling of the STECAMOSA petition, shirking its obligations under Guatemalan law to do so. Had the Labor Ministry established the facts, *a precedent would have been set with which many Guatemalan and foreign employers in Guatemala's maquila sector would have been uncomfortable.* By refusing to enforce the law, the labor authorities maintained a status quo in which not one of Guatemala's overseas assembly plants operate with a collective contract and less than a handful tolerate independent unions (emphasis added).[93]

The Labor Ministry's actions displeased STECAMOSA, but not everyone was equally concerned. The U.S. Embassy in Guatemala has been a long-time, stalwart supporter of export-led development and the *maquila* industry.[94] Most Embassy personnel implement U.S. policies that favor free trade and foreign investment, but one official—the labor attaché—has responsibilities that could potentially interfere with that objective. The attaché examines the country's labor rights violations and reviews GSP petitions before forwarding them to the USTR in Washington, D.C. The person holding this position, therefore, could have played a crucial role in the PVH case by pressuring the Labor Ministry to conduct a more thorough investigation of the 25 percent issue.

U.S. Embassy Labor Attaché John Cushing did no such thing, however. He took the government and company's position, stating:

Cushing: The key problem right now is that the number of names [of union members] keeps changing. The company and government simply want the union to follow all correct procedures. The company and union agreed to a head-count [to verify the number of union members], but the union later opposed this. Why did they do that?

Question: Wouldn't this procedure [openly declaring union membership before company officials] be dangerous? Couldn't the workers lose their jobs?

Cushing: What could happen? The company is under a legal injunction that strictly forbids that type of activity.

Question: But the company has indirectly forced workers to quit by placing them on broken machines and lowering their wages and this is prohibited by the injunction.

Cushing: That might be happening. PVH says that they have a code of conduct and that they expect their suppliers to follow it. There have been a number of unsubstantiated allegations in this case. If workers are not happy at PVH they can leave—*they are not slaves.* Those businesses that treat their employees badly will shut down. We know that working conditions are not that great in the *maquilas,* but *this job is better than being a maid* (emphasis added).[95]

Cushing's comments demonstrate that the U.S. Embassy stood squarely behind PVH and the *maquiladora* industry. This position, combined with the company and government's anti-union activities, effectively blocked STECAMOSA from starting contract negotiations with PVH. The union and its transnational allies did not give up, however. STECAMOSA organized a rally outside *Camisas Modernas* II with the Coca-Cola Workers Union, linking together historical and present-day transnational labor solidarity campaigns (see Figure 2.6). Meanwhile, in the United States, U.S./GLEP helped mobilize activists from labor and human rights organizations such as Witness for Peace, the Campaign for Labor Rights, the Resource Center of the Americas, the Network in Solidarity with the Guatemalan People (NISGUA), the Support Team International for Textileras (STITCH), along with many others, to leaflet department stores, like J.C. Penney, that were major buyers of PVH products. These leafleting actions occurred during the high-volume holiday shopping season and they were designed to increase consumer pressure on PVH to begin contract negotiations with STECAMOSA. This strategy paid positive dividends as thousands

Fig. 2.6 PVH workers rally with Coca-Cola union members to seek contract negotiations (September 1996). Photo credit–U.S./LEAP.

of people called, faxed, or e-mailed messages to the company's headquarters in New York City, urging it to negotiate with the union.[96]

PVH did not budge, however. The campaign was still deadlocked because the union had very little, if any, leverage over the company and Guatemalan government. U.S./GLEP addressed this issue, using the "boomerang effect" again, by asking the USTR to continue its GSP review of Guatemala's trading benefits. The USTR temporarily delayed making its decision for several months, indirectly providing STECAMOSA with much needed leverage.[97]

U.S./GLEP's next target was PVH. The small, but savvy labor rights organization obtained information that Human Rights Watch had scheduled a fundraising dinner in November 1996.[98] PVH CEO Bruce Klatsky, a member of the Human Rights Watch board of directors, was the co-chair of the New York City-based event. U.S./GLEP criticized his involvement, given the company's on-going dispute with STECAMOSA in Guatemala. It planned to disrupt the dinner by passing out leaflets highlighting the contradiction between PVH's "socially responsible" image and its actual labor and human rights practices. Klatsky realized that the protest could have negatively affected the company's, along with his own, public image. Sensing potential shame and embarrassment, as well as defeat, Klatsky made a deal with U.S./GLEP. The compromise involved concessions from both sides—U.S./GLEP cancelled the demonstration, while PVH agreed to allow Human Rights Watch to investigate the 25% issue and to respect its findings.[99]

In January 1997, two Human Rights Watch (HRW) investigators completed a nine-day study of the PVH case. After examining the union's membership list and conducting dozens of interviews with company, government, and union officials, they determined that more than 25 percent of all *Camisas Modernas* were, in fact, union members.[100] This finding was a tremendous victory for STECAMOSA. It led Klatsky to finally agree to begin contract negotiations with the union in March 1997.

Talks began one month later, but U.S./GLEP and STECAMOSA still feared that the company might shut down its two factories and shift production overseas or to its other sub-contractors in Guatemala. This was a real possibility because the USTR lifted its review of Guatemala's GSP trading benefits in May 1997, cutting off one source of hard-earned leverage.[101] The union also worried that the company might co-opt its members by creating a *solidarismo* (company-union) organization. As Byron Padilla, STECAMOSA Director of Organizing, said:

> When Bruce Klatsky came here, he told us, 'we are all members of the same family.' We knew that this was not true. He only said that because he wanted our members to leave the union and join the *solidarismo* organization. We knew this organization did not want to negotiate a contract, so we held meetings with our members to tell them what the company was trying to do.[102]

Another union member mentioned, "we had a hard time keeping up our spirits, but we had meetings, *plácticas* (informal talks), and *manifestaciones* (demonstrations) in front of the factory to show the company that we were not giving up."[103]

The union's members and leaders created relatively strong bonds of internal solidarity and cohesion through these activities. Their efforts finally bore fruit. On August 14, 1997, after four months of contract negotiations and eight long years of struggle and sacrifice, the union finally ratified a two-year contract with PVH. The contract included wage increases (11 percent for the first year and 12.5 percent for the second), a grievance procedure, subsidies for transportation, lunch, and child care, clear wage guidelines, resources for an off-site union office, space for union bulletin boards within the factory, and a clause stating that employment and production levels would be maintained as long as "basic productivity levels" were met.[104]

Byron Padilla discussed what happened next:

> We had a party. We danced and were proud that we had won after so many years. This was a hard fight, but we overcame tremendous pressure

and in the end, thanks to our members, leaders, and international supporters, we won. The supervisors thought that this was a disaster. They were angry, but for us, it was beautiful. We had finally won.[105]

Mónica Felipe Alvarez, STECAMOSA General Secretary for most of the 1995–1997 campaign, spoke about the wider implications of this victory:

We are now the best paid workers in the *maquila* sector, but the most important thing about achieving this contract is that it opens up a new space for us and for the workers in other *maquila* factories.[106]

As this statement indicates, the PVH workers' triumph was a major achievement for them, as well as for Guatemala's eighty thousand *maquiladora* workers. Their victory was widely praised within the newly emerging contemporary anti-sweatshop movement. The PVH workers overcame great odds and ratified the only contract in the entire Guatemalan *maquila* industry. How did they and their transnational allies accomplish this remarkable feat?

Like the 1991–1992 campaign for recognition, the PVH workers' union faced two targets—one "primary" one (PVH) and the other "secondary" (the Guatemalan government). It had very little leverage over both when the contract negotiation drive began in 1995. STECAMOSA and its transnational allies obtained power (or leverage) using five types of "politics"—information, symbolic, leverage, accountability, and organization-building. The latter strategy involves strengthening the capability and viability, through financial and technical assistance, of "domestic non-state actors" (e.g., unions). Keck and Sikkink overlook organization-building politics because they seemingly assume that transnational advocacy networks can independently generate social change for relatively "powerless" organizations.[107]

This model, while useful, contains some flaws and weaknesses. During the 1989–1992 campaign for legal recognition, for instance, labor, solidarity, and human rights organizations (the "transnational advocacy network") within the United States successfully pressured the Guatemalan government into recognizing STECAMOSA. The union was weak, however. It and the transnational advocacy network had no leverage over the primary target—PVH. This situation made contract negotiations impossible.

The union languished for several years before the ITGLWF, UNITE, and U.S./GLEP developed a clandestine organizing model to strengthen it in 1995. The newly rejuvenated union could not, however, pressure PVH, *by itself*, to begin contract negotiations. At this point, U.S./GLEP and other solidarity organizations began holding demonstrations, passing out informational leaflets and holding up signs and posters that called symbolic attention to the plight of PVH workers (see Figure 2.7). Information and symbolic politics were only marginally effective, however. Renewed GSP pressure and attacks on the

Fig. 2.7 U.S. labor rights activists protest PVH labor rights practices in the Mid-West (January 1997). Photo credit–David Bryden. Photo appears in US/LEAP, *Fighting for Worker Justice in the Global Economy* (10 Years of Leadership) (1997), p. 6.

company's "socially responsible" image, which highlighted the glaring contradiction between PVH's human rights violations and its involvement with human rights organizations, in contrast, did have an impact. These strategies gave the union and the transnational advocacy network leverage over both targets—"material" leverage (potential loss of trading benefits) over the Guatemalan government and "moral" leverage over PVH.

Gaining moral leverage, as Keck and Sikkink point out, can be crucial because "target actors" (governments, corporations, etc.) want the public to think highly of them.[108] Corporations, for instance, spend millions of dollars every year on advertising, telling consumers, "image is everything," or that their products are recyclable or that they participate in human rights, environmental, or women's organizations. When transnational advocacy networks disrupt these "tropes" by pointing out the "accountability gap" between image and reality, the financial damage can be enormous. Sensing this kind of impact, as well as public humiliation, PVH capitulated and began contract negotiations with STECAMOSA. Contract talks were difficult, but the union and transnational advocacy network were strong and maintained close ties with each other. The PVH workers finally got what they wanted—better wages and working conditions, respect, dignity, and more opportunities for their children (see Figure 2.8).

The outcome of the recognition and contract phases of the PVH campaign illustrate that transnational advocacy networks can autonomously achieve "limited" change on behalf of domestic non-state actors. In the 1989–1992 campaign, for instance, the transnational advocacy network was strong, but the union was weak. What was the end result of these two factors? The union obtained recognition, but it could not negotiate a contract. In the 1995–1997 campaign, the union was much stronger and its ties with the transnational advocacy network were solid. What was the result this time around? The union ratified a two-year contract that included better wages and working conditions. These two outcomes indicate that the strength of the union made a difference and that organization-building politics was perhaps *the* decisive factor in the contract negotiation phase of the campaign.

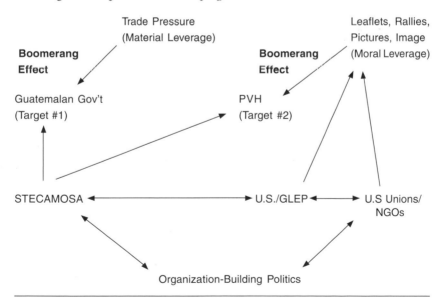

Fig. 2.8 Negotiating the Contract (The PVH Campaign, 1995–1997).

The broader lesson, I believe, of this campaign is that it shows that transnational advocacy networks and domestic non-state actors can have a more "far-reaching" (better wages and working conditions, not just legal recognition) impact when they both have strength and close links with each other. As FITTIV Representative Bruce Fieldman said:

> Solidarity organizations can only do so much. For real change to take place the workers have to be committed and they have to be organized. When you have a strong union working with solidarity organizations, the chances are more likely that you will succeed.[109]

The Day of Reckoning: December 11, 1998

The PVH workers were victorious, but only for a brief moment. On December 11, 1998, just fifteen months after they signed their two-year contract, *Camisas Modernas* shut down. The company claimed the loss of a "major client" left it "no other choice." Fending off criticisms from anti-sweatshop activists that "union-busting" was the driving factor, PVH Vice-Chairperson Allen Sirkin, explained the company's unexpected decision in the following manner:

> This was a very difficult and painful step for our company, but one that was unavoidable. Unfortunately, this year [1998] we lost a major dress shirt customer. This was the purchase of the Mercantile Group by Dillard's department stores who do not carry our dress shirts. This loss of volume required PVH to reassess its sourcing plan. We cut back with several contractors, but also decided that we had to further reduce our owned capacity. The commitment to keep owned factories open is difficult to maintain in any erratic, declining market where flexibility is needed. We had only three fully-owned factories and are committed to our last remaining facility in Alabama and to be fair, we selected the last opened plant, unfortunately, *Camisas Modernas*.
>
> Contrary to what you have been told, the closing decision was not influenced at all by the presence of the union in that factory. We have enjoyed a very amiable relationship with the union. The officials have been very cooperative and extremely reasonable. It's unfortunate that business conditions are not better. We regret that this step had to be taken, but our company had *no choice if we are to remain healthy and stay in business* (emphasis added).[110]

Sirkin's comments seem quite straight-forward, even remorseful ("it's not our fault, the market 'made' us do it"), but how accurate were they? Upon examining PVH's 1998 Annual Report, U.S./GLEP found that its profits on men's dress shirts, which were produced at *Camisas Modernas, increased* from $45 million to $50 million. The report also showed that just $15 million (1.6 percent) of the company's $910 million sales volume in 1997 came from Mercantile Stores.[111]

U.S./GLEP also discovered that after PVH closed down *Camisas Modernas*, the company expanded production with four sub-contracting factories— *Corporación Mercantil del Caribe* (CMC), *Cardiz*, *Bluca*, and *Camisas Miltas Alpas*. U.S./GLEP found that whereas *Camisas Modernas* workers earned about nine dollars a day, worked forty-four hours a week, and had proper ventilation, protective equipment, on-site medical care, potable water, and a sufficient number of bathrooms, workers at *CMC, Cardiz,* and *Bluca* only received five dollars a day, worked fifty-five hours a week, and had none of the health and safety measures that the *Camisas Modernas* workers enjoyed.

The wages and working conditions within these four sub-contracting factories, along with the company's annual report, contradict PVH's claim that it had "no other choice" but to close down *Camisas Modernas*. PVH was, in fact, doing quite well in 1998—profits and sale of men's dress shirts had gone up and company CEO Bruce Klatsky earned $2 million for the year. Why, then, did PVH close down *Camisas Modernas*? Byron Padilla answered this question:

> The company never really wanted us here. They fired workers, gave them less work, and hired armed guards to eliminate the union. In 1997, they were forced to negotiate with the union, but they never accepted it as a real [legitimate] force. So in 1998 they began moving some production and equipment to other factories and finally they totally shut down. They moved to these other factories because the wages were much lower and the working conditions were much worse. It's really not that difficult to understand, it's very easy to see what they were doing.[112]

U.S./GLEP Executive Director Stephen Coats echoed these sentiments:

> The true facts are simple: PVH shut down its high-wage union factory in Guatemala to concentrate production at sweatshops that pay poverty wages. Indeed, PVH is continuing to produce in Guatemala, but at a factory (sic) that pays substantially less than what was paid to PVH union members. Last year [1997] PVH took a big step toward setting standards for the apparel industry in Guatemala. Now it has taken an even bigger step back.[113]

As these comments make clear, PVH did not close *Camisas Modernas* because of "erratic, declining markets." The company essentially dismantled the factory in order to lower production costs and get rid of the union.

The Fight To Reopen The Factory, January–July 1999

The union did not disappear, however. Some members held a spontaneous rally outside the factory immediately after it was shut down. STECAMOSA took this action to stop PVH from selling off its sewing machines and other equipment, a decision that would have forestalled a quick re-opening of the factory. In January 1999, the union organized several more protests outside the factory. On three separate occasions, three hundred former *Camisas Modernas* workers blocked roads near the factory.[114] As these actions were taking place, CUSG filed an *amparo* (legal action) charging PVH for not filing a legally mandated thirty-day notice before shutting down *Camisas Modernas*. The company later acknowledged this violation and stated that it had not provided union leaders, pregnant workers, and nursing mothers with their proper severance pay.[115]

Despite admitting these infractions, PVH did not reopen the factory. The company's intransigence led STECAMOSA to organize a twenty-four-hour, seven-day a week vigil outside the factory. Given the harsh economic reality that most Guatemalan workers face every single day, the vast majority of *Camisas Modernas* workers did not join the round-the-clock protest. These workers accepted their severance payments and began looking for new jobs. A "core group" of approximately fifty workers remained active within the union. They took shifts (sometimes with their children) and maintained the vigil.

As the protest continued in Guatemala over the first few months of 1999, U.S./GLEP and other solidarity organizations (e.g., STITCH, Campaign for Labor Rights, NISGUA, etc.) organized leafleting actions and rallies in San Francisco, Eugene, Portland, Des Moines, New York City, Chicago, Los Angeles, Boston, Hamilton, Ontario, and many other cities across the United States and Canada.[116] The United Students Against Sweatshops (USAS) also called for a National Student Week of Action Against PVH in April 1999. Students from the University of North Carolina (Chapel Hill), Purdue, Indiana University, the University of California, Santa Barbara (UCSB), and many other campuses passed out flyers and set up "informational tables" with petitions about the PVH campaign. Hundreds of students, consumers, and concerned citizens took this information and sent letters, faxes, or e-mails to PVH, asking it to reopen *Camisas Modernas*.[117]

Most of the letters and petitions highlighted the fact that PVH had signed and violated the Apparel Industry Partnership's (AIP), "Workplace Code of Conduct," which states, "employers shall recognize and respect the right of employees to freedom of association and collective bargaining." U.S./GLEP stated that the company could not call itself a "leader" of the anti-sweatshop movement when it was, in fact, using sweatshop labor. As Stephen Coats said:

As a member of the Fair Labor Association (FLA) [the organization cre-ated to oversee compliance with the AIP Code of Conduct], PVH prom-ised the White House, its shareholders, and the public that it would help lead an industry-wide effort to reverse the race to the bottom in this industry and set a floor of decency for the workers that sew the clothes we wear. In Guatemala, PVH has made a mockery of this promise.[118]

The leafleting actions and the new attacks on the company's "socially re-sponsible" image did not influence PVH. *Camisas Modernas* remained closed, but the company did state that it would look for a new buyer that would rehire workers, recognize STECAMOSA, and negotiate a new contract. This proposal gave the union renewed hope.

PVH dragged its feet over the next several weeks. The campaign, therefore, responded boldly. On June 15, 1999, STECAMOSA General Secretary Marisol López personally delivered a stinging report issued by U.S./GLEP (renamed the United States/Labor Education in the Americas Project or U.S./LEAP dur-ing this time period), USAS, and the People of Faith Network, an alliance of religious activist groups, outlining labor rights violations at PVH's four sub-contracting facilities, to Bruce Klatsky. She also asked him for permission to speak at the company's annual shareholder meeting in New York City on June 17. Klatsky rejected her request. Later that same day, the New York City-based Global Sweatshop Coalition held a protest outside the PVH shareholder meet-ing where López made a statement, asking the company to reopen *Camisas Modernas*. During the demonstration, the Global Sweatshop Coalition gave its annual "golden rat" award to Bruce Klatsky for the company's anti-union ac-tivities (see Figure 2.9).[119]

The day after the protest, López's husband, Marío Naves, received a death threat from a caller, saying that she and the STECAMOSA members holding the vigil should immediately stop their organizing activities or they all would be killed.[120] U.S./LEAP filed a new labor rights petition, based on the report that López gave to Klatsky, with the USTR, asking it to review Guatemala's GSP benefits, later that same day.

These strategies, which combined information (leafleting, the investigative report on PVH's four sub-contractors); symbolic (the "golden rat" award); lev-erage (GSP pressure and attacks on the company's image); and accountability politics (highlighting the gap between PVH's involvement in "anti-sweatshop" organizations while it uses sweatshop labor in Guatemala) were ultimately unsuccessful. The factory remained shut down. Why wasn't it reopened?

Corruption and internal divisions within STECAMOSA are two possible explanations. Marisol López, along with some of the union's other leaders, ended the vigil outside the factory on July 9, 1999. This action came after these individuals

Fig. 2.9 PVH CEO Bruce Klatsky was presented with the "Golden Rat" award by the Global Sweatshop Coalition outside of PVH stockholders' meeting in New York City (June 17, 1999). Photo credit–Diane Greene Leaf. Photo appears in U.S./LEAP Newsletter (August 1999), p. 1.

received rather large severance payments, which some later called "bribes" (*mordidas*), from PVH.[121] This controversial decision hit the remaining active union members hard. Many walked away feeling "angry and confused," while a smaller contingent adopted a different approach. This group condemned López, along with several other union leaders, and established a loose, ad-hoc committee to continue the fight to reopen the factory.

One worker from this committee described how she felt after she heard López called off the vigil:

> I was really angry and surprised. We struggled for seven months to re-open the factory and for six years to negotiate a contract and now we have nothing. I think that some of the members of the *junta directiva* [executive committee] and the Secretary-General [López] are traitors. I don't understand what they did. They said that they were fighting for us and working for social justice, but then they took the *mordidas* and now there is nothing left inside the factory. They [PVH] sold all the machines.[122]

Another former *Camisaş Modernas* worker talked about López's actions:

Many members thought that something was wrong before the factory closed. Marisol made *pactos* (deals) with company supervisors that made us suspicious. For example, after Hurricane Mitch [in October 1998], the company said that things were not going too well and so it fired some workers. Another time, the company fired some workers and moved others around inside the factory and lowered their salaries [wages]. What did Marisol do? Nothing. She allowed the company to do what it wanted.[123]

These statements indicate some significant conflicts existed within STECAMOSA before and after the factory shut down. One former union member discussed this issue:

The problems began in 1997 after Marisol replaced Mónica [Felipe Alvarez] as Secretary-General. Marisol had a different style than her. She was enthusiastic and committed when she began, but later she "crossed-over" and took sides with the company.[124]

Other representatives from U.S./LEAP and COVERCO,[125] a Guatemalan-based independent monitoring group, privately expressed similar opinions about López, stating that she received "bad advice" about handling firings and other work-place related grievances from CUSG. CUSG Secretary-General Juan Francisco Alfaro denied these accusations, claiming STECAMOSA was not internally divided.[126] STECAMOSA Director of Organizing Byron Padilla confirmed these conflicts existed, however:

This is a very sensitive issue. There were problems within the union. Some members did not trust the Secretary-General [López]. They thought that she was too close with the supervisors. After the factory closed down, some members accepted their severance payments and did not participate in the *paro* [vigil]. This made the union weaker. I think that if we didn't have these problems, then the factory *might* be open today. We had support from unions and students in the United States, but it was not enough.[127] [emphasis added]

Padilla's comments support my earlier argument that transnational advocacy networks can only achieve limited social change without strong domestic non-state actors. During this segment of the campaign, for instance, U.S./LEAP and other labor, human rights, and solidarity organizations in the United States used a variety of strategies or politics (mentioned above) to put pressure on PVH and the Guatemalan government to reopen the *Camisas Modernas* factory. They did not produce a more favorable outcome because the union was slowly falling apart. To be sure, the company bears the most responsibility for the final result, but the union's lack of strength cannot be ignored.

Table 2.2 The PVH Campaign, 1989–1999

Campaign Phase	Union Strength	Level of Unity Within TAN	Types of Politics (Strategies)	Outcome
1989–1992 (#1)	Low	High	Material Leverage (GSP)	Union Recognition
1995–1997 (#2)	High	High	Org.-Building, Material and Moral Leverage	Two-year Contract
1998–1999 (#3)	Low	High	Moral Leverage	Factory Closure

Analysis: Putting The Pieces Together

The PVH workers' movement was a roller-coaster affair. There were victories and defeats that occurred during different phases of the campaign. Table 2.2 illustrates the stages of the campaign. In phase one, the union was weak and it had very little influence over the two main targets—PVH and the Guatemalan government. U.S./GLEP and other U.S.-based labor unions and solidarity organizations (the "transnational advocacy network"), nevertheless, gained "material" leverage through the GSP review process, pressuring the Guatemalan government into recognizing STECAMOSA. The union did not have enough members, however, and so it could not compel PVH to begin contract negotiations.

U.S./GLEP, UNITE, and the ITGLWF recognized the union's weaknesses. They developed a clandestine organizing model that strengthened it by expanding its membership base during phase two of the campaign. Organization-building politics were not enough, however. Trade pressure and attacks on the company's "socially responsible" image provided STECAMOSA and the transnational advocacy network with "material" and "moral" leverage, prompting PVH to finally agree to start contract negotiations with the union. The talks took some time, but the union remained strong and eventually signed a collective bargaining agreement with PVH. This was an astonishing victory that was achieved as a result of the strength of the union, the high degree of unity within the transnational advocacy network (TAN), and the skillful use of leverage-based politics.

During the third phase of the campaign, STECAMOSA and the union used a wide variety of strategies—leafleting, investigative reports, protests, symbolic awards, trade pressure, and a new offensive on the company's image—but they all failed for two reasons—inefficient union leadership and capital mobility. Without a strong union, the TAN could not, by itself, work any "miracles" like it did during the 1991–1992 drive for legal recognition. GSP pressure, for instance, was not as effective this time around because the USTR lifted Guatemala's review status in May 1997, thus taking away a crucial source of material leverage. The TAN had moral leverage over PVH, but that was not enough.

The TAN could have obtained material leverage by calling for a boycott of PVH, but it is not likely that this strategy would have been successful given the internal problems within STECAMOSA. Without a stronger union and more leverage, U.S./LEAP and the other labor and solidarity organizations in the United States, Canada, and Europe could only do so much. This phase of the campaign ended unsuccessfully. The factory remained shut down and a new buyer was never found.

Based on this "final" outcome, the PVH campaigns looks like a dismal failure. It was perhaps. Five hundred workers lost their jobs. The only (until recently) unionized factory with a collective bargaining agreement in the entire Guatemalan *maquiladora* industry was closed down.[128] On a broader level, this was a devastating blow for *maquila* workers throughout the entire Central American region. Nonetheless, one cannot forget that the campaign produced some important victories—wages and working conditions were improved, respect and dignity were obtained, and a sense of hope was created.

Seen from this perspective, the PVH campaign cannot be simply classified as a clear-cut "victory" or a "defeat." It was both. I think that this is a realistic interpretation that recognizes the campaign's complexity and nuances. The campaign's mixed outcomes provide activists and academics with many lessons. Two crucial ones include:

- Strong domestic non-state actors and well-unified TANs, working in collaboration with each other, are more likely to generate more "substantial" social change (e.g., a collective bargaining agreement with better wages and working conditions). This situation corresponds with the second phase of the PVH campaign.
- Weak domestic non-state actors and well-unified TANs can achieve "limited" social change (e.g., union recognition), but this may not occur without some degree of material leverage. Moral leverage is not enough. This scenario corresponds with the first and third phases of the PVH campaign.

I believe that these two points highlight this observation: strong garment worker unions, whether they are in the developed or developing world, are essential for eliminating sweatshops and overcoming the "race to the bottom." When STECAMOSA was weak, for instance, it could not improve the wages and working conditions of its members. After the union gained strength, it managed to do so before it crumbled. I think that the PVH campaign illustrates that strong unions can make a major difference and that the anti-sweatshop movement should make bolstering them one of its highest priorities.

Conclusion

The *Camisas Modernas* workers struggled for two years before they obtained legal recognition. They continued fighting for six more years until they signed one of the few contracts that have ever been negotiated in the Guatemalan *maquiladora* industry. PVH eventually closed *Camisas Modernas*. STECAMOSA and the transnational advocacy network worked hard for several months, but the factory never reopened.

After coming across that clandestine meeting behind the *tienda* and talking and spending time with some of the organizers of this campaign, I have great respect for what they achieved. These "sweatshop warriors" (in Mirian Ching Yoon Louie's words) made great sacrifices and literally put their lives on the line for themselves and their loved ones. They challenged one of the most powerful transnational corporations in the world and accomplished something intangible (greater self-esteem/personal empowerment) that no one could ever take away. They also gained better wages and working conditions.

These victories were not sustained over time, however. Until cross-border labor solidarity campaigns target entire company production systems or geographical regions, positive results will be ephemeral. Sweatshop labor practices will persist. Those are the broader implications of the PVH case. How can successful campaigns be maintained and their scope widened over time? The next chapter raises and addresses that question.

3

The Salvadoran Maquiladora Industry and Cross-Border Labor Solidarity
Bridging the Gap Between Image and Reality

Mandarin International and the Gap Campaign

The San Marcos Free Trade Zone lies just outside the southern edge of San Salvador. The *Zona* includes fifteen *maquiladora* factories and ten thousand workers. Low wages and poor working conditions inside one of these plants—named Mandarin International—sparked two "general" strikes in 1995 that crippled production within the entire free trade zone. The Mandarin International Workers Union (*Sindicato de Empresa de Trabajadores de Mandarín Internacional*—SETMI) organized the work stoppages, hoping that they would bring the Taiwanese-owned company to the negotiating table.

That did not happen. Mandarin vigorously opposed the strikes as well as the overall unionization campaign. Company supervisors, for instance, fired hundreds of workers and physically assaulted several union members. These repressive strategies triggered widespread media attention, generating concerns about the wages and working conditions in El Salvador's booming *maquiladora* industry. Before the end of the country's violent twelve-year civil war in 1992, there were very few *maquila* factories in El Salvador. In the mid-1990s, as political conditions shifted, the industry took off and became the country's largest source of exports, surpassing the long-influential and powerful coffee industry. The United States government praised these trends and on the eve of the *huelgas* (strikes) at Mandarin, Salvadoran President Armando Calderón Sol, a member of the neoliberal, right-wing ARENA (Nationalist Republican Alliance) party, stated that he wanted to turn El Salvador into "one big free trade zone."[1]

While some U.S. garment manufacturers like the Gap and Liz Claiborne may have found this statement appealing, most *maquila* workers took a more nuanced approach, neither condemning nor praising the jobs the industry created. As one woman said:

> I was happy when I first started working for the *maquila*. I had two children and I needed to work. The salary was sufficient, but our supervisors made us work overtime and they never paid us. If we didn't work hard enough, they would yell at us. I began to feel like one of the machines inside the factory and so I left and went to look for a new job. I found one, but it was the same. They didn't yell as much, but I never earned enough money.[2]

Sentiments like this spawned numerous *maquila* union organizing drives in the early and mid-1990s, but most failed. The result was that, when the strikes took place at Mandarin, there were less than a handful of unions and no collective bargaining agreements in the country's six free trade zones, which employ over twenty-five thousand workers. The stakes surrounding the Mandarin campaign, therefore, were very high.

SETMI was initially quite strong. The union had several hundred members, but firings, physical intimidation, and fear led it to fall just short of the required legal threshold to begin contract negotiations. Faced with an anti-union employer and unsympathetic government, SETMI organized two strikes that shut down the whole San Marcos Free Trade Zone. The company responded with massive force, firing all the union's members. SETMI was essentially eliminated through these measures.[3] By mid-1995, the campaign looked like it was over.

In July 1995, the National Labor Committee (NLC), a U.S.-based labor rights organization with deep, long-standing ties with Salvadoran labor and human rights groups, began targeting Mandarin's largest supplier, the Gap, for labor rights violations. The NLC highlighted, through leafleting actions, videos, and worker testimonies, the "gap" between the company's "socially responsible" image and the reality that its workers faced in El Salvador. These savvy tactics breathed new life into the campaign. The Gap denied all allegations of wrongdoing and claimed that its code of conduct provided its workers with certain labor rights, such as the right to organize. The NLC, along with human rights, labor, and women's organizations in El Salvador, challenged the Gap's assertions and called on it to rehire the fired union members and to allow "independent monitors" to inspect whether or not Mandarin was complying with Salvadoran labor law and the company's code of conduct.

The NLC's relentless public relations campaign backed the Gap into a corner, leading it to change its position. It briefly suspended its contract with Mandarin and requested that the company and the Salvadoran government protect basic labor rights. Finally, in March 1996, after more firings, foot-dragging, and pressure from the NLC and the Gap, Mandarin backed down and signed a historic independent monitoring agreement with four Salvadoran-based organizations. The Independent Monitoring Group of El Salvador (*Grupo Monitoreo Independiente de El Salvador*—GMIES) emerged from the agreement to monitor Mandarin's compliance with Salvadoran labor laws and the Gap's code of conduct.

This was a tremendous victory because it marked the first time that a garment manufacturer or retailer had agreed to allow independent monitors to inspect and investigate its contracting shops. By all accounts, independent monitoring has been relatively successful so far—working conditions, for instance, have improved within Mandarin over the past five years, but instead of "showcasing" the factory for the *maquiladora* industry, it remains highly fortified behind closed doors.

I had heard many stories from workers and activists that free trade zones and *maquila* factories resemble "panoptic-like" prisons, but nothing prepared me for the "real thing." While waiting for an interview with Pedro Mancíllas, Mandarin's corporate director, I observed the free trade zone's security guards carrying shotguns, Mandarin's guards armed with hand-guns, a pistol-packing company supervisor, plain-clothes cops wearing gun holsters and talking on cell phones, civilian police officers with side-arms, and traffic officers wielding batons. Six different levels of security blocked the "masses" (including me) from casually entering the San Marcos free trade zone.

After making these mental notes and absorbing the landscape's surreal atmosphere, I sat down (thinking quizzically about Foucault's *Discipline and Punish*) on the hot concrete pavement. Thirty minutes passed before Mancíllas' car pulled up. The free trade zone's security officers opened the gates and waved him through. He finally came out and told me, "let's go inside." We passed through several locked doors before entering Mancíllas' spacious, air-conditioned office where he talked about why the company hired so many guards after signing the independent monitoring agreement:

> We have nothing to hide, but we have to watch out for people that do not tell the truth because they can hurt the country, the industry, and the workers. I know that some of these groups in the United States, like the National Labor Committee, say that they are telling the truth, but in 1995 they lied about what was happening in the factory. They said that we fired pregnant workers, hired children, and did other things that weren't true. At first we did not want to sign the monitoring agreement, but we didn't have much choice. So we signed it and now *everything* is better. There are a lot fewer problems than we had before (italics added).[4]

SETMI leaders and members view these issues in a less sanguine manner. While they acknowledge the positive impact of independent monitoring, they pointedly claim that "everything" is *not* better. Wages, for example, remain very low. SETMI feels that the only way that they can be increased is through collective bargaining. As the union's secretary of organization said:

> We support independent monitoring and have good relations with GMIES. We think that they have done good work, but there are some things that they cannot do. For example, they cannot improve our wages. That is *our* responsibility, but we cannot do that right now because we do not have a contract. We need a contract, but we do not have enough members right now (emphasis added).[5]

This point illustrates an on-going debate within the anti-sweatshop movement between independent monitoring and collective bargaining. As chapter 1 indicated, some labor and human rights organizations contend that independent monitoring can effectively combat low wages and poor working conditions, especially in authoritarian societies where labor laws are not properly enforced and unionization efforts are routinely crushed. Most labor unions hold a similar viewpoint—they generally support independent monitoring, under certain conditions, but some fear that this strategy will undercut their legitimacy and create confusion and complacency among workers.

The discussion revolving around these two strategies is crucial because it raises a larger question—how can workers and labor, human rights, and women's organizations challenge sweatshop labor practices over the long-haul? Is independent monitoring, collective bargaining, or some other strategy more effective? In the Gap case, the Mandarin workers took an important step toward answering these questions by improving their working conditions, but their wages did not increase. These results indicate that it is difficult to state whether or not independent monitoring or collective bargaining is *the* definitive solution for creating meaningful, sustained social change in the global apparel industry. Both strategies, I believe, are useful, but unfortunately the two key groups (the NLC and UNITE) involved in the Gap campaign cast them in stark "either–or" terms. This dualistic outlook generated intense conflict between these actors, making deeper progress at Mandarin virtually impossible.

The Gap campaign's final results thus were rather mixed. On the one hand, the Mandarin workers obtained some significant achievements through independent monitoring. The first half of this chapter describes and explains how these gains were made. On the other hand, internal divisions between the actors within the transnational activist network limited the scope of these accomplishments. The dynamics surrounding this conflict are analyzed in the second half of the chapter. Before embarking on these tasks, however, I briefly examine the history and trajectory of the Salvadoran labor movement and the *maquiladora* industry. This overview, I believe, is critical for understanding the broader context of the Gap campaign.

The Salvadoran Labor Movement, 1900–2000

The Salvadoran labor movement emerged during the late nineteenth and early twentieth centuries. These initial organizations were based on mutual assistance and were fairly apolitical. During the conservative (pro-coffee oligarchy, pro-United States) Meléndez-Quiñónez dynasty (1913–1927), the labor movement became more militant and class-conscious. Workers organized strikes and demonstrations, and established the country's first nation-wide labor organization, the Regional Federation of Salvadoran Workers (*Federación Regional de Trabajadores de El Salvador*—FRTS) in 1924. The FRTS grew fairly rapidly in the late 1920s and formed close ties with the Salvadoran Communist Party (*Partido Comunista de El Salvador*—PCS) in 1930.[6]

In the early 1930s, coffee prices declined sharply, sparking high unemployment and the radicalization of the rural and urban working class. Despite government repression, membership within the FRTS and PCS grew dramatically. After a "liberal" president was overthrown and PCS electoral victories were overturned through fraud, an armed popular insurrection, led by indigenous people, farm workers, students, and FRTS and PCS activists, against the military dictatorship of General Maximilano Hernández Martínez erupted on January 22, 1932.[7] The military viciously crushed this short-lived uprising, killing 15,000–30,000 people. The *matanza* (massacre), as it became known, eliminated the labor movement over the next decade.[8]

Martínez was finally overthrown in 1944, but El Salvador remained in the hands of the military and coffee oligarchy.[9] Over the next twenty five years, very little space existed for labor organizing, although some unions from a wide variety of ideological and political perspectives were established during that time period.[10] In the early 1970s, a coalition of moderate and leftist political parties was created. It won the 1972 presidential election, but the ruling, pro-military Party of National Conciliation (*Partido de Conciliación Nacional*—PCN) threw out the results and held onto power.[11] This decision generated widespread outrage, facilitating the rise of five "popular/revolutionary" organizations.[12]

These organizations combined civil disobedience with armed struggle. They gained increasing popularity in the mid-1970s, organizing massive demonstrations and strikes.[13] While all five organizations maintained ties with broad-based "popular front" groups of workers, students, teachers, women, and religious activists, only three worked directly with the labor movement. The Popular Liberation Forces (FPL), for instance, was linked with the Revolutionary

Table 3.1 Links Between Labor and Revolutionary Movement Organizations, 1970–1980

Labor Federation	Popular/Revolutionary Organization	Year Labor Federation Established
Revolutionary Trade Union Federation (FSR)	Popular Liberation Forces (FPL)	1979
National Federation of Salvadoran Workers (FENASTRAS)	National Resistance (RN)	1972
Unitary Trade Union Federation of El Salvador (FUSS)	Salvadoran Communist Party (PCS)	1965

Trade Union Federation (FSR), the National Resistance (RN) with the National Federation of Salvadoran Workers (FENASTRAS), and the Salvadoran Communist Party (PCS) with the Unitary Trade Union Federation of (FUSS) (see Table 3.1).[14] FENASTRAS was, arguably, the largest, most militant, and well-respected federation among these three organizations.[15]

The rapid development of the popular and revolutionary movements in the middle and late 1970s sparked a violent backlash.[16] The armed forces and paramilitary death squads responded with arrest, torture, and assassination, but these tactics did not stifle dissent; they actually intensified it.[17] In October 1979, a "revolutionary junta," which included military officials, social democrats, and members from the moderate Christian Democratic Party (PDC), took power. The Salvadoran military and conservative elements within the PDC, with the blessing of the United States, gained control of the junta before it could carry out progressive socioeconomic reforms and halt human rights abuses, however.[18] This decision indirectly facilitated the unification of the five popular/revolutionary movement organizations in January 1980.[19]

On January 22, 1980, exactly forty-eight years after the failed 1932 popular insurrection, two hundred thousand people marched in the largest protest in Salvadoran history. The military fired into the crowd, killing nearly fifty and injuring hundreds.[20] Three months later, Archbishop Oscar Romero, a disciple of non-violence, peace, and reconciliation, was assassinated while celebrating mass.[21] His death unleashed an intense cycle of repression and resistance that left tens of thousands of people dead between 1980 and 1983.[22] During that time period, five thousand labor activists were killed and leftist labor federations like FENASTRAS, FUSS, and the FSR were driven underground.[23]

Over the next few years, as the civil war raged on between the military and the Farabundo Martí National Liberation Front (FMLN), labor organizations from across the ideological spectrum resurfaced (see Table 3.2). The AFL-CIO's

Table 3.2 The Salvadoran Labor Movement, 1980–1992

Umbrella Organization/Labor Federation	Key Members	Ideological Perspective	Year Established
Democratic Popular Unity (UPD) (AIFLD-linked)	Construction and Transport Workers Federation (FESINCONSTRANS), Salvadoran Communal Union (UCS), CTS	Center-Right (initially)	1980
General Confederation of Labor (CGT)	N/A	Conservative	1983
Democratic Workers Central (CTD) (AIFLD-linked)	N/A	Center-Right	1984
National Unity of Salvadoran Workers (UNTS)	CTS, UPD, FENASTRAS, FUSS	Center-Left	1986
National Union of Workers and Campesinos (UNOC) (AIFLD-linked)	FESINCONSTRANS, UCS, UPD, CTS, CTD	Center-Right	1986

regional arm, the American Institute for Free Labor Development (AIFLD), for instance, established and funded a coalition of centrist-oriented unions, known as the Democratic Popular Unity (*Unidad Popular Democrática*—UPD), which initially included the Salvadoran Workers Central (*Central de Trabajadores Salvadoreños*—CTS), a labor federation affiliated with the Christian Democratic Latin American Confederation of Workers (CLAT).[24] The UPD originally had close ties with José Napoleón Duarte's ruling Christian Democratic government in the early 1980s, but the party's strong links with the military and the economic elite created a rift between these two organizations.[25] AIFLD exacerbated this split by demanding that UPD affiliates join the "non-political" (pro-U.S.) Democratic Workers Central (*Central de Trabajadores Demócraticos*—CTD) in the mid-1980s.[26]

AIFLD's policies generated intense controversy, crippling the CTD and facilitating a political shift within the UPD.[27] In 1986, the UPD and CTS, along with the vast majority of the country's centrist and leftist unions, joined the National Unity of Salvadoran Workers (*Unidad Nacional de Trabajadores Salvadoreños*—UNTS).[28] The UNTS quickly became the country's leading opposition force, organizing huge demonstrations, calling for peace negotiations, and demanding AIFLD's expulsion from El Salvador for its "shameful practices."[29] AIFLD dangerously responded, given the country's polarized political climate, that the UNTS was a "guerrilla front."[30] It created the National Union of Workers and Campesinos (*Unión Nacional de Trabajadores y Campesinos*—UNOC), which included the CTD and the conservative General Confederation of Labor (*Confederación General de Trabajo*—CGT), an extremely small, pro-government federation formed in 1983, as "center-right" alternative to the UNTS in 1986.[31] UNOC had very close ties with the PDC. The UPD and CTS, for different reasons, eventually left the UNTS and joined UNOC in the late 1980s.[32]

During this time period, peace negotiations, which began in the mid-1980s, resumed. As the deliberations moved forward, the civil war continued. On October 31, 1989, the military bombed the offices of FENASTRAS, killing ten of its key leaders.[33] Two weeks later the FMLN launched its so-called "final offensive" in wealthy neighborhoods of San Salvador. Several days later, the military replied, brutally assassinating six Jesuit priests and their two assistants.[34] These killings provoked international fury, pressuring Alfredo Cristiani's ruling ARENA party into more serious talks with the FMLN.[35] On January 16, 1992, the peace accords were finally signed, ending the twelve-year civil war that claimed over one hundred thousand lives.

In the post-war era, one might assume that the labor movement might "take off," given the country's "democratic transition." That has not happened, however. The labor movement is weaker *today* than it was during the civil war. Mark Anner suggests there are two reasons for this paradox.[36] The first one is that the links that existed between the labor and revolutionary movements collapsed after the war. FENASTRAS, for instance, left the RN and UNTS in 1993 and moved sharply toward the right in the mid- 1990s.[37] The once-radical labor federation has reportedly signed favorable contracts with several *maquiladora* factories over the last few years and is now perceived as a "company union."[38] In contrast, other left-leaning labor federations such as FUSS, the Federation of Associations and Independent Unions of El Salvador (FEASIES), and the Union Federation of Salvadoran Workers (FESTES), have remained on the "left," but they have not developed a strategic vision or new organizing model for dealing with the challenges of the post-war period. Consequently, their membership, which began declining in the mid-1980s, continued falling after the peace accords were signed.[39] These three federations are still active today, but they are very small and lack the resources to organize *maquila* workers on a widespread basis.[40]

The second problem facing the labor movement revolves around the demise of "centrist" unions and umbrella organizations like the CTD and UNOC.[41] In the early and middle 1990s, the AFL-CIO trimmed back its budget for AIFLD before completely shutting it down and replacing it with the American Center for International Labor Solidarity (ACILS) in 1995. This long overdue decision (given AIFLD's historical record between the 1960s and 1990s) negatively affected the CTD and UNOC, both of which, at one time, received significant funding from AIFLD. Fewer resources, combined with allegations that one of the CTD's leaders embezzled a major share of its funds, severely weakened the federation, leaving it with fewer than five thousand members in 1994.[42] The National Confederation of Salvadoran Workers (*Confederación Nacional de Trabajadores Salvadoreños*—CNTS) emerged from this context, filling the void left by the CTD and the still functioning, but extremely feeble CTS.[43] The CNTS includes the country's largest labor federation, the General Trade Union Federation of Salvadoran Workers (*Federación Unión General de Trabajadores Salvadoreños*—FUGTS), but it has not yet focused on organizing *maquila* workers.[44]

The fragmentation of the labor and revolutionary movements and financial cutbacks from AIFLD, combined with decades of military repression and internal divisions within the labor movement, explain why there were only 118,000 unionized workers in El Salvador in 1996.[45] These factors also explain why fewer than one thousand of the country's sixty thousand *maquila* workers were unionized in 1995.[46] There are several more reasons why the level of unionization in the *maquiladora* industry is so low. Before analyzing them, we must first grasp the structure and nature of the industry.

The Salvadoran Maquiladora Industry

The *maquiladora* industry and the country's first free trade zones emerged in the early 1970s, but political instability and civil unrest thwarted their growth.[47] This situation changed after ARENA's Alfredo Cristiani took over as president in 1989. Cristiani deepened already existing "structural adjustment programs," selling off state-owned enterprises and lowering tariffs in an effort to stimulate export-oriented growth.[48] As Anner notes, ARENA and the United States Agency for International Development (USAID) thought that incorporating El Salvador into the global economy through *maquiladora* production would offset the loss of jobs generated as a result of privatization.[49]

ARENA took the first step towards facilitating the development of the *maquiladora* industry by creating new free trade zones, as well as specially-defined areas, known as *recintos fiscales* (fiscal "precincts" or districts), outside the zones in the early 1990s. While some technical and legal differences exist between free trade zones and *recintos fiscales*, both offer foreign investors tax exemptions, duty-free import of machinery and raw materials, and unlimited repatriation of profits.[50]

The U.S.-backed Caribbean Basin Initiative (CBI) and the Generalized System of Preferences (GSP), which provide trade benefits and "guaranteed access levels" of specific exports into the U.S. market based on the protection of international labor standards, also created a "favorable climate" for foreign investment during this time period.[51]

These policies, combined with the end of the civil war and ARENA's commitment toward maintaining a low-wage, union-free environment, stimulated the growth of the *maquiladora* industry in the middle and late 1990s. The total percentage of exports from the *maquila* sector rose from 18 percent in 1991 to nearly 48 percent in 1998, reaching almost $1.2 billion dollars.[52] In 1990, there were less than five thousand *maquila* workers in the entire country, but by 1996, there were just under sixty thousand.[53] Over 80 percent of these *maquila* workers produce clothing and apparel goods, most of which are exported into the United States.[54] Some of the biggest and most well-known labels that are produced in El Salvador include the Gap, Liz Claiborne, Bugle Boy, J.C. Penney, Fruit of the Loom, Macy's, Osh-Kosh, and Eddie Bauer.[55]

Table 3.3 provides more detailed information on the *maquiladora* industry. In 1997, there were 170 factories and 33,086 workers in the *recintos fiscales*, while there were 43 plants and 25,976 workers in the free trade zones.[56] The largest number of *maquilas* in the *recintos fiscales* are Salvadoran-owned (127) followed by U.S. (9), Korean (7), and Taiwanese (3) producers. Salvadorans also own the most factories (12) within the FTZs; U.S. (10), Taiwanese (3), and Korean (2) firms fall next in descending order. The vast majority (154) of all *maquila* factories in El Salvador produce clothing and apparel goods.[57]

Most *maquila* workers are women between the ages of sixteen and thirty. An International Labor Organization (ILO) study found that 78 percent of all *maquila* workers were women and 50 percent of them were single mothers in 1996.[58] The legal minimum wage in the maquila industry is 1,260 *colones* ($143) per month. Most workers earn that amount; however, the Salvadoran government has calculated that an average size family of 4.3 people must spend exactly that much to meet its daily food requirements. One report found this situation troubling, stating, "a family must spend 100% of one wage earner's income just to eat." This same document determined that a "living wage," which would enable an average size family to meet all its basic needs (e.g., food, housing, education, health-care, child-care, clothing, electricity, water, and transportation) would be 4,556 *colones* ($517) per month.[59] There are very few, if any, *maquila* workers that make this much income.

Beyond low wages, there have been numerous studies that show working conditions within the industry are highly strenuous and exploitative. Complaints

Table 3.3 Number of Factories and Employees in the Free Trade Zones and Recintos Fiscales

Production Location	Number of Factories	Number of Workers
Recintos Fiscales	170	33,086
Free Trade Zones	43	25,976
(Total)	213	59,062

Source: Quinteros et al. (1998), p. 26.

range from long hours to unpaid overtime to sexual harassment. In 1997, nearly 20 percent of *maquila* workers in the free trade zones reported that they worked more than fifty hours per week. 45 percent of all *maquila* workers also stated that they never received overtime pay.[60] In one glaring case of exploitation, *maquila* workers at a factory named Do-All, which produces clothes for Liz Claiborne in the San Marcos FTZ, claimed that they sometimes toiled fifteen hours a day and over one hundred hours per week.[61] In 1998, the office of the Ombudsperson for the Defense of Human Rights (PDDH) found that 69 percent of all *maquila* workers reported work-related illnesses (e.g., headaches, respiratory problems, etc.); while another 38 percent said that they had been mistreated and threatened on the job.[62]

Another study found that 13 percent of all women *maquila* workers had been sexually harassed.[63] The U.S. State Department Country Report on Human Rights Practices in El Salvador mentioned some of these issues, noting there were also "credible accusations" of pregnancy-based discrimination in 1998.[64]

The Salvadoran Constitution and Labor Code (along with several ILO Conventions that El Salvador has signed) provide workers with the right to organize. *Maquila* workers have periodically exercised this right, organizing themselves into unions in order to improve their wages and working conditions. In 1993 and 1994, there were eleven organizing campaigns.[65] Each one of these drives failed. There are currently only two "factory-level" unions in the entire *maquiladora* industry.[66] Both unions, incidentally, do not have a contract with their employer. There are no contracts in the entire industry.

There are four key reasons why so few unions exist in the *maquiladora* industry. First, when workers organize they are usually fired or pressured into quitting their jobs.[67] These activities have had a "chilling effect," creating fear and limiting the potential for organizing. Second, the weakness of the labor movement, along with its inability to develop a new strategic organizing model, has made unionization extremely difficult.[68] Third, as Julia Evelín Martínez and Carolina Quinteros have noted, most *maquila* workers are women who work "double-shifts"—on the assembly line and in their homes—leaving them little time to organize.[69] Fourth, the government's priority on attracting and retaining foreign investment has also limited organizing.[70] Despite these significant obstacles, two unions remain—the members of one work for Mandarin International.

Mandarin International and The Gap

Mandarin International opened its doors in the San Marcos Free Trade Zone in 1992. A majority of the factory's clothing and apparel items are produced for the Gap. Gap Inc. is a San Francisco-based transnational corporation that has production facilities in over 40 countries and annual sales of $4 billion. In 1998,

Gap Chairman Donald Fisher received $700 million in compensation and stock options. That same year, *Forbes* magazine estimated that the net worth of the Fisher family empire was $8 billion. The company owns 2,200 retail outlets. Its most popular and well-known labels include the Gap, Old Navy, Banana Republic, Gap Kids, and Baby Gap.[71]

The Gap has consistently claimed that it is a "socially responsible" company that cares about human, labor, and women's rights, and the environment. The company's workers in El Salvador quickly found out, however, there was a "gap" between this image and the reality that they faced at Mandarin. From the moment Mandarin opened up, workers complained of poor working conditions, such as forced overtime, regulated bathroom breaks, lack of drinking water, and poor ventilation. Mandarin workers also stated that the company's personnel manager, a retired army colonel, verbally and physically abused them, hitting them on top of their heads with his fists for alleged "mistakes" and "poor quality work." Pregnant workers were also mistreated and sexual harassment was reported. The Human Rights Office of the Catholic Archdiocese (*Tutela Legal*) and PDDH also found that Mandarin workers were denied health care and that their wages were extremely low.[72]

Early Organizing Efforts, 1993–1994

These conditions led some Mandarin workers to begin organizing and making plans to form a union in late 1993. One of the first things that they did was make contact with striking members of the powerful Construction Workers Union near the gates of the San Marcos Free Trade Zone. After a brief, impromptu discussion, the construction workers told them that their union was affiliated with FUGTS and that they should go to the federation's office to talk with Juan Hernández, General-Secretary of the *Sindicato de la Industria Algodón, Sintéticos, Similares, y Conexos* (STIASSYC), an industrial textile workers' union that is also affiliated with FUGTS. Hernández discussed what happened next:

> The workers said that the company did not respect them. They said that they did not have enough drinking water and that they had to ask to use the bathroom. They also mentioned that some pregnant women were being mistreated [fired without receiving their legally guaranteed severance payments]. The workers were very angry and they asked me for advice and assistance. I told them that the only thing that they could do was to fight back and organize. So they did that and on November 13, 1993 they formed a *seccu-ónal* (sectional).[73]

Under Salvadoran labor law, industrial unions, such as STIASSYC, can form *secciónales* (sectional unions) with only *seven* members.[74] In order to begin contract negotiations, however, sectional and factory-level unions (*sindicatos de empresa*), which can be created with *thirty-five* members, must represent more than 50 percent of all workers within a particular factory or worksite.[75]

At this moment, there were more than eight hundred workers inside Mandarin, but no more than fifty were members of the newly formed *seccional*.[76] This left the fledging union far below the 50 percent mark. Despite its relative weakness, Mandarin became concerned and fired many union members. Other members, after receiving tremendous pressure from the company, "voluntarily resigned," taking their severance payments with them. These anti-union activities effectively destroyed the first unionization campaign.[77]

The Mandarin workers did not give up after this setback. They remained angry about their low wages and poor working conditions, and began a series of talks with FENASTRAS General-Secretary Juan José Hueso in early 1994 about their next move. Hueso suggested that the workers form a new *seccional* with the *Sindicato de Trabajadores de la Industria Textil de Algodón, Sintéticos, Acabados, Textiles, Similares, y Conexos* (STITAS), an industrial textile workers union affiliated with FENASTRAS. The Mandarin workers took this advice, establishing a new *seccional* with FENASTRAS/STITAS, under the assumption that the federation would struggle for better wages and working conditions and the rehiring of their fired *compañeras/os*.[78]

FENASTRAS did no such thing, however. As previously mentioned, the former left-leaning labor federation underwent a sharp ideological transformation after the civil war ended in 1992, becoming more conservative and friendly toward the business sector, especially the *maquiladora* industry. Juan José Hueso is, in fact, one of its staunchest defenders. It has been widely reported that he has signed various "sweetheart" deals with *maquila* owners to establish, in exchange for bribes and financial gain, pro-management *seccionales* (i.e. "company unions," also sometimes called *sindicatos blancos*) that do not focus on improving the wages and working conditions of *maquila* workers. Many labor federations and nongovernment organizations (NGOs) have also claimed that FENASTRAS has deliberately created unrest and provoked "voluntary resignations" so it can receive a portion of the severance payments, which it obtains through negotiations with *maquila* owners.[79]

FENASTRAS used this latter strategy at Mandarin. After some of the workers involved with the STITAS/FENASTRAS *seccional* "resigned" and accepted their severance payments, Juan José Hueso allegedly collected 20,000 *colones* ($2,500) from Mandarin.[80] These activities stunned most of the workers that were involved in the campaign, leading it to eventually fall apart.

The Rise and Decline of SETMI, January–July 1995

Despite the FENASTRAS/STITAS debacle, the Mandarin workers did not give up hope—they continued organizing. This time they contacted the CTS and CTD, who at this time, despite their different ideological and historical trajectories, were working together as one "unified" body. After a series of strategy sessions, the CTS/CTD and the Mandarin workers decided that they should form a factory-level union, instead of a *secciónal*. CTS Organizing Director Otilio Candido explained the strategic logic behind this decision:

> *Secciónales* are too small. They do not involve enough affiliates (members). To make change you need more members. The Mandarin workers understood the labor code. They know that you need 35 members for recognition and over 50% for contract negotiations. So they began organizing just before the end of 1994. After a very short time, they had more than 35 members and formed a factory-level union (*sindicato de empresa*). The name of the union was the *Sindicato de Empresa de Trabajadores de Mandarin Internacional* (SETMI).[81]

This was a major step forward for the Mandarin workers, but the newly formed union, even though it had more than enough members, still lacked recognition. The process for obtaining legal recognition is fairly straightforward—unions with thirty-five or more members must file specific documents (e.g., affiliate names and addresses, organization meeting minutes and statutes, etc.) with the Labor Ministry's office. The Labor Ministry then determines whether or not the union has followed the appropriate legal guidelines.[82] Because Labor Ministry officials were concerned about scaring away foreign investors, they have routinely denied requests for recognition, or worked with management to weaken or eliminate the union.[83] This situation made gaining recognition nearly impossible—in fact, very few legally recognized *maquila* unions existed before SETMI was established.[84] Nevertheless, CTS General-Secretary Felix Blanco, an elected official with the Christian Democratic Party in the Salvadoran National Assembly, used his political connections and influenced the Labor Ministry to recognize SETMI in January 1995.[85]

The newly-recognized union initially had less than one hundred members. Despite its fairly small size, Mandarin took preemptive action, firing several dozen SETMI members.[86] The company thought that this strategy would generate fear and dampen enthusiasm for unionization like it did before, but it had the opposite effect. In February 1995, SETMI organized a three-day general strike that shut down the entire San Marcos Free Trade Zone. During that action, one union member was badly beaten by Mandarin's Chief of Security and another company supervisor. The next day talks between SETMI and Mandarin began. The company promised that it would not take retaliatory action against the workers that went on strike, but fifty were fired over the next few weeks.[87]

The union survived these attacks. In fact, SETMI *gained* three hundred new members between February and May 1995.[88] Since Mandarin had over eight hundred workers, during that time frame, the union still fell short of the required 50 percent mark to begin contract negotiations. SETMI's expanding membership base still concerned Mandarin though. It realized that mass firings alone would not undermine the union. The company therefore established a "company union," called the Mandarin International Workers Association (*Asociación de Trabajadores de Empresa Mandarin International*—ATEMISA), to contain worker dissatisfaction and marginalize SETMI.[89]

Almost immediately after ATEMISA was created, new conflicts emerged within the factory. Mandarin fired over two hundred workers between February and May of 1995. SETMI responded, organizing another strike. This time violent clashes broke out between SETMI and ATEMISA. Mandarin security forces also beat several SETMI members. The walkout lasted several hours before officials from the Ministries of Labor and Education and the Ombudsperson's Office for Human Rights intervened and negotiated a temporary "cooling-off" agreement between all three parties.[90]

The situation remained "hot," however. Mandarin continued firing and harassing workers. On June 26, 1995, SETMI activists blocked the gates of the San Marcos Free Trade Zone, while union members inside the factory simultaneously stopped working and cut off the electricity. They also prevented the company's supervisors from leaving the factory, and urged them to rehire their fired *compañeras/os* and to begin contract negotiations with SETMI.[91] Mandarin rejected these demands and called for the National Civilian Police, who threatened to forcibly remove the striking workers in order to "free" the "captured" supervisors. After a tense stand-off, the managers and workers left the building.[92]

The day after the strike, Mandarin launched an all-out offensive on SETMI, firing all remaining union members. Without its base, the union could not survive for very long. Mandarin took no chances. It blocked SETMI's leaders from entering the factory, stopping them from organizing, and nearly causing them to quit due to financial necessity. Mandarin also threatened to shut down and move someplace else unless the unrest subsided. These activities decimated SETMI, undermining its drive to negotiate the only contract in the country's free trade zones.[93]

The National Labor Committee and Independent Monitoring, July 1995–October 1996

Shortly after SETMI was essentially wiped out, the National Labor Committee (NLC) became involved in the campaign by conducting some "background research" on the U.S.-based companies that Mandarin produces for. In mid-1995, Mandarin was making clothes for J.C. Penney, Eddie Bauer, J. Crew, and Liz Claiborne. Most of the company's production orders came from the Gap, however. In fact, at certain points, 80 percent of Mandarin's production was for the Gap.[94] Given this situation, and the reality that it would be practically impossible to run multiple campaigns against all the companies that had ties with Mandarin, the NLC decided to target the Gap. Its plan was to force the Gap to pressure Mandarin to rehire the fired union members and to improve wages and working conditions within the factory.[95]

The Gap initially claimed that its own private monitors and investigators found no labor rights violations at Mandarin. The NLC challenged these assertions and launched a high-profile, three-pronged counter-attack, using various types of information, leverage, and accountability politics. The first part of this coordinated campaign involved flying two Central American women *maquiladora* workers, Judith Viera (a fired SETMI member), and Claudia Molina, to the United States for a speaking tour.[96] These women had never traveled outside their respective countries before. In July 1995, they gave their first presentation at the founding convention of the Union of Needletrades, Industrial, and Textile Employees (UNITE) in Miami. They talked about their wages and working conditions, galvanizing the audience with their *testimonios*.

The speaking tour put a "human face" on the campaign and served as a crucial organizing tool. Each stop along the twenty-five-city tour sparked local protests. In Chicago, for instance, activists from UNITE, Jobs with Justice, Women for Economic Justice, the Nicaragua Solidarity Committee, the Illinois Nurses Association, the Service Employees International Union (SEIU), and the Chicago Religious Leadership Network on Latin America (CRLN), calling themselves the "Gapatistas" after the mostly indigenous "Zapatista" movement in Chiapas, Mexico, picketed Gap stores, passed out informational leaflets, and urged consumers to call, fax, write, or e-mail the company to express their support for the Mandarin workers.[97] All across the United States and Canada, labor, student, fair trade, religious, and women's organizations carried out similar activities, putting great pressure on the Gap, during the all-important "back-to-school" shopping season in August and September 1995.[98]

Like the speaking tour, the second element of the NLC-led campaign was based on information politics and raising public awareness. The NLC produced a short, powerful documentary called *Zoned for Slavery: The Children Behind the Label* about sweatshops and the Central American *maquiladora* industry. This video was seen widely all over the United States and Canada. In Minnesota, the Fair Trade Coalition and the Resource Center of the Americas showed it to six thousand students at eighteen high schools and five colleges. After viewing the film, hundreds wrote letters to the Gap, while others cut off the company's labels and made them into a mural that was sent to Gap CEO Millard Drexler. Students from a Catholic women's college also held an "alternative" fashion show, wearing clothes with price tags stating, "teen-age girls get 38 cents an hour to sew this garment," after watching the film.[99]

The video and speaking tour also unintentionally coincided with the infamous raid on the El Monte "slave sweatshop," triggering major press coverage in the *New York Times, Washington Post, Los Angeles Times,* and *Miami Herald.*[100] Sweatshops were, once again, after a decades-long absence, the subject of front-page columns and editorials. These articles, which were the third "leg" of the campaign, highlighted the contradiction between the Gap's progressive, trendy image and the reality that its workers faced in El Salvador. The NLC wisely recognized from the very beginning of the campaign that the Gap's public image was its "soft spot."[101] It exploited that weakness in every single leaflet, press release, and public statement. Through these attacks, the NLC gained "moral leverage" over the Gap, holding it accountable to its lofty rhetoric.

As these activities proceeded across the United States and Canada, a wide cross-section of Salvadoran-based labor, human rights, women's, and religious organizations, including SETMI, the Center for Labor Studies (CENTRA), the University of Central America (UCA), the CTD, UNTS, Mélida Anaya Montes Women's Movement, the International Solidarity Committee (CIS), and the FMLN met and wrote a letter to the Gap in mid-October 1995.[102] The letter stated that there was "sufficient and abundant" evidence that labor and women's rights violations existed at Mandarin. It called on the Gap to conduct an "independent and objective" investigation of these charges. The Salvadoran government sharply criticized the activists that signed the letter. President Armando Calderón Sol called them "bastards," while Interior Minister Mario Acosta ominously said, "they deserve the death penalty." Acosta also claimed that the letter would lead Mandarin to shut down, forcing women workers to "turn towards prostitution."[103]

The Gap's response was much more favorable. It temporarily suspended its contract with Mandarin until the Salvadoran government enforced its labor laws and the company upheld the Gap's code of conduct.[104] These actions, stated in a letter from Gap Vice-President Stan Raggio, were surprising because the Gap did not permanently terminate its contract with Mandarin. It did not, as so many other garment manufacturers have done when confronted with labor unrest, "cut and run," rather, it admitted the existence of labor and women's rights violations and clearly stated under what conditions it would resume placing orders with Mandarin. The Gap, therefore, used, as the NLC and transnational advocacy network hoped for, its "material leverage" over the company to resolve the conflict and create change.

How would change come about? Who would insure that Mandarin complied with Salvadoran labor law and the Gap's code of conduct? The NLC suggested that, given SETMI's weakness and the Salvadoran government's ineptitude, an independent monitoring group should carry out these tasks.[105] On December 15, 1995, in a meeting in New York City, the Gap signed a historic agreement with the NLC calling for independent monitoring, the reinstatement of the fired SETMI members, and the resumption of "productive and humane" employment based on the Salvadoran government's "just and prompt" resolution of labor conflicts and Mandarin's compliance with the company's code of conduct.[106] NLC Director Charles Kernaghan praised the Gap's action, stating, "[it] listened to the consumers and did the right thing."[107]

Although this accord was an unprecedented breakthrough, things remained the same inside Mandarin. Despite facing extreme pressure from company supervisors, all seven SETMI executive board members continued working inside the factory after the June 1995 strike. However, several days after the December 15th meeting in New York, five of the seven union officers received death threats, stating that they would be killed if they did not resign. These warnings came from "anonymous callers and unknown men that appeared at the workers' doors."[108] The five union leaders eventually quit. When the Gap became aware of this situation, it threatened to permanently leave. Mandarin finally understood the stakes—either accept independent monitoring or face the loss of its largest supplier. On March 22, 1996, Mandarin signed a new agreement that called for the reinstatement of all SETMI leaders and members and the establishment of an independent monitoring group.[109]

The Independent Monitoring Group of El Salvador (*Grupo Monitoreo Independiente de El Salvador*—GMIES), which includes representatives from the University of Central America Human Rights Institute (*Instituto Derechos Humanos Universidad Centroamérica*—IDHUCA), the Legal Aid Office of the Archbishop of El Salvador (*Tutela Legal*), the Archdiocese of San Salvador, and the Center for Labor Studies (*Centro de Estudios del Trabajo*—CENTRA), emerged from the accord. The agreement states that the objective of GMIES is to investigate and monitor Mandarin's compliance with Salvadoran labor law and the Gap's code of conduct.

The March 22 agreement stated that SETMI's leaders would be rehired by May 1, 1996. Mandarin claimed that "insufficient orders" prevented it from doing this, however. GMIES reminded the company that it could face possible financial losses if it did not fully comply with the agreement. It also met with the Gap and the Independent Monitoring Working Group (IMWG), a U.S.-based organization consisting of the Interfaith Center for Corporate Responsibility (ICCR), Business for Social Responsibility (BSR), and the NLC, to force Mandarin's hand.[110] These efforts failed, leading GMIES to temporarily suspend its monitoring activities. This decision prompted the Gap and IMWG to intervene and initiate a new round of negotiations. On September 12, 1996, another agreement was signed. Under the terms of this accord, Mandarin agreed to rehire the union leaders and the Gap pledged to provide the company with more production orders. Consequently, on October 15, SETMI's leaders resumed working inside the factory.[111]

Independent Monitoring: Results and Consequences

Over the next three months, GMIES worked towards locating and rehiring the three hundred workers who had been fired during the strikes in 1995 and carried out regular inspections inside Mandarin.[112] In April 1997, GMIES issued its first "progress report," indicating that working conditions had improved. The report found, for instance, no cases of physical or verbal mistreatment or abuse from company supervisors, and noted that workers had access to an on-site medical clinic and a cooperative, where they could buy low-cost consumer goods. On a less positive note, the report stated that just over 50 percent of the three hundred workers applied to be re-hired and that only twenty-eight got their "old jobs" back. After several more months, seventy-five of the previously fired workers had been rehired.[113]

In October 1997, GMIES, after interviewing one hundred and fifty of the factory's approximately five hundred workers, published its second "progress report." The findings, once again, were largely positive. Eighty-three percent of the workers stated that working conditions were better than they were in 1995, and 90 percent said that they were pleased with how company supervisors treated them. The study also found no cases of forced overtime and no complaints about lighting, ventilation, bathrooms, or drinking water. It also reported that workers had access to health insurance and that all were being paid at least the minimum wage.[114]

These two reports indicate that working conditions improved rather dramatically inside Mandarin between 1995 and 1997, and that independent monitoring has been quite effective. Another report, conducted by the University of El Salvador, "reconfirmed" the results of the previous two studies, finding that 78 percent of the workers that were interviewed stated that the involvement of GMIES improved working conditions as well as respect for labor rights. Over 70 percent of these workers also reported that GMIES had created greater stability and improved relations between management and labor.[115]

Moral Leverage and The Boomerang Effect

How did all this happen? What made Mandarin shift from near total intransigence for four years toward changing working conditions inside the factory? The crucial moment of the campaign came when a transnational advocacy network of organizations, under the leadership of the NLC, became involved and started targeting the Gap rather than Mandarin. Before this decision was made, SETMI had basically been eliminated—all its members had been fired, giving it absolutely no leverage. The NLC understood that SETMI had no influence over Mandarin, but realized that the Gap did.

The Gap initially did not want to use its "material leverage"—stopping production orders—to force Mandarin to improve wages and working conditions and negotiate with SETMI. Its "hands-off" approach led the NLC to launch a sophisticated campaign in the United States to put pressure on the Gap through the workers' speaking tour, *Zoned for Slavery*, leafleting, letter writing, consumer activism, alternative fashion shows, and media coverage. These strategies smeared the Gap's "socially responsible" image, giving SETMI and the NLC "moral leverage."

Because the company did not want to be associated with "sweatshops paying starvation wages,"[116] the Gap temporarily suspended its ties with Mandarin. Naomi Klein, author of *No Logo: Taking on the Brand Bullies*, calls this process the "brand boomerang."[117] The Gap is one of the most widely-recognized brands or labels in the entire world. Klein suggests that the larger the brand the more susceptible it is to consumer-based protests. As she says:

> Branding, as we have seen, is a balloon economy: it inflates with astonishing rapidity but it is full of hot air. It shouldn't be surprising that this formula has bred armies of pin-wielding critics, eager to pop the corporate balloon and watch the shreds fall to the ground. The more ambitious a company has been in branding the cultural landscape, and the more careless it has been abandoning its workers, the more likely it is to have generated a silent battalion of critics waiting to pounce.[118]

When the Gap stopped sourcing with Mandarin, it showed, in the words of the old Nike advertisement, that "image *is* everything." The NLC wisely realized that the Gap's image was the "key hook" of the campaign, using it over and over again to create a powerful "boomerang effect" (see Figure 3.1). Mandarin finally capitulated after realizing that it could lose its biggest supplier for good. It, therefore, accepted independent monitoring, rehired the union's leaders and some of its members, and improved working conditions inside the factory. These results are remarkable given how difficult it is to fight back and create social change in the Salvadoran *maquiladora* industry.

Independent Monitoring and Collective Bargaining: Either/Or?

Despite all the positive changes that have occurred inside Mandarin, one thing remains constant—low wages. Nearly all the workers that I spoke with discussed this issue and talked about how it affected their everyday lives. One ATEMISA member, for instance, said:

> My salary right now is 1300 *colones* a month. That's a little more than the minimum wage, but it's not enough. I have three children. I'm single. It's hard to buy all the things that we need to live, like food, clothing, and

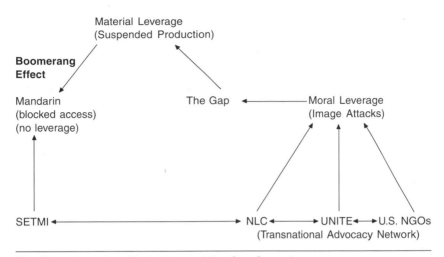

Fig. 3.1 Independent Monitoring and the Gap Campaign.

rent. I joined ATEMISA because my *compañera* told me that it would be safer than joining SETMI. Now I think that I should have talked with the other workers before I did that because ATEMISA doesn't fight for us. They sometimes make some noise, but our wages stay the same.[119]

Other workers voiced similar concerns about their wages and said that they felt that independent monitoring had not "gone far enough."[120]

The debate surrounding what mechanism—independent monitoring or collective bargaining—is "more effective" for improving wages and working conditions in overseas sweatshops is complex. In the Gap campaign, the two strategies were seen in dualistic, either–or terms. The NLC, for example, supported monitoring for resolving the Mandarin crisis, even though the three signed agreements did not include a "living wage" provision, which could have raised wages for all Mandarin workers. In all fairness, this was not the NLC's fault. The Gap's code of conduct does not include a living wage clause, so this issue fell outside the scope of the accords. The AFL-CIO, UNITE, and later the American Center for International Labor Solidarity (ACILS), in contrast to the NLC, favored strengthening SETMI's membership base. These organizations believed that a rejuvenated SETMI could improve wages and working conditions through collective bargaining.[121]

These two viewpoints underlie a long-standing disagreement between the NLC, the AFL-CIO, and UNITE. All three organizations theoretically support independent monitoring *and* collective bargaining. They do not see them as mutually exclusive strategies; rather, they complement each other. Officials from the NLC and UNITE, as well as the ACILS and AFL-CIO, have mentioned, for instance, that monitoring can open up space, by insuring that employers protect the right to organize, for unions to emerge and negotiate contracts.[122]

Consensus between the NLC, AFL-CIO, and UNITE existed, on the surface, during the Gap campaign. In reality, tensions ran high. It should be pointed out that all three groups did work together, but their strategic and historical differences generated unnecessary conflict. The NLC distrusted the CTD and CTS's involvement in the Gap campaign because of their previous ties with AIFLD. AIFLD's uncritical stance towards El Salvador's human rights abuses generated dissent within the AFL-CIO, sparking the establishment of the NLC in 1981.[123] The NLC worked closely with leftist and moderate labor federations like FENASTRAS, FEASIES, and FESTES in the 1980s and early 1990s.[124] If SETMI had affiliated with FEASIES or FESTES, the NLC would have probably supported collective bargaining more strongly. The NLC rejects working with all "corrupt," centrist unions like the CTD, CTS, and CNTS.

The ACILS, on the other hand, opposed working "exclusively" with FEASIES and FESTES, at that time, because they did not have the financial and technical resources to organize *maquila* workers on a sustainable basis. The ACILS, AFL-CIO, and UNITE also claimed that the NLC's campaigns are too "media-driven" and that they leave workers defenseless after they are inevitably fired. These organizations suggest that the NLC should work toward empowering workers and making them (rather than consumers, students, or Charles Kernaghan) the primary agents of change, on the ground, through unionization.[125]

Analysis

These perspectives highlight a crucial, although unstated, point: officials from the NLC, UNITE, the AFL-CIO, and ACILS generally mistrust each other. Long-standing disputes exacerbated strategic differences over independent monitoring and collective bargaining. In some ways, the debate about these two strategies was not the "real issue"—deeply-held doubts and suspicions stemming from the legacy of the Salvadoran civil war in the 1980s spilled over into the Gap campaign, limiting further progress from occurring. Had there been greater unity between the NLC, AFL-CIO, and UNITE, wages *and* working conditions might have improved inside Mandarin.

The NLC, AFL-CIO, and UNITE both admit that independent monitoring and collective bargaining are small pieces of a larger overall puzzle. Independent monitoring has had a positive impact inside Mandarin, but there is much to do (over 250 *maquila* factories remain unorganized) and it cannot be achieved until the NLC, ACILS, UNITE, and AFL-CIO sit down and discuss their differences in a candid and open manner. Many Salvadoran labor activists mentioned that, until the conflicts between these organizations are resolved, wages and working conditions in the *maquila* industry will probably not improve. While

perhaps overstated, this is a strong indictment, coming from Salvadoran unionists themselves.

The organizations that were involved in the Gap campaign should listen to
their Salvadoran sisters and brothers more carefully because their concerns have
theoretical and political ramifications. Keck and Sikkink suggest that
transnational advocacy networks (TANs) are more likely to create change when
there is unity and consensus amongst network actors.[126] The previous chapter
noted that the degree of change that occurs during a cross-border labor solidarity
campaign depends on the strength of the domestic non-state actor. Based on
these two points, I contend that strong domestic nonstate actors working together with unified TANs have the best chance to create meaningful and substantive change (e.g., better wages and working conditions).

The Gap campaign's mixed results illustrate this argument. After the massive firings in June 1995, SETMI was effectively eliminated. The NLC, UNITE,
and numerous solidarity, human rights, women's, and religious organizations
from the United States and Canada became involved in the campaign at this
point, forming a fairly cohesive transnational advocacy network. These groups
skillfully targeted the Gap. They attacked the company's image and obtained
moral leverage through various forms of information politics, such as passing
out leaflets, showing *Zoned for Slavery*, and sponsoring the *maquila* workers
speaking tour. These activities mobilized consumers and activists, and generated
extensive media coverage, driving another nail into the Gap's fragile public
image.

Sensing public concern about the issue of sweatshops, the Gap sought to
repair its tattered image by suspending its contract with Mandarin. This dramatic move unwittingly transformed the Gap into an "unofficial" member of
the transnational advocacy network, and led Mandarin to sign the first-ever
independent monitoring agreement in the entire Central American *maquiladora*
industry. Independent monitoring has produced some significant changes inside Mandarin. Workers are no longer physically and verbally abused; and there
is no forced overtime. They enjoy unrestricted bathroom use and have access
to safe drinking water. All workers are also paid the minimum wage and have
health insurance. These might seem like minor concessions, but given the anti-
union nature of the Salvadoran *maquiladora* industry, they are striking.

A relatively unified transnational advocacy network, under the direction of
the NLC, combined with the involvement of Salvadoran-based NGOs like
GMIES, made this outcome possible. Without a strong union, however, the
NLC and GMIES could not improve the wages of the Mandarin workers, which
still hover near or below the poverty level. Given the weakness of SETMI, one
might think that the NLC, AFL-CIO, and UNITE would have tried to work
together to strengthen it so it could negotiate a contract with wage increases.
That did not happen, unfortunately. Historical and strategic differences blocked

these two groups from fully collaborating with each other. The results of this bitter conflict are that SETMI remains weak and wages remain low inside Mandarin.

These "split" results demonstrate how crucial the relationship between domestic non-state actors and TANs is. In this case, when the three independent monitoring agreements were signed, the TAN was strong, but the union was weak. Monitoring enhanced working conditions, but left wages unchanged. After monitoring began, serious tensions within the TAN emerged. These divisions, combined with the weakness of SETMI, made increasing wages nearly impossible. Given the feeble nature of SETMI and the deep-seated clash between the NLC and UNITE, further progress seems unlikely.[127]

There are several important lessons that can be drawn from this case. First, independent monitoring can be effective, but it is not a "magic bullet." It cannot, in most cases, improve wages. Strong unions are necessary for achieving that objective. That is the second lesson of this case. The third one is that robust unions cannot be established until Salvadoran labor federations and U.S.-based organizations like the NLC, UNITE, the AFL-CIO, and the ACILS address their differences and begin working together in a more coordinated and strategic manner. That is what the situation in the *maquiladora* industry demands—a stronger Salvadoran labor movement and greater unity between U.S.-based labor, human rights, women's, and religious organizations.

Conclusion

The Gap campaign was relatively successful. After an intense four-year campaign, working conditions inside Mandarin International improved through independent monitoring. Wages remained low, however. They did so because Mandarin essentially wiped out SETMI. Strategic conflicts between the NLC and UNITE weakened the union even further, making wage increases virtually impossible. Unless those tensions are resolved, the chances for achieving more substantial changes at Mandarin and at other *maquila* factories look extremely remote.

The Gap campaign produced some incredible, although limited gains. This case should inspire anti-sweatshop activists, but also serve as a sobering reminder of the challenges that lie ahead. Thousands of *maquila* factories remain unorganized. Tens of thousands of workers are struggling economically. Hundreds of thousands, if not millions, of Central Americans are impoverished and malnourished. Independent monitoring and collective bargaining cannot address this larger reality; more sweeping changes are necessary. That is perhaps the ultimate lesson of the Gap campaign.

4

The Honduran Maquiladora Industry and Cross-Border Labor Solidarity

The Kimi Campaign

Continental Park and the Kimi Campaign

Just outside *Parque Continental* (Continental Park) lies a union office in a dusty, gritty working-class *colonia* (neighborhood) in La Lima, Cortes (Honduras). The "office" is not really an office though—it is a turquoise-painted house with wrought-iron windows, but no one lives there. Inside its doors are the organizer's "tools of the trade"—maps, tape, flyers, "strategy posters," butcher paper, chairs, tables, and a phone (but no fax machine or computer). These are the "weapons of the weak"[1] and this is one of their key "war rooms" in the on-going struggle for social and economic justice.

On the frontlines of this battle are tens of thousands of workers. On this particular warm and muggy evening in September 1999, there are about two dozen young women *maquiladora* workers, along with several *hombres* (men),[2] at the union office discussing wages, quotas, never-ending conflicts with management, and bold plans for organizing other *maquiladora* factories inside *Parque Continental*. These workers are members of the Kimi Workers' Union (*Sindicato de Trabajadores de Kimi de Honduras*—SITRAKIMIH). Kimi is one of eight *maquiladora* factories that are located inside *Parque Continental*.[3]

Between 1993 and 1995, Kimi workers began organizing over low wages and poor working conditions. As the campaign unfolded, the workers formed a union and started working with the U.S. garment workers' union, UNITE. Through clandestine organizing, the union gathered enough strength to file for legal recognition in July 1996. The Korean-owned factory bitterly opposed the union and fired over sixty of its members. This action sparked a rancorous two-and-half year campaign to negotiate one of the few collective bargaining agreements in the Honduran *maquiladora* industry. During this time period, the union held several strikes; a non-governmental organization, known as the Independent Monitoring Team (*Equipo Monitoreo Independiente*—EMI), was established; conflicts between SITRAKIMIH, EMI, UNITE, and the National Labor Committee (NLC) emerged; and in October 1998, Hurricane Mitch killed over five thousand Hondurans and caused hundreds of millions of dollars in damage. The hurricane damaged the factory, leading it to shut down for three months.

Despite all these events, SITRAKIMIH ratified a two-year contract in March 1999. Before anyone could pause and celebrate this achievement, however, *Parque Continental* owner, presidential candidate, and long-time powerbroker Jaime Rosenthal dropped the other shoe, announcing on national television that he would not renew Kimi's lease. Rosenthal eventually backed down, but Kimi remained concerned. It began holding a series of meetings with the union about moving the factory outside of *Parque Continental*.

These talks proceeded without any major conflict, until Kimi officials unexpectedly walked away from the negotiating table in August 1999. This move infuriated Kimi's workers and they responded with a strike that included nearly all of *Parque Continental's* six thousand *maquiladora* workers. This stunning display of solidarity crippled production and completely shut down the industrial park. Over one hundred riot-clad police officers crushed the short-lived general strike by beating and tear-gassing several workers. Kimi also filed criminal charges against the union's leaders.

These repressive measures backfired against Kimi. The U.S. and Honduran governments, along with solidarity groups from the United States, pressured Kimi into dropping the criminal charges and negotiating a settlement with SITRAKIMIH. With this agreement signed, production resumed inside the factory, although labor-management relations remained extremely tense.

Tension and excitement—those were the two key emotions that filled the Lima union office when I arrived in September 1999. The Kimi workers had just returned to work and they were buzzing over the establishment of a new union at a factory named Yoo Yang, inside *Parque Continental*.[4] Members from both unions spoke enthusiastically about organizing a park-wide union that would include all workers inside the sprawling complex, while others adopted a more cautious tone, warning that firings, managerial divide-and-conquer strategies, and Rosenthal's anti-union stance might thwart their ambitious plans.[5]

These latter concerns were prescient. Rosenthal withdrew Kimi's lease in February 2000. With eviction and joblessness hanging over their heads, Kimi and SITRAKIMIH made a deal—the company was allowed to move the factory under several key conditions. One of the most important stipulations was that Kimi would have to pay for the workers' transportation costs to the new facility.

Kimi accepted this provision and the factory re-opened with the union and contract still intact.

After five years, the Kimi campaign finally looked like it was a triumph—for both the workers and their cross-border allies. This victory turned into a tragic defeat, however, when Kimi closed down the factory on May 5, 2000. In an episode strikingly reminiscent of the Phillips Van-Heusen (PVH) campaign, Kimi claimed that "financial difficulties" prompted the decision, but the factory did not stay closed for very long. Kimi ironically, thanks to PVH, opened up a new factory in the union-free Guatemalan *maquiladora* industry. Over one hundred fifty Kimi workers protested the company's decision, calling on it to re-open in Honduras. It refused. Hundreds of workers were left unemployed.

This chapter examines the Kimi campaign's trajectory—from start to finish. It specifically seeks to explain two questions—what went "right" and what went "wrong?" In order to fully address these questions, which lie at the heart of this book, I initially analyze the Honduran labor movement and the incredible growth of the country's *maquiladora* industry. This contextual information is crucial for understanding the nature of the Kimi campaign. An in-depth overview of the actual campaign follows this section, while the final segment explores how it was won and why it was lost.

The Honduran Labor Movement, 1900–1995

The Honduran labor movement has a rich and relatively unknown history. In the early decades of the 1900s, banana workers, protesting low wages and poor working conditions, organized strikes against the United Fruit Company (UFCO) and Cuyamel Fruit Company.[6] These two U.S.-based corporations dominated Honduras in the early twentieth century, turning it into a virtual "Banana Republic."[7] In the early 1930s, as banana prices and wages fell in the midst of the global economic depression, more strikes in the Northern Coast and San Pedro Sula Valley regions broke out. The radical Honduran Syndical Federation (*Federación Sindical Hondureña*—FSH) organized these work stoppages, calling for the "downfall of the system of capitalist exploitation."[8]

These developments alarmed political and economic elites in Honduras and the United States. In 1932, they threw their weight behind newly-elected President Tiburcio Carías Andino. He ruled the country with an iron fist over the next fifteen years (1933–1948), banning all political parties and driving the labor movement underground.[9] Carías could not completely control the country, however. In 1944, Jorge Ubico (Guatemala) and General Maximiliano Hernández Martínez (El Salvador) were ousted. These events emboldened Honduran dissidents. In July 1944, they held a nonviolent demonstration in San Pedro Sula, calling for greater democracy, but government troops opened fire on the crowd, killing fifty people. These deaths sparked widespread outrage, precipitating Carías' eventual downfall.[10]

Juan Manuel Gálvez, a former UFCO lawyer and Minister of the Interior who was held "legally responsible" for the San Pedro Sula massacre, replaced Carías.[11] During his presidency (1948–1954), Gálvez surprisingly (given his record) introduced pro-labor legislation (e.g., the eight-hour day, paid holidays, and regulations for children and women's labor), but he blocked the unionization of banana workers until May 1954.[12] That month twenty-five thousand UFCO workers went on strike. Over the next several weeks, fifteen thousand Standard Fruit Company workers, along with thousands of miners, dock, textile, and railroad workers, joined them. The "great banana strike" lasted sixty-nine days, paralyzing the entire North Coast economy and generating huge financial losses for U.S. companies.[13]

The strike occurred shortly before the CIA overthrew Guatemalan President Jacobo Arbenz.[14] Arbenz expropriated hundreds of thousands of acres of UFCO land in the early 1950s, making him a "communist" in the eyes of the U.S. State Department, the CIA, and UFCO.[15]

Anti-communist rhetoric spilled over into Honduras during the work stoppage. Some strike committee leaders were labeled "communists" and arrested for their activities.[16] As these events unfolded, the AFL, CIO, and the Inter-American Regional Organization of Workers (ORIT) encouraged UFCO to negotiate a settlement with the committee's more "moderate" leaders.[17] The company heeded this advice, ending the strike in July 1954.[18]

The AFL-CIO, through the Inter-American Regional Organization of Workers (ORIT) and the American Institute for Free Labor Development (AIFLD), became deeply involved in the Honduran labor movement over the next decade. In the late 1950s, the Federation of Northern Workers of Honduras (*Federación Sindical de Trabajadores Norteños de Honduras*—FESITRANH) and the Central Federation of Free Trade Unions of Honduras (*Federación Central de Sindicatos Libres de Honduras*—FECESITLIH) were established, for example, with ORIT's support.[19] The country's first national labor *central*, the Confederation of Honduran Workers (*Confederación de Trabajadores de Honduras*— CTH), was created with assistance from AIFLD in 1964.[20]

These politically moderate federations did not initially concern the country's authoritarian-minded political leaders. Indeed, Honduras had the highest level of unionization in Central America in the late 1960s.[21] Nevertheless, over the next ten years, dissident forces, unhappy with the organization's close ties with AIFLD and the Honduran military, emerged within the CTH.[22] Most either left or were pushed aside and joined the General Confederation of Workers (*Confederación General de Trabajadores*—CGT), a "centrist" Christian Democratic-oriented *central* established in 1970.[23] More radical, former CTH activists, founded the left-leaning Union Federation of Honduran Workers (*Federación Unitaria de Trabajadores de Honduras*—FUTH) in 1981.[24]

Honduras experienced a "democratic transition" in the 1980s. The military stepped down from power and "free and fair" elections were held in 1981 and 1985.[25] Despite these events, the decade was not positive for the labor movement. The United States gave Honduras hundreds of millions of dollars to help the Nicaraguan Contras overthrow the Sandinista government.[26] U.S. aid strengthened the role of the military, giving it *de facto* power. Under the pretext of safeguarding "national security," the military embraced counterinsurgency techniques that included eliminating several small guerilla organizations and killing hundreds of "subversives."[27]

While the level of repression was not as severe as in El Salvador and Guatemala, opportunities for labor organizing declined. The CTH remained the country's leading labor federation in the 1980s, adopting mostly moderate, pro-government positions. The CGT, for its part, moved toward the right.[28] This shift upset some of its members who, in turn, created the Independent Federation of Honduran Workers (*Federación Indepediente de Trabajadores de Honduras*—FITH), in 1985.[29] The FITH and FUTH joined forces and established the leftist United Confederation of Honduran Workers (*Confederación Unitaria de Trabajadores de Honduras*—CUTH) in 1992.[30]

During the late 1980s and early 1990s, neoliberalism replaced counterinsurgency as the country's main political and economic project. Privatization of state-owned enterprises, higher sales and income taxes, tariff reductions, and the firing of thousands of public employees devastated the labor movement, but tens thousands of workers from the CGT, CTH, FUTH, and FITH held strikes and demonstrations, protesting these policies.[31] These activities, however, did not stem skyrocketing rates of poverty and unemployment.[32]

Two decades of counterinsurgency and neoliberalism left the labor movement reeling by the mid-1990s. The country has fewer than one hundred and twenty thousand unionized workers today.[33] Among the three *centrales*, CUTH is the country's strongest labor confederation, in terms of membership, followed by the CTH and CGT. Notwithstanding these categories, the Honduran labor movement is extremely weak and divided today (see Table 4.1 for a descriptive overview of its key tendencies).[34] This situation benefits the Honduran *maquiladora* industry because it thrives on feeble labor unions, low wages, and poor working conditions.

Table 4.1 The Honduran Labor Movement, 1964–Present

Labor Confederation (Central)	Ideological Perspective	Year Established
CTH	Moderate	1964
CGT	Conservative	1970
CUTH	Left	1992

The Honduran Maquiladora Industry and Labor[35]

The Honduran *maquiladora* industry is the strongest one in Central America. Facing spiraling unemployment, rising external debt, rapid population growth, and fluctuating commodity prices, as well as pressure from the United States Agency for International Development (USAID), the Honduran government, in the 1970s, adopted a "non-traditional" export model, which was primarily based on attracting foreign investment through the creation of special geographic areas known as "free trade zones" (*Las Zonas Libres*—ZOLIs).[36] The first ZOLI was established in 1976 in Puerto Cortes and three years later, ZOLIs were created in Tela, Omoa, La Ceiba, Ampala, and Choloma. ZOLIs are government-owned enterprises that lease out space for foreign investors, providing them with the ability to import raw materials and re-export finished goods without tariffs and duties, and with tax exemptions on profits.[37]

Despite Honduras' shift towards greater democratization in the early 1980s and its abundant supply of cheap labor, the ZOLIs and later, the "industrial export processing zones" (*Las Zonas Industriales de Procesamiento para Exportaciones*—ZIPs), which gave companies even more far-ranging benefits, including complete elimination of tariffs and duties, no payment of any taxes of any kind, and utility rate deductions, did not initially generate much foreign investment. In the late 1980s, there were less than twenty factories and ten thousand workers in the *maquiladora* industry. Political instability, inflation, corruption, and the violent civil war in neighboring Nicaragua scared off potential investors, thwarting the industry's growth.

In 1990, the Nicaraguan civil war finally ended and the National Party's Rafael Callejas became President. One of Callejas' initial tasks in office was managing the country's deep economic crisis. During the 1980s, average real wages fell every year, combined under and unemployment figures reached a staggering 70 percent, poverty and malnutrition levels climbed to over 50 percent, budget deficits soared, and foreign debt doubled, rising from $1.7 billion in 1981 to $3.4 billion in 1989. These figures indicate the Honduran economy was in serious trouble when Callejas assumed power.[38]

Under the Liberal Party administration of José Azcona (1985–1989), Honduras moved toward accepting the "Washington Consensus" model of IMF and World Bank-supported neoliberal reforms, such as, structural adjustment policies, privatization, cuts in social spending, export-oriented growth, incentives for foreign investors, and currency devaluation. During the subsequent administration (1990–1994), Callejas maintained and *expanded* these policies, selling off publicly-owned enterprises, laying off state employees, raising sales and income taxes, and reducing tariffs and investment regulations.[39]

These policies exacerbated poverty and misery, but they also stimulated increased foreign investment. Southeast Asian and U.S. garment producers found the entire San Pedro Sula Valley region attractive because of its world-class port (which facilitates quicker turn-around time), five ZOLIs and eight ZIPs (replete with tax, tariff, duty, and utility exemptions and unlimited profit repatriation), and plentiful supply of cheap labor.

These contextual factors accounted for the rapid growth of the *maquiladora* industry in the early and middle 1990s. The Honduran Apparel Manufacturers Association (HAMA) reports that the industry had 8,300 workers in 1989. Five years later, there 50,000.[40] In 1999, there were over 250 factories and 110,000 workers in the entire industry. In terms of exports, Honduras sent $87 million of apparel goods to the United States in 1989 and $646 million in 1994—a whopping 642 percent increase. In 1998, the export figure reached $1.8 billion (see Table 4.2). In 1994, Honduras was the seventeenth largest supplier of apparel goods in the entire world to the U.S. market and the third largest in Central America; in 1998, it moved up to fifth place in the world and to first place in Central America. Thus, in ten short years, Honduras became the regional leader in apparel exports and employment.[41]

In addition to these statistical indicators, several other key characteristics of the Honduran *maquiladora* industry are worth noting. First, the vast majority of industry's estimated two hundred and fifty factories are located in the northeastern cities of San Pedro Sula, Villanueva, Bufalo, La Lima, El Progreso, Choloma, and La Ceiba.[42] This spatial concentration is not too surprising given the area's rapid industrialization rate since the 1960s and its close proximity to Puerto Cortes. Second, most *maquila* factories are located inside either ZOLIs or ZIPs, although the privatization of the latter has made them more attractive for foreign investors than the former. Third, in 1998, approximately 41 percent of all *maquila* factories were U.S.-owned, 32 percent Honduran-owned, 14 percent Korean-owned, and 13 percent were classified as "other."[43] Some of the best-known U.S. labels that are produced in Honduras include Oshkosh B'Gosh, Phillips Van-Heusen, J.C. Penney, Sara Lee, Maidenform, and Jansport.

Women constitute the overwhelming majority of *maquiladora* workers in Honduras. Approximately 80–85 percent of the industry's 110,000 workers are

Table 4.2 Honduran Maquiladora Industry Exports

Year	Exports in U.S.$
1987	87.0
1994	646.0
1995	921.1
1996	1,219.5
1997	1,659.0
1998	1,855.1

Source: Honduran Apparel Manufacturers Association (1999), 2.

women between the ages of fourteen and twenty-four.[44] Many women *maquila* workers have very low levels of education, few know their labor rights, and 50 percent are new migrants from the *campo* (countryside).[45] Nelly del Cid, Carla Castro, and Yadira Rodríguez found that women *maquila* workers typically feel "liberated" from "traditional" gender roles, but that they also face constant pressure and threats of punishment and harassment from their male supervisors. They also report that many women *maquila* workers have no union experience and fear joining one might cause them to lose their jobs.[46]

Despite this very real, tangible concern, there many reasons why some *maquila* workers might take such a risk. Although the Honduran Labor Code explicitly limits the workday to eight hours and the work-week to forty-four hours, a typical shift runs ten to twelve hours a day.[47] Because of the piece-rate system, wages vary, but they range between 50–60 cents an hour.[48] Inside the factories, most workers are not allowed to talk with each other. Bathroom breaks are strictly timed and regulated. In some cases, women have been forced to take birth-control pills. Pregnant women have also been fired without receiving their legally guaranteed benefits. Many factories are also extremely hot and poorly ventilated, making breathing very difficult. Asthma, bronchitis, and other respiratory-related illnesses, along with fainting spells, have been widely reported as well. Stress-related health problems, such as insomnia, loss of appetite, spasms, and diarrhea are also quite common.[49]

These conditions have generated discontent. In the early 1990s, there were nearly thirty labor conflicts, involving nearly 25,000 workers.[50] There also have been numerous wildcat strikes, work stoppages, and union organizing campaigns over the past few years. The Honduran Labor Code stipulates that before unions can be legally recognized they must have at least thirty members.[51] This may sound like a low threshold, but it is not. Thousands of *maquila* workers have been fired for union activity.[52] Based on Honduras' neoliberal, export-oriented model that favors foreign investors, labor ministry officials have often turned over the names of union members to company representatives, who, in turn, have fired those workers. The 1999 U.S. State Department human rights report on Honduras described this common practice:

> When unions are formed, organizers must submit a list of initial members to the Ministry of Labor as part of the process of obtaining official recognition. However, before recognition is granted, the Ministry must inform the company of the impending union organization. The Ministry has not always been able to provide effective protection to union organizers. There were credible reports, particularly in the export processing zone sector, that some inspectors had gone so far as *to sell the names of employees involved in forming a union to companies that then dismissed union organizers before the Ministry could recognize the unions* [emphasis added].[53]

Despite these odds, *maquila* workers have organized nearly two dozen unions. The International Labor Organization (ILO) reports that there were twenty-eight unions and 42,000 unionized workers in the Honduran *maquiladora* industry, while the U.S. State Department study cited above claimed that there were forty-six unions, thirty-two of which had collective bargaining agreements.[54] These numbers are probably inflated. Officials from CUTH, FITH, FUTH, and the CTH, as well as other human rights activists and scholars, contend that there are about twenty *maquila* unions.[55] More than half of these unions are affiliated with FITH/CUTH and several of them have negotiated contracts.[56] The CUTH and the CTH allege that most other *maquila* unions are "solidarity associations" or "company unions" that do not represent their members' best interests.[57] These organizations may be included in the ILO and State Department reports, thereby accounting for the numerical discrepancies.

Based on interviews, primary and secondary sources, and direct observation, the level of unionization in the *maquiladora* industry is minimal (although it is higher in Honduras than other Central American countries). Various factors (such as capital mobility, unemployment, fear, and mass firings) make *maquila* labor organizing extremely difficult. These constraints, along with the labor movement's weaknesses, created a vacuum that some non-government organizations like the Committee for Defense of Human Rights in Honduras (*El Comité para la Defensa de los Derechos Humanos en Honduras*—CODEH) and the Collective of Honduran Women (*Colectiva de Mujeres Hondureñas*—CODEMUH) have partially filled. These two NGOs have conducted studies documenting labor and women's rights violations, as well as wages and working conditions in the *maquila* industry, and have held legal rights workshops for women workers.[58] These classes have personally transformed many workers and sporadically improved working conditions, but they have not yet had a widespread impact.[59]

This synopsis illustrates that challenging sweatshop labor practices in the Honduran *maquiladora* industry is no easy task. Notwithstanding all the barriers and limitations, some workers—like those at Kimi—successfully fought back, albeit for a short time. The gains that they made evaporated over time. What factors explain these disparate results? That story comes next.

The Kimi Workers Campaign: Fighting For Recognition, 1993–1996

Kimi de Honduras (Kimi for short) is one of eight *maquila* factories located in *Parque Continental*, in the city of La Lima, Cortes. Kimi is a Korean-owned factory that opened up in 1990. Its six hundred to eight hundred workers, mostly young women between the ages of eighteen and twenty-five, produce women's and men's shirts for J.C. Penney's, Macy's, and the Gap. Other U.S.-based companies that source from Continental Park include Kohl's, Dayton-Hudson, Salant, Phillips Van-Heusen, and American Eagle.

The Kimi union organizing campaign began in 1993. SITRAKIMIH General-Secretary Sara Aguillón recalled those early days:

I started working for Kimi in 1993. There were people inside already organizing workers. At first, I wasn't interested—I was scared. Over time, some friends began talking with me about organizing and little by little, I became less frightened. During this time period, we met in each other's houses because it was safer and people talked about why we needed to organize. A few workers also told stories about how their fathers and uncles were involved in the great banana strike. Over time, more and more people, like myself, lost their fears and so that's how it all began.[60]

Why did the Kimi workers begin organizing? Sara Aguillón stated:

The Korean supervisors always treated us badly. They yelled, 'faster, faster,' and hit some workers if they did not. Sometimes they did not give us our paychecks. They also forced us to take urine tests, didn't allow us to use the bathroom, and forbade us from talking to each other. They searched us every time we entered and left the factory. They were very, very strict. The conditions were very bad.[61]

During late 1994, the fledging union's membership expanded. Union executive committee member Yesenia Bonilla claimed that the union actually organized nearly all the *maquila* workers inside Continental Park. Before the union filed for legal recognition, however, the company fired every single member of the union's executive committee.

While this was a major setback, Bonilla noted:

We did make some gains. We got purified water; the company started to pay for transportation; and they also fixed the road to the factory, which used to be horrible. They put in lights so it wasn't dark for the workers who had to walk home late at night. But it didn't take long before they forgot all that and started treating us badly again. They took away our transportation and the other things that we gained.[62]

These anti-union activities did not derail the campaign; rather, they sparked a new round of organizing. In 1995, the Kimi Workers Union, which was not affiliated at that time with any Honduran labor confederation, began working with UNITE Representative Bruce Fieldman (a long-time U.S. labor activist in Central America), on a clandestine organizing plan to strengthen its membership base. The plan was based on the factory's production lines. Each line contained three to five "delegates" or organizers that were responsible for recruiting and signing up new members through private house visits. This organizing model eased workers' fears that they might be fired for joining the union. These

Fig. 4.1 Continental Park sign (note, Kimi is located mid-center). Photo credit—U.S./LEAP.

savvy tactics ultimately worked—more than one hundred fifty workers became new members between 1995 and 1996.[63]

The broader strategy behind this model was to build a resilient and sustainable organization with a deep, committed membership and leadership base that could withstand the company's anti-union policies. Previously, most *maquila* unions filed for legal recognition with few more than thirty members, but company officials often obtained their names from the labor ministry and fired them, thereby stopping the campaign. The Kimi Workers Union and UNITE thought that they might avoid this outcome by signing up so many members that the company could not fire them all. As long as the union had enough members, they believed, Kimi could be legally compelled to recognize the union *and* negotiate a contract at the same time.[64]

Those were the campaign's two key objectives. After months of clandestine organizing, the union came out into the open and presented its membership list to the labor ministry on July 27, 1996. Later that day, more than four hundred Kimi workers, along with hundreds of Continental Park *maquila* workers, held a work stoppage and gave the company the same exact list. These were exciting times for the newly established Kimi Workers Union (SITRAKIMIH). However, two weeks later, sixteen workers were fired, including most members of the union's executive committee (or *junta directiva*). SITRAKIMIH General-Secretary Sara Aguillón described what happened next:

We knew that the company was trying to eliminate the union, but we could not let that happen. The fired workers began demonstrating outside the park. Inside the factory, the workers began protesting—they held up signs, chanted slogans, pounded on tables, and stopped working for thirty minutes. Our main demands were—rehire the workers and recognize the union. The company didn't listen—they were hard-headed, like *burros*. They then fired forty-eight more workers. They thought that would stop us, but it did not. We continued fighting.[65]

Indeed, they did. After the second wave of firings, union executive committe members, rank-and-file activists, and UNITE, along with officials from FITH/CUTH, met and planned their next move—a strike. For five days—between October 7 and 12—nothing moved inside the factory. This action finally produced the results that the union was looking for. Kimi rehired almost all the fired workers and agreed to recognize the union—in six months.[66]

This was a major triumph for the Kimi workers. How was it achieved? During this phase of the campaign, SITRAKIMIH and UNITE were the two main actors—the two unions worked closely together. UNITE provided SITRAKIMIH with technical and strategic advice as well as financial assistance, thereby strengthening the union. I call this process *organization-building politics* (see Figure 4.2). Keck and Sikkink (1998) do not discuss this strategy because they position the transnational advocacy network as the "key agent" of social change. In this specific case, the TAN (which essentially included only one organization—UNITE), provided the domestic nonstate actor with much-needed support, but it was the high degree of unity and solidarity within SITRAKIMIH, and the workers' courage that triggered this victory. "Sweatshop warriors" like Sara Aguillón, Yesenia Bonilla, and many others like them took great risks. UNITE could not have produced this outcome without them. Unlike the PVH and Gap campaigns, information, leverage, and accountability politics were not used, although pressure on U.S. retailers may have indirectly facilitated Kimi's decision to recognize the union.

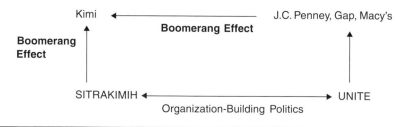

Fig. 4.2 Union Recognition and the Kimi Campaign–Part I.

Independent Monitoring Versus Unionization, 1996–1998

The July and October 1996 strikes at Kimi helped generate a debate in Honduran-based regional and national newspapers about the country's booming *maquiladora* industry. Meanwhile, in the United States, at nearly the same time, the Kathie Lee Gifford scandal and the infamous Thai slavery case prompted President Clinton to establish an anti-sweatshop task force known as the Apparel Industry Partnership (AIP) in 1996.

The AIP initially involved garment manufacturers, government officials, NGOs, and unions. The AIP drafted a voluntary code of conduct stating that corporations that ousource production overseas should not employ anyone under fifteen years old; limit the work-week to sixty hours; pay local, "prevailing" minimum wages; and protect the right to organize.[67] The code also stated that garment manufacturers like Nike, Liz Claiborne, and Phillips Van-Heusen should hire "independent monitors" to insure proper implementation of its provisions.

After intense internal debate, UNITE and several NGOs within the AIP left the organization on the grounds that its code would perpetuate, rather than eliminate, sweatshop labor practices.[68] The National Labor Committee expressed similar concerns about the AIP code of conduct. Despite these shared views, a rift between the NLC and UNITE opened up over the efficacy of independent monitoring versus unionization. Both organizations rhetorically supported these two strategies. On the ground, in this specific case, they were seen in dualistic, either–or terms, however, with the NLC supporting independent monitoring and UNITE backing unionization.

How did this dispute affect the Kimi campaign? After the July and October strikes, SITRAKIMIH was independent, although FITH/CUTH provided it with some support. The left-leaning CUTH is not affiliated with the International Confederation of Free Trade Unions (ICFTU), but the CTH and the AFL-CIO are. Based on these long-standing historical and ideological ties, UNITE and the American Institute for Free Labor Development (AIFLD) advised SITRAKIMIH to join a CTH-linked labor federation—the Unified Federation of Honduran Textile Workers (FESITRAINCOH).[69] Over the next year, SITRAKIMIH maintained ties with FESITRAINCOH, but it worked more closely with UNITE, along with the International Textile, Garment and Leather Workers Federation's (ITGLWF) regional affiliate, the Inter-American Textile and Garment Workers' Federation (FITTIV) and the American Center for International Labor Solidarity (ACILS), which in 1997 replaced AIFLD (for glossary of these terms see Appendix A).

During late 1996 and early 1997, SITRAKIMIH anxiously waited for Kimi to legally recognize the union and begin contract negotiations. The Honduran

Labor Code states that employers must negotiate with legally recognized unions, no matter how many members they might have.[70]

After several months passed, the NLC contacted CODEH, CODEMUH, Caritas Diocesana (a community-based organization affiliated with the Catholic Church), the Mennonite Church, and the Jesuit-linked Reflection, Research, and Communication Team (ERIC) in El Progreso about the possibility of creating an independent monitoring team to investigate labor rights violations inside Honduran *maquila* factories.[71] UNITE was apparently not involved in these conversations. NLC Executive Director Charlie Kernaghan, in fact, sharply criticized UNITE for maintaining ties with the CTH, calling it "corrupt" and "tainted by AIFLD and the Cold War."[72]

The talks between the NLC and the Honduran-based NGOS mentioned above finally bore fruit with the establishment of the Independent Monitoring Team (EMI) in June 1997. The NLC had several previous discussions with Kimi and knew that it was interested in independent monitoring and in resolving the problems inside the factory. These talks laid the basis for the signing of the first-ever independent monitoring agreement in the Honduran *maquiladora* industry on June 2, 1997 (only one other such agreement, incidentally, existed in Central America [El Salvador] at that time).

The agreement focused on four specific issues: managerial misconduct (specifically activities involving Kimi personnel manager Rigoberto Echeverría); poor treatment of pregnant workers; legal recognition of the union; and rehiring illegally fired union members and workers.[73] EMI informed Kimi that it had three weeks to resolve these issues and that if it did so, it would work with garment companies to "reestablish contracts" with the company. This language is revealing because when labor unrest broke out at Kimi, some feared that J.C. Penney, Macy's, and the Gap, three of its most high-profile buyers, would simply cut and run. J.C. Penney did cut back some production orders with Kimi for "business reasons," but did not pull out one hundred percent; neither did Macy's. The Gap did leave, however.[74]

Over that three-week time period (late June through early July 1997), J.C. Penney called Kimi several different times to resolve the dispute.[75] After nearly a year, Kimi capitulated and recognized SITRAKIMIH in July 1997. This outcome indicates that EMI and the NLC, along with the United States/Guatemala Labor Education Project (U.S./GLEP), which was also involved in negotiations with J.C. Penney,[76] more than likely used the U.S.-based retailer's concerns about its public image being smeared with allegations of sweatshop labor to put pressure on Kimi to recognize the union. In Keck and Sikkink's (1998) terminology, the TAN gained "moral leverage" over the "secondary target" (J.C. Penney), which pressured the "primary target" (Kimi) to grant concessions to the "domestic non-state" actor (SITRAKIMIH) (see Figure 4.3).

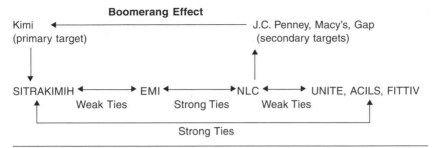

Fig. 4.3 Union Recognition and The Kimi Campaign—Part II.

Having temporarily resolved the recognition issue, SITRAKIMIH and EMI turned toward improving wages and working conditions inside the factory. EMI's regular, unannounced visits curtailed mass firings and verbal assaults on workers. SITRAKIMIH initially praised these results, but later agued that EMI "took over" its customary role, conducting informal bargaining sessions with Kimi personnel. SITRAKIMIH also maintained that collective bargaining was more effective than independent monitoring, while EMI claimed that the latter strategy could open up "space" for the former.

These tensions slowed down contract negotiations between July 1997 and November 1998. EMI representatives suggested that Kimi officials (especially Echeverría) exacerbated this conflict, dividing workers that supported either SITRAKIMIH or EMI. Making this situation even worse was the split between the NLC on one side and the UNITE, FITTIV, and the ACILS on the other. The NLC distrusted UNITE's involvement with CTH-FESITRAINCOH, calling it "incompetent" and "practically useless" (SITRAKIMIH eventually broke off and became independent, once again, based on internal discussions and advice from Bruce Fieldman, who began working with FITTIV in 1997). Meanwhile, UNITE officials asserted that EMI's members did not have the "expertise or experience" that was needed for monitoring Kimi. UNITE, FITTIV, and ACILS representatives also criticized the NLC for fostering a "paternalistic" approach that turns *maquila* workers into victims who depend on "benevolent intervention."[77]

This raw, although largely hidden conflict,[78] negatively affected this all-important phase of the campaign. SITARKIMIH obtained earlier gains when the TAN was largely united and had a strong membership base. When internal divisions emerged within the TAN, Kimi exploited them, making further progress nearly impossible.

Tragedy Turns Into Victory Turns Into Defeat, 1998–2000

In the midst of this "man-made" storm, a real natural disaster struck—Hurricane Mitch. Mitch came ashore in late October 1998, causing floods and landslides that destroyed crops, homes, and entire villages. The massive, category five hurricane left more than five thousand people dead and hundreds of thousands homeless. Southern cities like Choluteca and Tegucigalpa were hit the hardest, but Mitch eventually traveled north, pounding San Pedro Sula with torrential rains that flooded rivers and sent residents rushing for higher ground.[79]

Mitch devastated the entire country, but how did the hurricane specifically affect the Kimi campaign? Company supervisors shut down the factory for ninety days (November 1998–February 1999) for cleanup and repair. The workers finished the job in two weeks. Despite this fact, the plant remained closed down. Sara Aguillón blasted this decision on the popular El Progreso radio station:

> When we finished cleaning the factory, they closed the doors and told us that we should show up [for work] on February 3rd. They only wanted to take advantage of us to do the cleaning work. We cannot accept that. We rise up against them and say, 'we need these jobs because Mitch did not kill us, but Hurricane Kimi will kill us of hunger!' We have the only union in Continental Park. We have made tremendous sacrifices over these past few years, but we have succeeded and now we are fighting for a contract.[80]

With this salvo, the confrontation between Kimi and SITRAKIMIH reached a new height. The union wrote a letter to the NLC, requesting that it talk with Kimi's main buyers (especially J.C. Penney) to reopen the factory and to send it more production orders. This action indicates that despite earlier tensions between SITRAKIMIH, EMI, UNITE, and the NLC, some degree of cooperation was maintained in the middle of this crisis.

As more time passed, UNITE raised the possibility of placing Honduras' Generalized System of Preferences (GSP) benefits "under review." The GSP is a U.S.-based policy that provides recipient nations hundreds of millions of dollars in trade benefits, provided that they protect internationally recognized worker rights standards, like the right to organize and collectively bargain.[81] Given Honduras' intransigent stance toward *maquila* unions like SITRAKIMIH, UNITE believed that GSP pressure could provide the Kimi workers with a key source of "material leverage." GSP pressure had been used before in the campaign.[82] Indeed, it may have led the Labor Ministry to lean on Kimi to begin contract negotiations with SITRAKIMIH in 1998. However, those talks never got off the ground.

UNITE understood that the potential loss of GSP benefits might have exacerbated Honduras' economic woes after Hurricane Mitch, so it momentarily backed off. As the country slowly recovered, UNITE raised the issue again.[83] This time around trade pressure, a letter-writing campaign, regular production orders from J.C. Penney, rank-and-file pressure from SITRAKIMIH, and hopeful, though tenuous, bonds of solidarity between UNITE, U.S./LEAP (the United States/Labor in the Americas Project, formerly U.S./GLEP), and the NLC broke the logjam in January 1999. Fearing potential trade sanctions, the Labor Ministry, the Honduran Apparel Manufacturers Association (HAMA), and J.C. Penney leaned on Kimi to begin contract negotiations with SITRAKIMIH.[84] Finally, after six long years, on March 19, 1999, Kimi workers ratified a two-year contract, calling for a 10 percent pay increase, bonuses, health benefits, and vacation and holiday pay.[85] Through organization-building, information, and leverage politics, the TAN *and* the domestic non-state actor generated this remarkable outcome—one of the few contracts in the Honduran *maquila* industry as well as the entire Central American region (see Figure 4.4).

This victory was short-lived. After the contract was signed, Continental Park owner Jaime Rosenthal declared that he would not renew Kimi's lease in August 1999.[86] This move led Kimi to begin looking for a new production site located miles away. Faced with this new predicament, SITRAKIMIH fought back. Union members slowed down production, chanted slogans, and hung banners inside the factory. SITRAKIMIH also contacted U.S./LEAP and the Campaign for Labor Rights (CLR) in the United States. These two NGOs coordinated a letter-writing, fax, and e-mail campaign against Rosenthal and Kimi. In a related move, EMI suspended its monitoring activities after Kimi blocked it from conducting surprise visits on the shop floor.[87]

These strategies backed Rosenthal into a corner. He eventually relented, renewing Kimi's lease for one more year. Kimi then called off its proposed move. SITRAKIMIH praised this decision, but also raised concerns about the company's violations of the collective bargaining agreement during negotiations

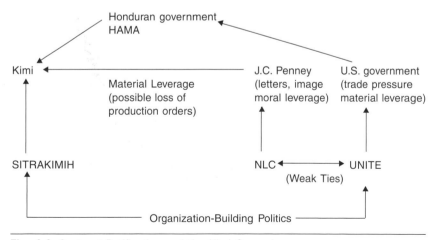

Fig. 4.4 Contract Ratification and the Kimi Campaign.

with Kimi. Talks revolving around this latter issue proceeded amicably until mid-August 1999, when Kimi suddenly walked out of the meetings and retracted a verbally agreed upon pay increase that would have raised the factory's minimum wage from 49 cents to 55 cents an hour.[88]

This latter move was the symbolic last straw. The Kimi workers went on strike for two days in late August 1999. On the third day, the entire Continental Park work force joined the work stoppage, making it a virtual general strike. The police broke up the action with tear gas, batons, and shields. Several Kimi workers were injured during the violent melee.[89]

This violent clash ignited a severe backlash against Kimi and the Honduran government. U.S./LEAP and the CLR immediately disseminated action alerts, requesting that letters, faxes, and e-mails be sent to the Honduran Ambassador to the United States and the Korean Ambassador in Honduras. The U.S. government also began discussions regarding Honduras' GSP benefits, which prompted the Labor Ministry and HAMA to actively intervene to resolve the conflict. Confronted with pressure from virtually all sides, Kimi backed down, raising the factory's minimum wage and accepting all provisions of the March 1999 collective bargaining agreement.[90]

This was a major victory, but it did not last very long. Jaime Rosenthal pulled Kimi's lease in February 2000. Before this action was made, the company and union both agreed to move the factory to a new location. This move was made

Fig. 4.5 Kimi workers rally outside the office of the Honduran Labor Ministry to reopen factory—May 2000. Photo credit—U.S./LEAP.

without incident.[91] Three months later, on May 5, 2000 Kimi shut down, however, citing "financial difficulties" and "intractable problems with the union's leadership."[92] Did these claims have any legitimacy? U.S./LEAP discovered that just after Kimi signed the March 1999, two-year contract, the company began moving production to a non-union plant in Guatemala called Modas Cielo. It appears that J.C. Penney, which earlier played a positive role in the campaign, stopped sourcing from Kimi after the August 1999 strike.[93] J.C. Penney transferred its orders to Modas Cielo, but it soon pulled out, leaving the company to find new buyers[94]

After Kimi shut down, more than one hundred and fifty workers later signed a petition to re-open the factory. The ITGLWF, U.S./LEAP, and the United Students Against Sweatshops (USAS) made similar requests.[95] Kimi rejected their pleas. Company officials may yet change their minds, but that is extremely unlikely.[96] Kimi de Honduras remains officially closed.

Analysis

How did this campaign end so tragically? How did this once stirring victory turn into defeat? Before analyzing those questions, let us first examine the gains that were made. SITRAKIMIH obtained legal recognition through organization-building politics. In Keck and Sikkink's (1998) model, domestic non-state actors establish ties with NGOs, creating transnational advocacy networks (TANs), who, in turn, put pressure on their respective states to bring about social change.[97] This model, as we have seen, is quite useful, but it inadvertently places too much emphasis on TANs, making them seem like they are the "saviors" of the "poor, downtrodden, masses."

This may not be Keck and Sikkink's intent, but their model gives one the impression that domestic non-state actors cannot independently determine their own fates without "outside assistance." As the previous two chapters have illustrated, transnational advocacy networks can only do so much on their own. Strong domestic non-state actors and relatively unified transnational advocacy networks, working together, are more likely to create far-reaching results.

What does this mean for the Kimi campaign? The Kimi workers initially organized themselves without any assistance and directly challenged the company, but they had very little leverage. SITRAKIMIH eventually asked UNITE for support. The two unions developed close ties with each other and mapped out a clandestine organizing plan. This model considerably strengthened SITRAKIMIH. Despite suffering several early setbacks, the union's members pressed Kimi to promise to recognize SITARAKIMIH six months after the October 1996 strike. Organization-building politics (e.g., the "strategic alliance" between SITRAKIMIH and UNITE) made this phase of the campaign successful.

Fig. 4.6 Kimi workers rally outside the office of the Honduran Labor Ministry to reopen the factory in May 2000. The sign reads, "For violating our constitutional rights, we ask for international sanctions. SITRAKIMIH—for the protection of our rights." Photo credit—U.S./LEAP.

The union was not recognized within six months, however. While SITRAKIMIH continued organizing inside and outside the factory, the NLC became involved in the campaign, establishing links with Honduran NGOs. These latter organizations created the Independent Monitoring Team (EMI). EMI, the NLC, and U.S./GLEP pressured J.C. Penney, one of Kimi's main buyers, to not "cut and run" when the campaign became public. The retailer probably feared that such a move would damage its reputation and reinforce the notion that it condoned sweatshop labor practices. J.C. Penney (the secondary target) therefore used its "material leverage" (the potential loss of production orders) over Kimi (the primary target) to essentially force it to recognize SITRAKIMIH. This outcome illustrates what strong domestic non-state actors and fairly well-unified TANs can achieve.

The next stage of the campaign revolved around contract negotiations. Kimi's stalling tactics delayed them from starting, but so did the conflict between the NLC and UNITE. This battle, stemming from mutual distrust, strategic differences, and the after-effects of the Cold War, became quite heated (even though it was not visible) and nearly derailed the campaign. Thus, despite the involvement of a very capable and active domestic non-state actor (SITRAKIMIH), splits within the TAN made further progress almost impossible.

Contract talks were still halted when Hurricane Mitch hit the factory in November 1998. After waiting several months, UNITE raised the issue of Honduras' GSP benefits to break the impasse. The NLC and U.S./LEAP, for their part, urged J.C. Penney, through informal negotiations and a letter-writing campaign, to use its influence over Kimi to settle the conflict. Trade pressure gave the Kimi workers "material leverage" over one of its targets—the Honduran government—and letter-writing provided them with "moral leverage" over their other key target—J.C. Penney. Rank-and-file pressure from SITRAKIMIH, technical assistance from FITTIV, UNITE, and the ACILS, a fragile transnational advocacy network, and the fear of losing one of its main buyers placed Kimi in an untenable position. Feeling heat from all sides, Kimi gave in, negotiating a two-year contract with SITRAKIMIH on March 19, 1999. This time, organization-building, leverage, and information politics were the key factors that generated this stirring victory.

Before the ink was dry of the contract, however, the Kim workers faced a new challenge—Jaime Rosenthal. Rosenthal's anti-union stance exacerbated tensions within the factory. That pressure bubbled over in late August 1999, with Kimi workers organizing a three-day strike and the police responding with tear gas. These violent tactics generated a new round of leafleting, trade pressure, and grass-roots activism, prompting Kimi to raise the factory's minimum wage and comply with the collective bargaining agreement.

J.C. Penney did not play a positive role during this phase of the campaign. In fact, it started shifting production to Kimi's Guatemala-based factory shortly after the August 1999 strike. Without pressure from J.C. Penney, SITRAKIMIH and its transnational allies lost an important source of material leverage, giving Kimi more freedom to do as it pleased. Feeling unencumbered, company supervisors permanently shut down the factory on May 5, 2000.

What factors explain this outcome? One strategy for addressing this question might be to make an arbitrary distinction between "external" and "internal" forces. The former would include corporate intransigence and capital mobility, while the latter involves conflicts within domestic non-state actors or transnational advocacy networks.

Kimi was clearly anti-union throughout the entire campaign. Company officials did all that they could to crush SITRAKIMIH. The union's leaders and rank-and-file members never gave up, however. They continued fighting with assistance from UNITE, FITTIV, ACILS, NLC, and EMI. Internal conflicts within the transnational advocacy network emerged, however, slowing down contract negotiations and limiting the effectiveness of the campaign to reopen the factory.

Were these divisions ultimately responsible for the factory's closure? I do not believe so. Greater unity between UNITE, FITTIV, ACILS, and the NLC might have been slowed down Kimi, but broader "external" forces, like capital mobility and the dispersed nature of production, gave the company the "ultimate" upper-hand. Given this situation, the campaign's gains were extremely hard to sustain over time.

SITRAKIMIH and its transnational allies, ultimately, successfully pressured four targets—Kimi, J.C. Penney, and the U.S. and Honduran governments—for a brief moment. The outcome of this very complex process was a two-year contract. Long-standing conflicts within that transnational advocacy network, however, gave J.C. Penney some space to "cut and run." Without the threat of losing production orders, SITRAKIMIH's main source of material leverage over Kimi evaporated. The union's remaining members fought valiantly to reopen the factory, but they could not reverse this decision.

The most optimal conditions for a successful cross-border labor solidarity campaign include the participation of a strong local union and a fairly unified transnational advocacy network (TAN). The Kimi campaign illustrates that both conditions are not always necessary—despite divisions within the TAN, a collective bargaining agreement was signed. Conflicts within the TAN weakened the campaign's efficacy, however. Yet, even if the TAN's members were united, it probably would not have made a significant difference.

The Kimi campaign was one where capital mobility trumped all other factors. A strong local union and cohesive transnational advocacy network may have temporarily prolonged the final outcome, but this would not have stopped Kimi. This is a bleak assessment, but it does not mean that challenging sweatshop labor practices is impossible. It can be done over short periods of time, yet in order for long-lasting gains to be made, cross-border labor solidarity campaigns need to take occur on a region-wide basis so companies like Kimi, J.C. Penney, and PVH, for that matter, have no place to run or hide.

Conclusion

The Kimi campaign cannot be classified as a clear-cut victory or defeat. Sara Aguillón, Yesenia Bonilla, and all the Kimi workers took great risks and made tremendous sacrifices before they finally won. They eventually lost their jobs, but they were not really defeated. These sweatshop warriors motivated their sisters and brothers at Yoo Yang and other Continental Park-based *maquilas* with their passion, humility, and *ganas* (desire) and inspired anti-sweatshop activists all over the world.

Long-standing historical, political, and strategic conflicts between U.S.-based solidarity groups and unions affected the campaign, but hopefully they will reflect upon and openly discuss those differences and begin working more closely together. The only chance that *maquila* workers and their cross-border allies have of eliminating sweatshops is through dialogue, debate, and consensus. These factors may not be enough, but they are absolutely crucial for creating a more sustainable and successful movement.

5

Ni Un Paso Atrás!
Not One Step Back!
Chentex and Cross-Border Labor Solidarity in the Nicaraguan Maquiladora Industry

The company calls us "terrorists," but we ask them, "who are the *real* terrorists?" They are the ones that fired young workers, with children. These workers have made tremendous sacrifices. Sometimes their children don't even eat. Why? Because the company won't pay them a just salary. That's not right. They're the terrorists, not us.[1]
 —Gladys Manzanares, General Secretary, Chentex Workers Union

Doña Gladys and the Chentex Campaign

Miriam Ching Yoon Louie calls "sweatshop warriors" neither "victims nor super-women." They are "simple everyday women in our communities who have much to tell and teach."[2] Gladys Manzanares is one of those women. She is a short, energetic, warm, middle-aged grandmother, mother, garment worker, and union leader. She is passionate, empathetic, generous, and unassuming. Her family, friends, neighbors, and co-workers deeply respect and admire her humble, yet resolute demeanor (calling her Doña Gladys).

Manzanares has struggled for social and economic justice for the past thirty years. As snipers stood on rooftops with their machine guns aimed on the crowds below them, she boldly marched against Somoza in the early 1970s. Several years later, she helped organize strikes and unions in clothing factories under the Sandinistas militant red-and-black banner.[3] Finally, after forty long years, the U.S.-backed Somoza dictatorship fell and the Sandinistas took power, introducing land redistribution and socioeconomic programs that turned long-standing class and power relationships upside down.

Manzanares strongly supported the Sandinista Revolution and remained politically active throughout the 1980s. Not everyone, of course, rallied around the new regime. The United States government, under President Reagan, and former members of Somoza's National Guard created a counter-revolutionary army, known as the *Contras*, to overthrow the Sandinistas. The Contras and Sandinistas fought for ten years, leaving tens of thousands of Nicaraguans dead and the country in shambles, with massive inflation, poverty, and unemployment.

Feeling numb, frustrated, and tired of war, the Nicaraguan people shocked the world, voting the Sandinistas out of power in 1990. The new conservative government overturned many of the Sandinistas' policies and opened up the country for foreign investment, establishing a free trade zone,[4] called Las Mercedes, complete with tax exemptions and unlimited profit repatriation, in 1991. Investors from the United States and Taiwan found these incentives, along with the country's abundant supply of cheap labor, appealing, and, in the 1990s, built dozens of export-oriented clothing assembly factories, known as *maquiladoras*.

Chentex is one of those factories and Gladys Manzanares is one of its nearly two thousand workers who produce brand-name jeans like Arizona, Faded Glory, Route 66, Sonoma, Bugle Boy, and Gloria Vanderbilt for J.C. Penney, Kmart, Wal-Mart, Target, and Kohl's. Given staggering levels of unemployment and very few job opportunities, other than working in the *campo* (countryside) or the informal sector, Manzanares like most of her *compañeras* (sisters) and *compañeros* (brothers) in the *maquiladora* industry, initially welcomed her new job. Her enthusiasm waned over time, however, as she became increasingly aware of the low wages and poor working conditions inside Chentex.

As we sat outside the doorway of her dirt-floor house in the working-class *colonia* of Waspan Norte, Manzanares talked about working for the company:

> I had worked for other companies before, but these were the worst conditions that I ever saw. The supervisors treated us badly and called us bad names. They timed us when we went to the bathroom and did not let us visit the medical clinic when it was open. We started working at seven in the morning and worked until 5:15 in the afternoon, but sometimes they made us work overtime, without paying us, until 7 or even 10 PM. The factory minimum wage is 800 *cordobas* ($64) a month. Workers can sometimes earn a little more than that, but no one live like this. The workers finally decided that they could not take these conditions any longer. We were suffering—so we started to organize.[5]

The campaign got off the ground in 1997. Manzanares was one of its key leaders, becoming General-Secretary of the Sandinista-linked Chentex Workers Union. As the union slowly built up its membership base, the National Labor Committee (NLC) helped produce a three-part exposé on the wages and working conditions inside Chentex for the television series, *Hard Copy*, in November 1997.[6] This series created a major scandal in Nicaragua and the United States, mobilizing thousands of consumers to send letters, faxes, and e-mails to Wal-Mart, Kmart, and J.C. Penney to resolve the problems inside the factory.

Several weeks later, the Chentex Workers Union filed a petition for legal recognition with the Nicaraguan Labor Ministry in January 1998. The Ministry apparently gave Chentex the petition because the very next day twenty-one workers were dismissed. This decision inflamed the union's members. They organized two large, militant strikes, forcing Chentex to rehire all the fired workers and the Labor Ministry to grant the union legal recognition.

Both concessions were major victories for the fledgling union. Only one other legally recognized union existed, at that time, in the Las Mercedes Free Trade Zone (FTZ).[7] After obtaining recognition, the union tried to start contract negotiations with the company. Chentex refused, forming ties with a less combative "company union" (or *sindicato blanco*).[8] Company supervisors also threatened to shut down and open up under a new name.

Faced with this new predicament, the Chentex Workers Union, along with and social justice groups in Canada and the United States, passed out leaflets and held rallies and demonstrations against the company. In August 1998, Chentex backed down, signing a contract that improved working conditions within the factory, but left wages intact. The company promised that it would talk about a wage increase the following year when the contract was scheduled for re-negotiation. The union accepted this condition and waited patiently.

Chentex never carried out its pledge. As more and more time passed, the workers grew restive and began demanding a "living wage." In March 2000, the company increased wages thirty-two cents *per week*, but that was not enough to live on. Chentex workers were still subsisting on a steady diet of beans and rice, with little left over for housing, health care, clothing, and other basic needs.

Having exhausted all available options, the Chentex Workers Union held a one-hour work stoppage on April 27, 2000. The company responded swiftly and harshly. It fired Gladys Manzanares and eight other union leaders, and installed barbed wire and video cameras around the entire factory compound. On May 2, the union went on a three-day strike, calling for the reinstatement of their fired leaders, no retaliatory measures against strike supporters, and salary negotiations. In late May, the Labor Ministry upheld the company's decision to fire the nine union leaders, claiming that the one-hour strike was "illegal." Over the next three months (June–August 2000), Chentex continued its anti-union offensive, firing more than seven hundred workers.

These repressive measures nearly destroyed the union, but it remained resolute. Rank-and-file members received extensive support from Canadian, U.S., European, and Taiwanese labor, human rights, student, anti-sweatshop, and faith-based organizations. Chentex workers also held demonstrations outside the factory, defiantly chanting, "*Ni Un Paso Atrás! Ni Un Paso Atrás!*" (Not One Step Back! Not One Step Back!). Over the next seven months every possible strategy was utilized. On April 4, 2001, the Managua Court of Appeals ordered Chentex to rehire the nine fired union leaders. The company opposed the decision, but eventually hired four of the nine leaders (not including Gladys Manzanares). Chentex pressured them into resigning, however. In June 2001, the union stopped functioning. The campaign was over.

These events had far-reaching consequences for Nicaraguan, as well as Central American, *maquiladora* workers. Between 1998 and 2000, four *maquila* unions in Nicaragua,[9] along with one in Honduras (Kimi) and another one in Guatemala (Camisas Modernas/PVH), were eliminated. The Chentex Workers Union was the strongest one among them. Its demise highlights the power of transnational corporations and the challenges that the anti-sweatshop movement faces.

This chapter examines the overall trajectory of the Chentex campaign—its origins, achievements, and set-backs. It seeks to explain why it initially succeeded, but later failed. In order to address this issue, I begin the chapter with a brief synopsis of the Nicaraguan labor movement and the country's *maquiladora* industry. A detailed chronology of the Chentex campaign follows these two sections, while the last one explores its outcomes and broader lessons.

The Nicaraguan Labor Movement, 1900–2000

The Nicaraguan labor movement emerged in the early twentieth century.[10] During that time period, U.S. corporations dominated the country's banks, banana plantations, gold mines, lumber companies, and railroads. The U.S. Marines also occupied, with some short interruptions, Nicaragua between 1912 and 1933.[11] Strikes targeting U.S. corporations were organized and violently repressed in the late 1920s.[12] Growing hostility toward near-colonial rule sparked a guerrilla uprising, led by Augusto Sandino. Sandino's bold and militant call for land reform and the removal of U.S. forces attracted workers, *campesinos*, and activists from radical labor unions and political parties throughout Nicaragua and the Americas.[13]

The Sandinistas forced the Marines to flee in 1933, but the U.S.-trained National Guard, under Anastasio Somoza García, captured and assassinated Sandino one year later.[14] Somoza gained tremendous power over the next several years, wiping out the Sandinistas and repressing leftist labor unions and political parties.[15] During his two-decade rule (1936–1956), Somoza tightly controlled the labor movement, although he supported the establishment of the pro-government General Confederation of Workers (*Confederación General de Trabajadores*—CGT). The CGT was the country's leading labor union in the early 1950s.[16]

After Anastasio Somoza was assassinated in 1956, his older son, Luis Somoza, became president. Under his rule (1956–1967), the Nicaraguan economy became more diversified and industrialized. The middle class expanded and demands for social change grew.[17] In the early 1960s, two non-Somoza controlled unions, the Nicaraguan Autonomous Union Movement (*Movimiento Sindical Autó-nomo de Nicaragua*—MOSAN) and the General Confederation of Workers-Independent (*Confederación General de Trabajadores-Independiente*—CGT-I), a break-off from the Somoza-backed CGT, were formed.[18] The Confederation of Union Unification (*Confederación de Unificación Sindical*—CUS) was organized several years later with financial support from the AFL-CIO's American Institute for Free Labor Development (AIFLD).[19] CUS was staunchly pro-U.S. and pro-Somoza.

The emergence of oppositional labor unions like the CGT-I and MOSAN (later renamed the Nicaraguan Workers Confederation—CTN) symbolized growing dissatisfaction with the Somoza regime. These organizations disturbed Somoza, but they were not his biggest concern. In 1961, radical students, workers, and intellectuals formed the Sandinista National Liberation Front (*Frcntc Sandinista Liberación Nacional*—FSLN). The FSLN favored removing Somoza through armed struggle. It was nationalist, anti-imperialist, and revolutionary.[20]

Like his father, President Anastasio Somoza Jr. (1967–1979) called on the National Guard to eliminate the Sandinistas, but after he took funds earmarked for victims of the massive 1972 earthquake that left twenty-five thousand people dead, support for the FSLN grew. Over time, the anti-Somoza movement expanded, with workers from the CGT-I, CTN, and Sandinista-linked labor and *campesino* organizations leading the way.[21] After the assassination of opposition newspaper editor Pedro Joaquín Chamorro in January 1978, the movement gained more strength. Over the next few months, popular, multi-class-oriented social movement organizations held several massive demonstrations.[22] The Sandinistas eventually overthrew Somoza and took power on July 19, 1979.

During the Sandinista period (1979–1990), the Nicaraguan labor movement split into three factions—ultra-left, left, and conservative (see Table 5.1).[23] "Ultra-left" unions, like Nicaraguan Communist Party-linked Union Action and Unity Central (*Central de Acción y Unidad Sindical*—CAUS) and the Marxist-Leninist Popular Action Movement-affiliated Workers Front (*Frente Obrero*—FO), rejected, sometimes using violence, the FSLN's ban on strikes, which was introduced after the U.S.-backed *Contras* began attacking the

Table 5.1 The Nicaraguan Labor Movement, 1979–1990

Labor Organization (Confederation)	Ideological Perspective	Year Established
CAUS	Ultra-Left	1973
FO	Ultra-Left	1974
ATC	Left	1978
CST	Left	1979
CGT-I	Center-Left	1963
CUS	Conservative-Right	Mid-1960s
CTN	Conservative-Right	1972

Sandinistas in the early 1980s.[24] Leftist unions, like the Sandinsta Workers' Central (*Central Sandinista de Trabajadores*—CST) and the Rural Workers' Association (*Asociación de Trabajadores del Campo*—ATC), strongly backed the FSLN, while the CGT-I did so as well until the late 1980s. Conservative unions, such as the CTN and CUS, sharply criticized the FSLN's ban on strikes, calling the measure "totalitarian."[25]

Despite these divisions, the percentage of unionized workers rose from 11 percent in 1979 to over 50 percent in 1986.[26] The CST and ATC had the most members, with the CGT-I coming in third. Sandinista-backed limitations on the CTN, CUS, CAUS, and the FO, along with declining popularity amongst workers for their ideological and political views, hampered their growth, keeping their membership rates very low.[27]

As the decade wore on, the situation for the labor movement and the entire country worsened. More than fifty thousand people lost their lives because of the war between the Sandinistas and Contras, which also sparked capital flight, lower living standards, and hyperinflation. Faced with this deep economic crisis, the FSLN, in the late 1980s, introduced a series of International Monetary Fund (IMF)-like austerity measures, devaluing the national currency and laying off public sector employees. These policies created a rift between the FSLN and the CST, although the two remained close allies.[28]

After witnessing death and destruction and experiencing tremendous economic hardship, the Nicaraguan people were ready for change. In 1990, they voted the Sandinistas out and elected a U.S.-financed coalition of opposition political parties, known as the United National Opposition (UNO), led by Violeta Chamorro. Her election shook up the labor movement (see Table 5.2). CAUS, CUS, CGT-I, and the Autonomous Workers Federation of Nicaragua (CTN-A),[29] an off-shoot of the right-wing CTN, created the UNO-linked, AIFLD-funded Permanent Congress of Workers (*Congreso Permanente de los Trabajadores*—CPT) in 1987, while FSLN-affiliated labor federations, including

Table 5.2 Nicaraguan Labor Movement, 1990–2000

Umbrella Organization	Key Members	Ideological Perspective	Year Established
CPT (linked with UNO)	CAUS, CGT-I, CTN-A, CUS	Center-Right	1987
FNT (linked with FSLN)	CST, ATC	Center-Left	1990

(Note: The CTN is not affiliated with either the CPT or FNT, although it tends to lean toward the former. Also ties between linked organizations are not always smooth.)

the CST, formed a new umbrella organization, the National Workers Front (*Frente Nacional de los Trabajadores*—FNT), in May 1990.[30]

Chamorro initially challenged the Sandinistas' land redistribution policies and effectively froze living standards (by raising prices and salaries at the same time). Sharply disagreeing with these policies, the FNT called for a general strike. In early July 1990, FNT activists, workers, and students erected barricades and seized radio and television stations. Water and electricity were later turned off. For a short time period, a new civil war looked imminent. Chamorro and the FSLN started tripartite negotiations, known as *concertación*, involving government, labor, and business officials, before open hostilities broke out, however. The talks generated a series of agreements, calling for job security, wage increases, the protection of collective bargaining agreements, and the creation of new jobs.[31]

These policies looked good on paper, but none were ever put into practice. In fact, in 1991, the Chamorro government moved in the *exact opposite direction*, implementing IMF-backed structural adjustment programs, including the privatization of state-owned enterprises and cuts in social spending, in order to obtain more loans to help pay off Nicaragua's staggering debt.[32] These policies weakened the labor movement, especially the CST and other FNT-affiliated labor unions.

The FSLN, eager to shed its "radical" past and gain electoral credibility, supported Chamorro's neoliberal reforms and urged the FNT and CST to remain patient. At first, rank-and-file members listened to their leaders, but health care workers and teachers eventually broke ranks, holding several militant strikes between 1991–1994. Dissidents within CTN-affiliated unions also joined these strikes over their leaders' objections. FNT and CTN leaders finally supported these work stoppages, which shut down, at various times, a majority of the country's hospitals and schools, illustrating cooperation across ideological lines.[33]

Despite these positive steps, the labor movement crumbled in the middle and late 1990s. Under the conservative and extremely corrupt Arnoldo Alemán administration (1996–2001),[34] privatization and spending cuts for health care and education continued, but Nicaragua's foreign debt *increased*, rather than decreased, reaching $6.4 billion dollars, defying IMF predictions. Nicaragua spent a whopping 48 percent of its budget on debt repayments in 1998.[35] During that same year, as these life-sustaining resources flowed out of the country, 86 percent of the population lived below the poverty line, 48 percent were under or unemployed, and 40 percent of all children under the age of five were malnourished.[36] Fifty percent of all households, moreover, had no drinking water or electricity—25 percent had toilets, while 61 percent had a latrine and the rest had no services at all.[37]

On top of all these tragic statistics, union density fell dramatically over the past ten years. The CST, for example, lost over 50 percent of its members between 1990 and 1999.[38] The CTN and CUS expanded their membership base over that ten-year period, however. Despite this fact, the CST remains the country's strongest labor confederation.

This overview indicates that the Nicaraguan labor movement has slipped badly over the past decade. It is weaker today, in some respects, than it was during the Somoza dictatorship. The key labor confederations have declined and remain ideologically divided. A fragile, fragmented labor movement ultimately benefits the interests of capital because without strong, powerful unions, companies can pay their workers lower wages and mistreat them more easily. As we shall see, *maquiladora* workers know this reality all too well.

The Nicaraguan Maquiladora Industry

The Nicaraguan *maquiladora* industry grew dramatically between 1995 and 2000. Faced with a massive foreign debt of $10.7 billion dollars, President Chamorro signed a "structural adjustment" program with the IMF in 1991.[39] This agreement diverted scarce resources from health care and education, redirecting them for debt repayments. Chamorro also privatized state-owned enterprises, lowered tariffs and trade restrictions, and converted, the *government-run* Las Mercedes Free Trade Zone, which focused on nationally-oriented production in the 1980s, into an export-oriented platform, complete with generous tax exemptions, water and electricity subsidies, and a huge pool of cheap labor.[40] IMF experts suggested that these free-market ("neoliberal") oriented policies would generate foreign investment, economic growth, employment, higher living standards, and lower rates of inflation.

These heady predictions were not fully realized. Over the next decade, inflation dropped dramatically from 13,000 percent in 1990 to less than 10 percent in 1999; and the total value of exports increased, with some minor exceptions.[41] These macro-economic gains are impressive, but they overlook the fact that hunger, infant and maternal mortality, malnutrition, poverty, and unemployment rates also rose throughout this same time period.[42] Eight out of every ten Nicaraguans currently live in poverty and one out of every two is under or unemployed.

Seen from this perspective, the IMF's structural adjustment policies look like a dismal failure. Foreign investors view these programs much differently, however. For them, Nicaragua, with its free trade zone, tax exemptions, utility subsidies, low wages, high unemployment, and weak labor movement, is an almost ideal location. With the country's neoliberal, pro-business policies, profits seem almost guaranteed. Consequently, foreign investment began pouring into Nicaragua throughout the nineties.

In 1991, for instance, seven *maquiladora* factories employed thirteen hundred workers and produced $3 million worth of exports in the Las Mercedes Free Trade Zone. By 1999, there were thirty factories within the zone that employed over twenty thousand workers and produced over $200 million in exports to the U.S. market.[43] U.S., Taiwanese, Korean, Nicaraguan, and Italian investors own most of these factories.[44] They manufacture clothing for major U.S. retailers and labels like J.C. Penney, Sears & Roebuck, Kmart, Wal-Mart, Montgomery Ward, Target, Kohl's, Bugle Boy, and Tommy Hilfiger. Four other privately-owned free trade zones exist outside of Las Mercedes.[45] Factories within these locales employ several thousand workers.

More than 80 percent of all *maquiladora* workers are women between sixteen and thirty years old.[46] Fifty percent of these workers are single mothers with four or five children.[47] Single or married, most women work a "double-shift"—one inside the factory (typically lasting ten to twelve hours) and the other outside (looking after their children).[48] Conditions within the factories are harsh. Bathroom and lunch breaks are timed and regulated. Forced overtime is widespread. Safety equipment is rarely provided. Health-related problems include arthritis, asthma, and back-related injuries. Workers also have trouble visiting the zone's medical clinic because officials often block them from doing so. Breastfeeding mothers report that the zone lacks proper facilities to feed their infants as well. The zone's minimum wage is $65 a month; studies have shown a "living wage" for an average size family of four is $169 a month. No worker, no matter how many extra hours she works, earns that much. Most *maquila* workers, therefore, live near or below the poverty line.[49]

These conditions have sparked, despite the fact that hundreds of workers have been fired or blacklisted for doing so, numerous organizing campaigns. Unions, for example, were established inside five Las Mercedes-based factories—Fortex, Chih Hsing, JEM III, Mil Colores, and Chentex—between 1996 and 1998. All five had ties with the CST-linked Nicaraguan Textile, Garment, Leather, and Shoe Workers Federation.[50] Union organizing within the zone continued the following year. Wicker and Wimberley describe the results of those efforts:

By August 1999, eleven unions with 1,187 members were registered in seven different factories. Collective bargaining agreements had been negotiated in four of these seven factories, covering about 5,000 workers— one-fourth of the export processing zone's work force and approximately 13 percent of Nicaragua's *maquiladora* workforce. In short, Las Mercedes was the most unionized EPZ in Central America.[51]

These achievements, while remarkable, were short-lived. The companies with unions launched a full-scale counter-offensive in 2000. Chih Hsing, a Taiwanese-owned factory that produces for J.C. Penney and is owned by Nien Hsing, the same consortium that owns Chentex, for example, fired all the union's leaders in July 1999.[52] The union inside JEM III, a U.S.-owned factory that produces for Wal-Mart, crumbled next after mass firings in January 2000.[53] Around that same time, Mil Colores, a U.S.-owned factory that makes clothing for Kohl's and Target, fired over two hundred workers and filed criminal charges against sixty-eight of them, including Pedro Ortega, General Secretary of CST Textile Workers Federation. After receiving extensive international pressure from anti-sweatshop organizations within the United States, the company retreated, dropping all the charges against the fired workers and Ortega in August 2000.[54]

This was a major step forward, but the company delayed rehiring the fired workers and union leaders. Mil Colores finally rehired over two-dozen workers and recognized the union in November 2000. Pedro Ortega "felt that this was a victory for both parties and should be publicized as such." Several months later, the CST union stopped functioning inside the factory, however. A CTN-A affiliated union took its place and negotiated a collective bargaining agreement with Mil Colores management.[55]

The elimination of these three unions—Chih Hsing, JEM III, and Mil Colores—represented a major setback for Nicaraguan *maquiladora* workers and the CST. The left-leaning confederation and the more conservative CTN-A are virtually the only labor organizations, other than the María Elena Cuadra Women Workers' Movement,[56] that have actively targeted *maquiladoras* workers. The CST and the CTN-A were both involved in the Chentex campaign. Of all the Las Mercedes-based unions, the CST Chentex Workers Union was the strongest and best organized one. The union's trajectory, as well as its gains and setbacks, are examined below.

The Chentex Campaign: The Battle For Recognition, 1997–1998

Chentex opened its doors in the mid-1990s. It is owned by Nien Hsing, the powerful and politically well-connected Taiwanese-based consortium that owns two other *maquiladora* factories in Las Mercedes and has close ties with the Alemán Administration. Chentex employs nearly two thousand workers, the majority of whom are women. They produce over thirty thousand pairs of jeans a day for Wal-Mart, Kmart, J.C. Penney, Kohl's, and Target. The labels produced within the factory include Faded Glory (Wal-Mart), Route 66 (Kmart), Arizona (J.C. Penney), Sonoma (Kohl's), Bugle Boy, and Gloria Vanderbilt.

In 1996, Nicaragua's entire national budget was $585 million. That same year, Wal-Mart's sales were $105 billion ($3 billion in profits), Kmart's were $31.4 billion, and J.C. Penney's were $24.3 billion ($565 million in profits).[57] Despite these staggering numbers, all three U.S. retailers paid no corporate, sales, or municipal taxes because they operate in the free trade zone.

Chentex might have escaped widespread attention had it not been for the National Labor Committee (NLC). After obtaining labels, pay stubs, and company documents from garbage dumps and talking with workers from Chentex and seven other *maquila* factories, as well as the CST, the Nicaraguan Center for Human Rights (CENDIH), Nicaragua Network, Witness for Peace, and several other non-governmental organizations (NGOs), the NLC contacted the television series, *Hard Copy*, in October 1997.[58] *Hard Copy* broke the Kathie Lee Gifford scandal the year before and decided to do a follow-up piece on the Nicaragua *maquiladora* industry to determine whether or not wages and working conditions in "overseas sweatshops" had improved.

Posing as blue jean manufacturers, *Hard Copy* investigators entered the Las Mercedes Free Trade Zone armed with hidden cameras and microphones in late October 1997. They visited dozens of *maquila* workers' homes and talked with them about their wages and working conditions. They discovered the following:

- Average wages between 15–30 cents per hour.
- Twelve hour work shifts, six days a week.
- Forced overtime, with no additional pay.
- Verbal and physical abuse of workers.
- Overwhelming sense of fear and pressure to work faster.
- Sexual harassment.
- Body searches.
- Exposure to dangerous chemicals (used for dyeing jeans).
- Fired for being sick.
- Living in overcrowded stick and tin-roof homes, with cardboard walls, dirt floors, no running water, and outdoor latrines.
- Fired for union organizing.[59]

The three-part report that described these conditions aired on November 11–13, 1997. The program generated major headlines in the major Nicaraguan newspapers, enraging company officials. While watching a videotape of the *Hard*

Copy series, Chentex supervisors, for instance, saw Julieta María Alonzo and fired her for appearing on the program.[60] Eight other *maquila* workers were also fired after the show was broadcast; five of them, including Gladys Manzanares, had been involved in previous union organizing campaigns.[61] In the middle of these unfolding events, a twenty-two year old *maquila* worker named Oscar José Rivas Artolo tragically died after a machine that he reported was malfunctioning, but was never repaired, electrocuted him.[62]

Despite this overwhelming evidence, Free Trade Zone Executive Director Gilberto Wong claimed that the *Hard Copy* report was totally false. Labor Minister Wilfredo Navarro, after making a pre-announced visit to personally inspect conditions within the zone, concurred, stating, "there are no labor rights violations in the factories." Navarro also mentioned that the fired workers were terminated for participating in a mysterious, unidentified "conspiracy" to limit foreign investment in Nicaragua. The FSLN and the CST, for their part, asserted that although the free trade zone generates necessary employment, investors must treat their workers with respect and follow the Nicaraguan Constitution and Labor Code.[63]

Meanwhile, in the United States, Wal-Mart, Kmart, and J.C. Penney challenged the *Hard Copy* series, claiming that they had inspected their contractors' factories in Nicaragua and found that they met their "high standards."[64] Wal-Mart maintained its paid-for monitors (the Cal-Safety Compliance Corporation) actually inspected Chentex twice before the *Hard Copy* series ran. These so-called "independent" officials did not find the extensive violations that *Hard Copy* and the NLC uncovered.[65] The NLC suggested these findings illustrated the need for "transparent" monitoring.

Upon receiving negative publicity and being flooded with letters, faxes, and e-mails calling on the huge retailer to treat its employees more humanely, Wal-Mart initially threatened to sue *Hard Copy*, but it later backed down and rather surprisingly announced that it would not "cut and run." This was a key turning point in the campaign because while the brewing scandal was unfolding, Chentex workers were organizing themselves into a union.

The original organizing campaign actually began *before* the *Hard Copy* series aired. Gladys Manzanares explained the drive's origins:

> Pedro Ortega and I talked several times about organizing factories within the free trade zone before I started working for Chentex. We talked about the problems inside the factory and decided that we would start there because we knew the conditions there were not good. . . . After quietly observing and talking with several workers, we began organizing. We were very careful. The supervisors heard us talking, however, and said, 'shut up or you will be fired.' That scared most of the workers. It was difficult to organize after that.[66]

As these comments indicate, intimidation and fear stymied the initial campaign. After the *Hard Copy* series ran, however, the Chentex workers became more enthusiastic towards organizing. Gladys Manzanares described this shift:

> The workers were excited and angry after the report came out. I told Pedro, 'this is *the* moment—we have to take advantage of this situation—the people are excited (euphoric).' He said, 'are you sure?' I said, 'I'm sure, they are ready.'[67]

Manzanares was right—the workers were *listo* (ready)—they were fired up. Before she could start organizing, Manzanares and several of her *compañeras* were fired, however. The company thought that this would stop her, but it had the opposite effect. She and Harling Bobadilla, another Chentex worker, resumed clandestine talks with workers about forming a union.[68] Many were originally reluctant, but ninety eventually signed up as union members. At this time, the CST, the NLC, the American Center for International Labor Solidarity (ACILS), the regional arm of the International Textile, Garment, and Leather Workers Federation (ITGLWF), the Inter-America Textile and Garment Workers Federation (FITTIV), the Campaign For Labor Rights, Nicaragua Network, TecNica, the United States/Guatemala Labor Education Project (U.S./GLEP), and the Upper Westside/Tipitapa Sister City Project were working together with the fledging union on the campaign.[69]

The Nicaraguan Labor Code states that unions must have at least twenty members to be legally recognized.[70] On January 23, 1998, the Chentex workers (who had more than enough members) filed a petition with the Nicaraguan Labor Ministry asking for official recognition of the union. The Ministry presumably gave the petition to Chentex, because the very next day the company fired twenty-one of the ninety workers whose names appeared on it.[71]

Three days passed before the fired workers and union leaders made their next move. They walked into the factory and hoped many would stop working. Feeling energized by the *Hard Copy* series and frustrated by their low wages and poor working conditions, 90 percent of Chentex's two thousand workers heeded the call and walked off their jobs. Eighteen hundred workers were on a virtual wild-cat strike. Outside the factory gates, they chanted, "we want justice, we want recognition!" Armed security guards then threatened the striking workers and tried to keep the media out of the free trade zone. The workers bravely moved past the guards, however, and invited the press into the zone to cover the protest.[72]

Later that same day (January 26), Chentex and the Labor Ministry reinstated the fired twenty-one workers. The Ministry also agreed to process the union's petition for legal recognition and the company promised not to retaliate against any of the striking workers. Chentex immediately broke this pledge, however, firing several workers. Several days later, the Labor Ministry turned down the union's request for recognition and told it that it would allow Chentex to fire workers during another strike.[73]

These events infuriated the workers. They organized, despite the ministry's threats, another strike. Virtually the entire work force walked out on February 16. This time the Labor Ministry, which was being inundated with letters, e-mails, and faxes from the NLC, the Campaign For Labor Rights, and other anti-sweatshop organizations in the United States, backed down and granted the union legal recognition. At that time, it was the second legally recognized union in the free trade zone.[74]

This was a key victory for the union. How was it achieved? The Chentex workers initially had very little leverage over the company. That changed when they developed ties with a "transnational advocacy network" of solidarity and anti-sweatshop groups spearheaded by the NLC. The NLC understood that Wal-Mart, Kmart, J.C. Penney, and the Nicaraguan government were the "primary" targets, not Chentex. In fact, Wal-Mart, because of its prior involvement in the Kathie Lee Gifford scandal, was probably the most vulnerable target of them all.

Given this situation, the NLC launched a major attack on its public image based on the *Hard Copy* series. The program ultimately did two things—it disseminated information to the wider public about sweatshop abuses in Nicaragua and it "symbolically framed," through visual images, Wal-Mart, as well as Kmart and J.C. Penney, as the "villain" for allowing these problems to continue. By using information and symbolic politics, the Chentex workers gained "moral leverage" over Wal-Mart and the other two retailers.

Faced with more embarrassing attacks on its already battered image, Wal-Mart originally denied the *Hard Copy* allegations. J.C. Penney, embroiled in the Kimi campaign at the same time, and Kmart did likewise. These decisions sparked the NLC, the Campaign for Labor Rights, Nicaragua Network, Quest For Peace, Witness For Peace, and other solidarity groups to take action. They passed out hundreds of leaflets outside of Wal-Mart, Kmart, and J.C. Penney stores during the crucial holiday shopping season (named the "Holiday Season of Conscience To End Child Labor and Sweatshops" by the NLC).

Wal-Mart and J.C. Penney could have "cut and run" at this point, but this move would have further damaged their image. These retailers could not afford being called the "Grinch That Stole Christmas," laying off two thousand workers during the holiday season. With their backs against the wall, Wal-Mart and J.C. Penney reluctantly "joined" the transnational advocacy network and began putting pressure on Chentex to resolve the crisis.

Chentex initially refused. The company was soon confronted with two well-organized, militant strikes that involved over 90 percent of its workers, however. Chentex slowly realized that it could ill-afford to lose its two biggest buyers.

Feeling heat from below and above, Chentex capitulated, rehiring all the fired workers and union leaders (including Gladys Manzanares). Fearing more attacks and the possible loss of foreign investment, the Labor Ministry recognized the union.

This entire sequence of events illustrates that, like the Gap campaign, image was the key element of this phase of the Chentex case. Through the *Hard Copy* series, the NLC cleverly used information and symbolic politics to create a "boomerang effect" that generated some key concessions (see Figure 5.1). The *Hard Copy* video damaged the image of Wal-Mart, J.C. Penney, Kmart, and the Nicaraguan government, but mobilized the Chentex workers. Feeling pressure from U.S. retailers, a strong, unified transnational advocacy network, and a militant group of *maquila* workers, Chentex and the Labor Ministry backed down, reinstating the fired workers and recognizing the union.

Contract Negotiations: March 1998-August 1998

The Chentex workers rejoiced after their union was recognized, but they knew their work was not over yet. They developed a list of contract demands and called on the company to begin negotiations. Chentex rejected their offer. Instead, Chentex formed close ties with a pliant "company union" affiliated with the CTN-A. In marked contrast to the CST-linked union, the Labor Ministry took just three days to recognize this organization.[75] Two unions now resided inside Chentex. The Nicaraguan Labor Code states that more than one union can legally exist within a workplace. Companies can have only one collective bargaining agreement, however, so when there is more than one union, they must negotiate together.[76]

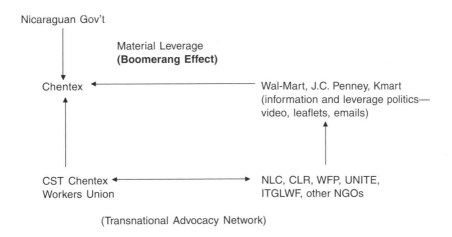

Fig. 5.1 Union Recognition and the Chentex Campaign.

Right after these events took place, Chentex told its workers that it would shut down in June 1998 and open up under a new name, hiring only those workers affiliated with the company union.[77] At this time, the CTN-A affiliated union had no more than fifty members, while the CST union had nearly one thousand.[78] This union clearly had majority support, but Chentex still refused to negotiate with it.

Over the next several months, a deadlock between Chentex and the CST union emerged. In the midst of this impasse, a broad-based coalition of solidarity, human rights, labor, and religious groups, including the NLC, the ITGLWF, ACILS, FITTIV, Witness For Peace, the United States/Labor in the Americas Project (U.S./LEAP), Nicaragua Network, the Campaign for Labor Rights, TecNica, the Westside/Tipitapa Sister City Project, and Quest for Peace, swung into action.[79] Its members sent hundreds of e-mails, faxes, and letters to the CEOs of Wal-Mart, Kmart, and J.C. Penney urging them to put pressure on Chentex to negotiate with the CST union. The coalition also handed out thousands of leaflets to U.S. consumers all around the country as they entered these retail stores.

Lingering image-based concerns prompted the U.S. retailers to lean hard on Chentex. In August 1998, the company finally relented, signing a two-year agreement with the CST and CTN-A that called for overtime pay, paid sick leave, the establishment of a health clinic inside the factory, company contributions for the birth or death of a family member, free school supplies for workers' children, subsidies for eyeglasses, and a credit fund. The contract did not include a wage increase, however. The union and company agreed to open up negotiations around that issue within a year.[80]

This contract, while not perfect, was a significant milestone for the Chentex workers. Through image-based attacks on U.S. retailers, the transnational advocacy network generated a positive "boomerang effect," opening up space for contract negotiations. Yet, without the presence of a militant, well-organized union, Chentex probably would have refrained from signing the agreement (see Figure 5.2). The combination of a unified transnational coalition and a strong local union temporarily overpowered the U.S. retailers and Chentex, paving the way toward the successful ratification of the collective bargaining agreement.

The Campaign For a Living Wage: September 1998–May 2000

As the months passed, the Chentex workers grew restless. They earned, after all, just twenty-two cents for every pair of $19.99 Arizona jeans they produced for J.C. Penney. This means that their wages constituted a little more than 1 percent of the total retail price of the jeans.[81] On a monthly basis, the Chentex

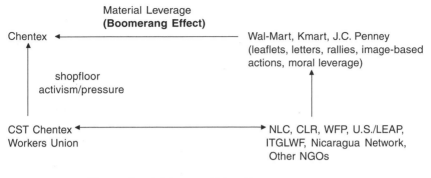

Fig. 5.2 Contract Ratification and the Chentex Campaign.

workers earned, on average, between sixty-five and ninety dollars. Researchers estimated a "living wage" for a family of five was $169 a month in 1999. The Chentex workers, therefore, could not afford one-half to two-thirds of their basic needs. Meanwhile, J.C. Penney made $336 million dollars in profits in 1999, while Kohl's were $258 million. Kmart CEO Floyd Hall paid himself four million dollars during that same year. That figure surpasses the annual salary of 2,400 *maquila* workers.[82]

These inequities concerned the Chentex workers. Many were struggling financially and emotionally—one worker told me her neighbor's daughter died from diarrhea because she could not afford the medicine.[83] The campaign for a living wage was thus not abstract; it was literally a life and death issue for the workers and their families. They waited for over a year, but Chentex remained silent. The company virtually ignored the CST union, but it negotiated a paltry thirty-two cent *per week* pay increase with the CTN-A-affiliated union.[84] The CST union called that raise "unacceptable" and asked the Labor Ministry, on four separate occasions, to intervene and mediate a settlement. It did so, but failed to put enough pressure on the company to begin negotiations with the CST union.

Having used all available legal strategies for resolving the conflict, the Chentex workers called for a one-hour strike on April 27, 2000. Once again, more than 90 percent of the factory's two thousand workers reportedly stopped working. The company's response was swift and severe. It fired CST Chentex Workers Union General Secretary Gladys Manzanares and eight other union executive board members. Chentex also threatened to shut down three production lines. Each line employs just over one hundred workers.

These actions sparked a three-day strike May 2–5. This time one thousand workers walked off their jobs. Chentex did not begin salary negotiations with the union as it hoped for, however. Instead, the company clamped down even harder, installing barbed wire and video cameras around the entire factory, turning it into a "panoptic-like prison." Chentex also asked twenty National Police officers to remain inside the factory during the strike and hired spies to intimidate the workers. Company supervisors told the workers, moreover, that they "would never receive a pay increase" and that the "union was dead."[85]

Chentex effectively crushed the strike through these repressive measures, but the CST union did not give up. Shortly after the work stoppage ended, it presented a petition to the company signed by over eight hundred workers, calling for the reinstatement of the fired union leaders, no production-line clos-ings, no repressive actions against strike supporters, and salary negotiations. The union also filed an appeal with the Labor Ministry to overturn the company's decision to fire nine of its leaders.[86]

These actions prompted Chentex's owner, Nien Hsing, to pull out its ultimate trump card. It threatened to shut down the factory and told the Nicaraguan government that if the fired union leaders were reinstated, it would suspend the planned construction of a new $100 million dollar free trade zone in León.[87] On top all of this, Chentex brought criminal charges for "rioting and threatening the freedom of commerce" against the fired union leaders.

Nien Hsing's machinations backed the Nicaraguan government into a corner. Fearing the loss of one of its most powerful and influential investors, Labor Ministry officials, on May 26, upheld the firing of the nine CST union leaders, ruling that the one-hour strike over the salary dispute was "illegal" and that the company, therefore, acted properly.[88] This decision came as no surprise because only three strikes have been declared legal within Nicaragua over the past thirty years.[89] The U.S. Embassy, overlooked this stunning statistic and backed the Labor Ministry's ruling.[90]

The Ministry's decision came as a crushing blow for the union. It was the largest and most militant union in the free trade zone. It had over eight hundred members, half of whom paid dues. The union's leaders and members, more-over, helped organize other *maquila* factories like JEM III, Chih Hsing, and Mil Colores. The union also participated in solidarity strikes when protests broke out at other factories in the free trade zone.[91]

The CST Chentex union was strong and well organized. After the unions at JEM III, Chih Hsing, and Mil Colores were effectively eliminated, the CST Chentex union had to go. Company unions like the CTN-A were fine, but the CST was not. It actually fought for the workers and their families' best interests. With the CST Chentex union out of the way, the labor movement in the *maquiladora* industry would be smashed and corporations and retailers like Nien Hsing, J.C. Penney, Kohl's, Target, Kmart, and Wal-Mart would be completely free to do whatever they pleased and to make even greater profits.

Ni Un Paso Atrás!: The Union and The Transnational Coalition Fight Back, May 2000–June 2001

The union and the transnational coalition of labor, solidarity, and religious groups that worked so well together during the campaign, however, was not about to let this happen. They knew how high the stakes were. The Chentex workers understood this too, stating, "this is really a life or death struggle. If Chentex is destroyed, it could be the end of the union movement in the *maquila* industry in Nicaragua."[92] A defeat would have also been devastating for Nicaraguan *maquila* workers, as well as for garment workers from all over the world.[93]

On May 31, therefore, the Chentex union, the CST-linked Textile, Garment, Leather, and Shoe Workers Federation, the Nicaraguan Center for Human Rights (CENDIH), and the NLC held a joint news conference to criticize the firings and violations at the factory. All the television stations and the two major daily newspapers, *El Nuevo Diario* and *La Prensa*, covered the event. NLC Executive Director Charles Kernaghan gained the most attention with these comments:

> We are going to launch an international campaign in support of the Chentex workers. On return to the United States, I will meet with members of Congress and with the media, with religious and labor groups of the U.S. and Canada, as well as with the retailers to tell them that in Nicaragua there is an attempt to destroy the union.[94]

Kernaghan also stated that the NLC would "challenge" Nicaragua's ability to receive trading benefits under the new Caribbean Basin Trade Partnership Act, also known as CBI Parity,[95] which states that recipient nations can export more apparel products into the United States on the condition that they protect international workers' rights standards, like the right to organize and collectively bargain.[96] The CBI Parity bill was passed on May 18, 2000, but it was not slated to be implemented until October 1, 2000. This time frame gave the CST Chentex union and the transnational coalition a more favorable "political opportunity structure" to obtain "material leverage."[97]

Kernaghan's statements ignited a nationalist backlash in Nicaragua. The conservative *La Prensa*, for instance, claimed that, "U.S. unionists were calling for a boycott of Nicaragua."[98] That was completely untrue, but this charge underscored a sensitive issue. If Nicaragua lost its CBI Parity benefits, then thousands of *maquila* workers could have possibly lost their jobs. The FNT and CST maintained that, while some urgent action in the *maquilas* was necessary, using CBI Parity, at that particular juncture, was simply too risky.[99]

This strategic disagreement created some tensions within the transnational coalition. Some groups claimed, for instance, that the NLC was operating on its own without consulting them or the Nicaraguan workers and that it was fanning the flames of "protectionism." This rift did not emerge into a full-blown conflict.[100]

The transnational coalition was still fairly well-unified and active. Coalition members, for instance, held 134 leafleting actions in 104 U.S.-based cities in May and another ninety-five actions from June 17 through July 16.[101] In the midst of these protests, Pedro Ortega, labeled a "terrorist" by the U.S. Embassy, was refused a visa to travel to the United States until solidarity groups pressured the State Department to back down. Ortega went to the Midwest, on a trip organized by the Nicaragua Network and the Campaign For Labor Rights, to try to personally speak with the CEOs of Kohl's and Target to resolve the conflicts at Chentex and Mil Colores.[102] Despite the repeated efforts of the Justice and Peace Office of the Sisters of St. Assisi (Milwaukee, Wisconsin) to set up a meeting with Kohl's and the Resource Center of the Americas (Minneapolis, Minnesota) to arrange a meeting with Target, both companies refused to meet with Ortega and members of local fair trade, labor, and religious organizations.[103]

This was another set-back, but it did not derail the campaign. In mid-July 2000, a "high-level" delegation, consisting of Congressman Sherrod Brown (Democrat–New York), Charles Kernaghan, Alan Howard (Assistant to the President of UNITE), and representatives from the United Steelworkers of America, the United Students Against Sweatshops (USAS), the American Center for International Labor Solidarity (ACILS), and other U.S.-based solidarity organizations, traveled to Nicaragua to investigate working conditions at Chentex and Mil Colores.[104]

The delegation visited Tipitapa, a Managua-based *barrio* where many *maquiladora* workers live. Delegates talked with Chentex workers about their low wages and poor working conditions. They learned that Chentex had effectively fired seven hundred workers since the three-day strike in early May. Most of these workers had been given the "option" of resigning from the union, with full severance pay, or being "laid off," with no pay. With children and families to support, many opted for the former.[105] Despite these firings, the union organized a rally outside the factory on July 14. The delegation attended the protest, holding picket signs and chanting, "*Ni Un Paso Atrás, Ni Un Paso Atrás!* (Not One Step Back, Not One Step Back!)," alongside the Chentex workers.[106]

Less than a week later, on July 21, Congressman Brown and three other congressional representatives sent a letter to new Taiwanese President Chen Shui-bian asking him to meet with Nien Hsing's owners to settle the Chentex conflict. That same day, Brown and sixty-three other congressional members delivered a similar letter to U.S. President Clinton stating:

> We request that the administration direct the U.S. Department of Labor and the U.S. Embassy to conduct an immediate and objective investigation

of the mass firings of union leaders and members, and other systematic human and worker rights violations at the Chentex and Mil Colores factories.[107]

The letter also talked about the possibility of using CBI Parity as a lever for resolving the conflicts at Chentex and Mil Colores.

At that moment, almost every conceivable strategy was being used—worker-led rallies and demonstrations, trade sanctions, congressional pressure, leafleting actions, and consumer activism. In the middle of this coordinated attack, a potentially serious disagreement arose within the transnational coalition. Coalition members claimed that the NLC was still acting alone and jeopardizing the entire campaign. For a brief moment, the NLC looked like it might be ousted from the coalition. That never happened—the coalition stayed intact, although Witness for Peace momentarily pulled out of the "core working group."[108]

In late July, Gladys Manzanares, Pedro Ortega, ITGLWF General Secretary Neil Kearney, FITTIV General Secretary José Ramirez, and other officials from the CST Chentex Workers Union, FITTIV, and the ACILS met behind closed doors. They developed a new strategy to specifically select Kohl's over Target and the other retailers that Chentex produces for. Kohl's was chosen because it was scheduled to open up a number of new outlets in the Midwest and Northeast in mid-August.[109] The transnational coalition thought that Kohl's would move quickly to settle the crisis at Chentex in order to avoid negative publicity during these "grand openings."[110] This assumption seemed reasonable since Kohl's did not have the deep pockets and resources that Target did to fight a long drawn-out battle.

Before publicly announcing this new strategy, on August 1, Pedro Ortega met with a Witness for Peace (WFP) delegation, which included the author and nine other people from all over the United States, and stated that unless Nien Hsing resolved the Chentex crisis, the union and the international garment workers' secretariat would launch campaigns against the consortium's factories in Taiwan, South Africa, Mexico, and the United States.[111] The next day ITGLWF General Secretary Neil Kearney repeated the same warning, stating that unless Chentex, along with Chih Hsing, JEM III, and Mil Colores, took steps to work with the Nicaraguan government to respect labor rights "it would be difficult [for Nien Hsing] to sell [its] products anywhere in the world."[112] The secretariat, it should be recalled, has over two thousand affiliates in 130 countries.

Shortly after Secretary Kearney made his comments, the WFP group met with U.S. Embassy Labor Attaché Mario Fernández about the Chentex case. He repeated the Nicaraguan Labor Ministry's ruling that the one-hour strike on April 27, 2000 was "illegal" and that the company, therefore, "legally" fired the nine union leaders. He also claimed that despite the elimination of unions at Chentex, Mil Colores, JEM III, and Chih Hsing he felt that *maquila* workers still had the right to organize and that reviewing or suspending Nicaragua's trading benefits under CBI-Parity would be "inappropriate."[113]

In mid-August, the NLC organized another "prestigious" delegation. This time the group included religious leaders from the United States. Detroit Bishop Thomas Gumbleton headed the delegation. Other members included Sister Mary Frances Heimann of the Sisters of St. Francis of Assisi (Milwaukee), Sister Teresa Terns of the Sisters of the Sacred Heart of Mary of Detroit, Reverend David Dyson from New York City with the People of Faith Network, and Barbara Briggs and Charles Kernaghan from the NLC.[114] The group met with *maquila* workers and tried to hold religious services inside the free trade zone, but zone officials blocked them from doing that. They conducted the services, therefore, just outside the zone. Hundreds of workers attended. Two days later, on the eve of the arrival of Taiwanese President Chen, the delegation was "expelled" and its members were told they would not be allowed to return to Nicaragua. The Nicaraguan government also added that it would not allow similar groups to enter the country because they "incite the people to do violence against the state."[115]

After the religious delegation was ousted, it returned to the United States with Gladys Manzanares and Rosa Esterlina Ocampo (a fired union leader from Mil Colores). Starting on August 18, the two women, along with Barbara Briggs and Charlie Kernaghan, went on an eight-day speaking tour, stopping at Kohl's "grand openings" and college campuses. The trip garnered major news coverage. National Public Radio (NPR) and Pacifica's *Democracy Now* program, for instance, ran stories on the Chentex and Mil Colores cases.[116] After the tour ended, U.S. Under Secretary of Labor Andrew Samet went to Nicaragua on August 29 to investigate the conflicts at Chentex and Mil Colores. Samet reportedly said that he was concerned about labor rights violations within the zone and told the Nicaraguan government that they were serious problems that had to be addressed.[117]

One day later, the 7th District Criminal Court of Managua, under pressure from the Nicaraguan Labor Ministry agreed to stop the criminal proceedings against the nine fired Chentex union leaders.[118] This was a step forward, but the campaign was not over yet. The union leaders, along with seven hundred workers, were still out on the streets and wages remained pitifully low.

In early September, the situation took a turn for the worse after Nien Hsing made new threats to shut down the factory. Chentex General Manager Lucas Huang then went one step further, saying he would commit suicide before rehiring the union leaders.[119] Despite these dramatic tactics, the Chentex workers and the transnational coalition remained optimistic. In late September-early October 2000, a new round of leafleting actions, strategically timed around the September 26 (S26) protests against the IMF and World Bank meetings in Prague, took place in over eighty cities.[120] Numerous USAS activists and affiliates passed out leaflets primarily against Kohl's. Ten University of Michigan students were arrested in one protest that Zenayda Torres and Angelica Pérez (two fired Chentex union leaders who were on a national speaking tour), along with Barbara Briggs and Charles Kernaghan, also attended.

One day after these arrests, on October 3, 2000, U.S. Trade Representative Charlene Barshefsky, responding to Representative Sherod Brown's July 15 letter, sent a letter to the Nicaraguan foreign minister, stating, "failure to improve the labor rights situation could well put at risk Nicaragua's access to preferential treatment under the Caribbean Basin Initiative."[121] Barshefsky's statement bore fruit. On October 10, Lucas Huang called for talks with the CST Chentex Workers Union. The negotiations were initially delayed. They later began, with Huang verbally agreeing to rehire the fired union leaders, but he refused to sign a written agreement at a later date. These tactics continued over the next several months. Huang made several verbal agreements, but he never signed any written documents.[122]

In November–December 2000, more leafleting actions, complete with activists singing "sweatshop carols," took place.[123] UNITE, the Steelworkers, Jobs for Justice, and many other organizations were involved in these protests. Fifteen people were arrested in one action in Minnesota.[124] Two weeks before these activities took place, Taiwanese labor and solidarity organizations held demonstrations outside Nein Hsing's corporate headquarters in Taipei. Taiwanese activists also interrupted the corporation's annual meeting with information about the Chentex campaign.[125]

Several weeks later, the Campaign for Labor Rights, the AFL-CIO, ACILS, and the ITGLWF met with the Taiwanese Representative to the United States, Chien-Jen Chen.[126] Chen later sent Nien Hsing a letter asking it to rehire the fired union leaders. On January 2, 2001, the Taiwanese Parliament held a special hearing on the Nien Hsing conflict, with almost all government officials taking the Chentex workers' side.[127]

One week later, on January 9, U.S. Embassy Labor Attaché Mario Fernández suggested that a written agreement between Chentex and the union was near, but Lucas Huang disagreed, calling him a "liar."[128] Chentex and the CTN-A union then organized two demonstrations, with over five hundred workers, outside the U.S. Embassy and Sandinista Party headquarters demanding that they intervene and stop the campaign. The NLC labeled these actions "puppet protests," pointing out that the company gave the workers a paid day off and provided them with small stipends and transportation.[129]

These events did not derail the broad-based transnational advocacy network (TAN), which included social justice organizations from Taiwan, Nicaragua, Canada, the United States, Africa, and Europe.[130] It maintained constant pressure on Chentex from a wide variety of angles. The United Steelworkers union, UNITE, and the Center for Constitutional Rights (CCR) sued Nien Hsing, which had a U.S.-based subsidiary, in U.S. District Court in Los Angeles, for using sweatshop labor at Chentex.[131] Meanwhile, Congressional Representative Cynthia McKinney (Democrat-Georgia) criticized the Pentagon for buying Chentex-made goods sold on military bases.[132]

These strategies finally paid off. After the May 2000 mass firings, the Nicaraguan Center for Human Rights (CENDIH) filed a lawsuit against Chentex for labor rights violations. On April 4, 20001, the Managua Court of Appeals, in a 2–1 decision, ruled that Chentex must rehire the nine fired union leaders.[133] The ruling was handed down on the same day that Chentex and the CST union were supposed to sign an agreement that would have included hiring two of the nine leaders and twenty of the seven hundred fired workers.[134]

This proposed accord clearly favored the company. When news of the court decision arrived, Chentex was stunned. Pedro Ortega told Lucas Huang, "there is no appeal, you have to obey."[135] He refused, however, and threatened to close down the factory. After several more weeks, Chentex and the CST union hammered out an agreement. Chentex agreed to rehire four of the nine union leaders, along with twenty-one fired workers.[136] Gladys Manzanares was not among those that were reinstated.

Those four leaders started working inside the factory on May 14, 2001, culminating a year-long battle for reinstatement. They faced constant harassment, however. Union leader Maura Parsons described her treatment:

> We arrived at 6 AM, but were forced to wait at the main entrance to the free trade zone until 9:25 AM, when the assistant manager of Chentex Carlos Yin and Nien Hsing legal advisor Doris Escalona picked us up in a vehicle to take us to the factory. We thought it was strange that they drove us to the factory in their vehicle, but they claimed that they were protecting us from the workers who did not want us to return to work.
>
> They took us to the reception office and told us the rules: that we could not be organized as we had been before, we couldn't talk with anyone at all, and that we were to act as brand new workers. By Friday, May 18, 2001, eight workers had been fired. They had all been affiliates of our union and were fired for getting near us.
>
> Santiago (another union leader) and I resigned from Chentex on June 13, 2001, just one month after our rehiring. The management wanted us to write on our resignation forms that we were not forced to quit. We refused to write that, but instead stated we were resigning for "personal reasons." We resigned because we wanted there to be labor stability at the factory. We didn't want more workers to lose their jobs just because of our presence. We didn't want the company or the government to be able to say that the CST is only a destabilizing presence in the free trade zone. They always called us terrorists, but we only wanted workers' rights to be

respected. We decided that it would be better for us to leave than to stay and have every single worker who had once known us to be fired. We wanted at least some of the workers who knew what it was like to have the union at the factory to keep their jobs so that perhaps in the future, at a better time, they can reorganize the union and we can help from the outside.[137]

This painful decision exemplified the spirit, drive, and never-ending sense of solidarity within CST Chentex Workers Union. The company finally, after four long years, defeated the union, but it could not take away everything. Its members remained proud, hopeful, defiant, and grateful. As "sweatshop warrior" Maura Parsons said:

> To the international community who supported us, I want to communicate my heartfelt thanks for the immense moral support you provided us throughout this long struggle. I hope you do not feel disappointed in us. Our struggle up until now has been for the workers, and we could not stand by and watch hard working people lose their jobs because of us. Given the grave economic situation in Nicaragua, it is extremely difficult to organize unions and there are many obstacles in our way. We have not given up and will continue the struggle until workers' right to organize and to a decent job are respected. We are continuing to organize unions in other factories and hope that the time will come at Chentex when workers shed their fear to rebuild the union there.[138]

Analysis

The Chentex factory remains open, but the CST-linked union is gone. Given this "final" outcome, the tumultuous four-year struggle looks like a clear-cut "defeat" for the Chentex workers and the wider anti-sweatshop movement. This assessment makes sense from a relatively narrow viewpoint, but a broader, more complex, and nuanced analysis reveals the campaign was not just another "failure." The Chentex workers obtained some stirring victories—they established a strong, militant union, won legal recognition, and negotiated a contract that improved working conditions within the factory.

How did they attain these results? The Chentex workers initially organized themselves and battled the company without any assistance, but intimidation and repression squelched this effort. Afterwards, they established a transnational coalition with the NLC and other solidarity organizations. The NLC realized that the Chentex workers lacked leverage. It understood that if it could shift the focus of attention to Wal-Mart, Kmart, and J.C. Penney, then a "window of opportunity" could be opened up to improve wages and working conditions within the factory.

Based on the *Hard Copy* series, the NLC symbolically "framed" Wal-Mart, Kmart, and J.C. Penney as corporate "villains." In the three-part exposé, the three retailers were blamed for low wages, unsafe working conditions, sexual harassment, dirt-floor homes, and a wide variety of other abuses. Wal-Mart, K-mart, and J.C. Penney became tagged with "sweatshop labor." In order to shed that label and to repair their sullied public image, the companies pressured Chentex to recognize the union.

These strategic moves generated a positive "boomerang effect" that gave the Chentex workers much-needed "moral leverage." Chentex probably would not have done anything, however, unless the workers mobilized and organized themselves. Feeling pressure from above (the U.S. retailers) and below (the union and transnational coalition), Chentex and the Nicaraguan Labor Ministry moved to recognize the union.

This outcome indicates, as I have mentioned before, that strong local unions and relatively well-unified transnational advocacy networks (TANs) are crucial for successfully challenging sweatshop labor practices. One side of the equation is not enough—both factors are important. During this phase of the campaign, the organizations within the transnational coalition were united and the CST union was strong and extremely well organized. By using information, symbolic, and organization-building politics (leafleting actions, the *Hard Copy* video, and two militant strikes), the CST Chentex Workers Union gained even more leverage and obtained recognition.

The CST union and the transnational coalition used the same formula—leafleting, continuing fall-out from the *Hard Copy* series, and rank-and-file pressure—to negotiate a contract. This agreement improved working conditions within the factory, but wages remained the same. The CST union held two strikes to pressure Chentex to raise wages. The company refused, firing seven hundred workers and nine of the union's leaders. These repressive activities sparked leafleting actions, congressional pressure, high-level delegations, a workers' speaking tour, positive media coverage, worker-led rallies and protests, a workers' rights petition, and the possibility of trade sanctions.

These strategies did not work. The union's members were never rehired and the campaign ended dismally. What factors explain this outcome? I contend that while strong local unions and well-unified TANs are crucial, they are not "necessary and sufficient" factors for creating a successful cross-border labor solidarity campaign. These two factors can generate crucial gains (i.e. legal recognition, better wages and working conditions, and collective bargaining agreements), but various "external" forces—capital mobility, mass firings, and state repression—can undermine these achievements.

The PVH and Kimi campaigns illustrate this argument. In these two cases, strong local unions and relatively well-unified TANs worked together and obtained better wages and working conditions through collective bargaining. These same two elements were present in the Chentex campaign, but the results were not the same—working conditions improved, but wages did not. These three outcomes indicate that strong unions and well-unified TANs can generate positive gains, but sustaining and broadening them over time is extremely difficult. This case study demonstrates that these two factors, while crucial, cannot automatically produce desired results.

Given this situation, what can garment workers and their allies do? The previous chapter stated that region-wide organizing could possibly limit companies from "cutting and running." In this case, however, capital mobility was not the "enemy," a stubborn anti-union company was. Based on this reality, a transnational, not regional, organizing and solidarity campaign, involving Nien Hsing workers from all over the world, might work. The Chentex workers and their allies tried this innovative strategy, bringing together the company's Taiwanese and Nicaraguan workers, but Chentex remained steadfastly anti-union.

The Chentex workers and the transnational advocacy network tried every conceivable strategy, with the exception of establishing stronger links with Nien Hsing's Lesotho-based workers. A tri-continental alliance of African, Asian, and Central American workers would have had tremendous potential, but it probably would not have mattered. Chentex consistently opposed and eventually destroyed the union, although it could not wipe out the spirit and determination of its members. They never took one step back, displaying exceptional courage and humility. Chentex could not take these things away. It remains to be seen whether or not the seeds of resistance that were planted during this campaign will bear fruit. One can only hope that they will.

Conclusion

The Chentex campaign was a high-stakes affair. The workers organized themselves into the strongest union within Nicaragua's Las Mercedes free trade zone and they established ties with an impressive transnational coalition of labor, human rights, religious, and solidarity groups from the United States, Asia, Central America, and Europe. Over time, the union was recognized and negotiated a contract.

Those gains were fleeting, however. The company fired the union's leaders and hundreds of workers. Despite all their best efforts, "sweatshop warriors" like Gladys Manzanares and Maura Parsons, along with thousands of activists within the transnational coalition, could not turn the tide. Chentex could not be budged. The union's defeat was a major set-back for Nicaraguan *maquila* workers, as well as the entire anti-sweatshop movement. Given the broader consequences of the Chentex campaign, how can *maquila* workers fight back and improve their wages and working conditions over time? Where does the anti-sweatshop movement go from here? These questions are explored in the book's final chapter.

6

Globalization and Cross-Border Labor Solidarity
Is Another World Possible?

Spaces of Hope

Challenging sweatshop labor practices is no simple task. The previous four chapters illustrate that point very clearly. Under very difficult circumstances, *maquila* workers and their cross-border allies confronted some of the most powerful companies in the world—Phillips Van-Heusen, the Gap, J.C. Penney, Wal-Mart, Target, and Kohl's. They organized clandestine meetings; held rallies and demonstrations outside well-guarded factories, free trade zones, and shopping malls; passed out leaflets; filed worker rights petitions; shared *testimonios* and personal experiences; sang songs of solidarity and resistance; and inspired and motivated each other. After years of struggle and sacrifice, they finally obtained better wages and working conditions through collective bargaining or independent monitoring. They also gained self-confidence, respect, and dignity through these struggles for social justice.

These positive results were hailed within the anti-sweatshop movement because they showed, following David Harvey that "spaces of hope" existed and that there were, indeed, "limits to capital."[1] On a perhaps even broader theoretical and political level, these campaigns demonstrated that "corporate-led" globalization was not an inexorable process and that agency/resistance remained viable. These case studies also punctured the triumphalism and fatalism associated with two widely accepted, although highly contested phrases, "history is over" and "there is no alternative."[2] The *maquila* workers and social justice activists from these campaigns made history and they helped construct an alternative, more egalitarian vision of globalization that put, using their words, "people before profit."[3] For a brief, fleeing moment, the World Social Forum's hopeful and imaginative motto, "another world *is* possible," seemed tangible and real.[4]

However, that optimism slowly evaporated over time. Two unionized factories with collective bargaining agreements (Camisas Modernas and Kimi) closed down, while another one (Chentex) remained open after virtually eliminating the union. Working conditions improved in the last factory (Mandarin International), but wages did not increase. These four results indicate that transnational corporations remain powerful and that resistance is not limitless. This sober fact highlights Robin Cohen's instructive comments about the perennial debate between "structure" and "agency." Writing about debates within labor studies and social theory, he warns against "proletarian messianism" and "structural-determinism;" simply meaning, victories are possible, but scholars and activists must not exaggerate those achievements because they can be constrained or completely overturned.[5] The workers from these campaigns can all attest to this fact.

Given this situation, where does the anti-sweatshop movement go from here? What factors limit *maquila* workers and social justice activists from broadening and sustaining its impact? These case studies indicate that transnational corporations, capital mobility, and strategic divisions between movement actors are the main obstacles or "enemies" that it faces. Some anti-sweatshop and global justice activists take this analysis one step further, suggesting that sweatshops and the capitalist world-system are intimately tied together.[6] This perspective raises another key question, what is relationship between the anti-sweatshop and global justice movements? How have the tragic events of September 11, 2001 and the "war on terrorism" affected these two movements?

These questions deserve serious analysis and consideration. Before addressing them, however, there is a fundamental issue that warrants comparative and systematic inquiry. This book started out with a basic, straight-forward question: why do most cross-border labor solidarity campaigns targeting sweatshop labor "succeed" in the short-run, but "fail" in the long-run? The larger questions outlined above cannot be fully explored without understanding what complex factors and subtle nuances produced these disparate outcomes. Where the anti-sweatshop movement goes from here, for example, largely depends on analyzing what strategies and tactics had the most effectiveness and explaining why the gains that were made were not sustained over time. The movement's future direction is also contingent upon pinpointing what factor(s) might be considered the "enemy." The old labor aphorism "know thy enemy" seems more appropriate today than ever.

Based on this study's key question and the larger issues that these four campaigns raise, this chapter is divided into four parts. The first one analyzes the theoretical and empirical literature on social movement outcomes, emphasizing how scholars have defined or measured "success" on a longitudinal, holistic, and contingent basis. This brief overview sets up the second and third sections, which examine how and why these four campaigns achieved some degree of success before they encountered resistance and/or fell apart. The last section explores the broader theoretical and political implications of these cases. Using a short, medium, and long-range typology, I identify some of the obstacles (enemies) that have blocked cross-border labor solidarity campaigns from becoming more successful and make some observations and suggestions about the anti-sweatshop and global justice movements. I conclude with some final reflections about the dialectic between hope and despair.

Social Movement Outcomes: Measuring Success

The social movement literature has rapidly expanded over the past thirty years. Studies on the civil rights, feminist, gay and lesbian, and anti-war movements of the 1960s, the anti-nuclear and environmental movements of the 1970s, the Central American solidarity movement of the 1980s, and many more recent movements (e.g., global justice) now exist. Despite this growth, very few scholars have examined movement outcomes. This does not mean no one has researched this topic; indeed several studies have done so.[7] Marco Giugni notes, however, "work on the outcomes of social movements has rarely been pulled together and systematically surveyed and theorized."[8]

Widespread ambiguity over what constitutes success and failure is one of the reasons why this area remains relatively underdeveloped. William Gamson's well-known study, *The Strategy of Social Protest*, succinctly articulated this dilemma many years ago, stating, "success is an elusive idea."[9] Because social movements and campaigns often occur over time (longitudinally) and take place in dynamic, ever-changing environments, assessment and evaluation can be rather complicated. This situation can be addressed through disaggregating the movement or campaign into a series of discrete, time-specific periods.

Maquila workers could, for example, organize a militant wildcat strike that would cripple production for several days, but company supervisors might respond with mass firings, ending the campaign. Several years may pass before the workers try again—this time, they receive financial and technical assistance from labor unions and non-governmental organizations (NGOs) from the United States, Europe, Asia, Africa, and the Americas. The workers obtain legal recognition for their union, ratify a collective bargaining agreement, and receive better wages and working conditions, along with an intangible sense of respect, dignity, and empowerment. Based on these criteria, the campaign could be classified a short-term "success." Several months later the factory shuts down and moves to a non-unionized location, however, leaving the workers unemployed. Seen from this lens, the campaign could be labeled a long-term "failure."

Paul Almeida and Linda Brewster Stearns examined a local grass-roots environmental movement in Minamata, Japan that followed, more or less, this hypothetical example.[10] Almeida and Stearns divided this movement into four time periods. During the movement's first phase (1955–1963), some protest groups publicized corporate misdeeds (e.g., dumping toxic mercury into local waterways that caused hundreds of deaths and thousands of injuries and birth defects) and organized rallies, but they lacked "external allies" (e.g., student, labor, and religious groups, etc.) and political and economic elites were unified.[11] The "political opportunity structure" was, therefore, not conducive for achieving a more favorable outcome. Sidney Tarrow contends that "political opportunities" expand when external allies are present and elite groups are divided.[12]

Frances Fox Piven and Richard Cloward suggest that "poor people's movements" can exploit those conditions through disruptive tactics (e.g., marches, strikes, etc.).[13] The Minamata-based movement practiced disruption, but given the limited range of political opportunities, it initially failed to obtain its "stated goals" (corporate responsibility, governmental legislation, and financial compensation), although some victims' families received small monetary benefits.[14]

The Minamata movement gained prominent external allies and divisions within elite groups surfaced during phase two (1964–1968).[15] These conditions expanded the "political opportunity structure," giving activists more leverage for bargaining and negotiating a favorable settlement. In phase three (1969–1974), external allies and elite instability were high, disruptive tactics (e.g., sit-ins, marches, and shareholder resolutions) were utilized, and relatively extensive concessions (corporate public apology, favorable court ruling, and major financial awards) were granted.[16] In phase four (1975–present), external allies and elite instability waned, as did disruptive activity. Declining political opportunities prompted elite groups to significantly roll-back previous gains.[17] Given these mixed outcomes, Almeida and Stearns state that the final result constituted a "shallow victory" for the victims' families who worked "so long, for so little."[18]

This case study highlights some of the pitfalls that are associated with evaluating social movement outcomes. Outcomes can rarely, if ever, be neatly classified into rigid, dualistic, "either-or" categories. The Minamata campaign illustrates this argument—it was a "success" *and* a "failure," but not in some absolute, abstract sense. Based on contingent, conjunctural, and fluid circumstances, activists, victims' families, and local organizations obtained some important gains, but they were curtailed over time. Seen from this holistic lens, this campaign might be best labeled a "short-term success" and a "long-term failure."

The four cross-border labor solidarity campaigns examined in this study could be classified in a similar manner. Using the criterion of organizing and establishing a legally recognized union and obtaining better wages and working conditions, these four campaigns were mostly successful in the short-run. In the long-run, these victories proved to be ephemeral or "pyrrhic," however. Some factories shut down and moved elsewhere, while others stayed open after crushing militant labor unions. What theoretical frameworks help us understand how and why these campaigns experienced such divergent outcomes (short-term victories/long-term defeats)?

The Boomerang Effect, Political Opportunities, and Cross-Border Labor Solidarity: Breaking Down the Victories

How were the *maquila* labor unions organized and legally recognized in these four campaigns? How did wages and working conditions improve? In chapter 1, I described what Margaret Keck and Kathryn Sikkink call the "boomerang effect."[19] The "boomerang effect" often emerges in contexts where "domestic non-state actors" (e.g., unions, student, human rights, and women's groups) encounter relatively closed "political opportunity structures." Khagram, Riker, and Sikkink contend "Political opportunity structures are those consistent dimensions of the political environment that provide incentives for or constraints on people undertaking collective action. Political opportunities often provide resources for leverage and spaces for access."[20] Despite the term's tendency toward becoming, in William Gamson and David Meyer's words, an "all-encompassing fudge factor,"[21] political opportunities can be seen as a key "sensitizing concept" that expands or contracts based on certain conditions (e.g., elite instability, external allies, etc.).[22]

The four countries—El Salvador, Guatemala, Honduras, and Nicaragua—where these campaigns took place had very few political opportunities for domestic-based labor organizing in the 1990s. This claim may sound rather counter-intuitive given these countries' so-called "transition" toward democracy.[23] There can be no doubt that the level of political repression has declined within Central America over the past twenty-five years. Tens of thousands of people, many of whom were trade unionists, were killed, tortured, arrested, and disappeared in the 1980s.[24] Those days are largely gone. The generals have relinquished power and the mercenary and guerrilla forces have disbanded. "Free and fair" elections are commonplace today. Once "subversive" political parties and labor confederations can now operate, more or less, freely without fear that the government or paramilitary forces will target them.

The region's shift from authoritarianism toward democracy has been widely noted and praised, but some scholars remain skeptical. Bill Robinson, for instance, contends that the mere presence of "free and fair elections" does not constitute "democracy."[25] He argues that in the post-World War II era, the United States supported authoritarian dictatorships (toppling democratically-elected governments in Guatemala and Chile in 1954 and 1973) to protect its economic and political interests. Those regimes brutal tactics indirectly facilitated the rise of militant, revolutionary movements (e.g., the Nicaraguan Sandinista Party) that jeopardized those interests, however.[26] Thus, in the 1980s and 1990s, U.S. officials began promoting "democracy," which Robinson claims should be more accurately called "polyarchy."[27] Polyarchy is "a system in which a small group actually rules and mass participation in decision-making is confined to leadership choices in elections carefully managed by competing elites."[28]

Robinson's thesis is provocative because it challenges the fundamental premise behind the "democratic transitions" literature.[29] He alleges that a "polyarchic," not democratic, shift took place in Guatemala, El Salvador, Honduras, and Nicaragua in the 1990s. This perspective helps us understand why so few political opportunities existed within those four countries over the past decade. Because elite groups introduced (after receiving pressure and advice from the United States, International Monetary Fund [IMF] and World Bank) neoliberal, export-led development policies based on maintaining low labor costs as an incentive for attracting foreign investment, the "climate" for organizing unions and demanding better wages and working conditions was not conducive.[30] In all four countries, government officials and *maquila* owners regularly worked together, limiting the possibilities for labor organizing through bureaucratic delays, legal maneuvers, firings, repression, and capital mobility. Thus, even though the formal political (electoral) process "opened up" and clandestine labor organizations surfaced from the underground, the overall environment for mobilization and unionization remained fairly restricted in the 1990s.[31]

Another perspective that explains why so few political opportunities existed for labor organizing in all four countries in the 1990s comes from Paul Drake's book, *Labor Movements and Dictatorships*.[32] His tripartite model suggests that structural, institutional, and political factors can both facilitate and limit the potential for collective action and resistance.[33] In three Southern Cone-based case studies (Argentina, Chile, and Uruguay), Drake found that capitalist authoritarian regimes introduced neoliberal economic policies (structural), passed anti-labor legislation (institutional), and repressed pro-labor parties (political) after taking power through military coups.[34] These conditions made organizing strikes, demonstrations, and unions extremely difficult, but most labor confederations survived and gained greater autonomy, though not necessarily power or leverage, after the dictatorships fell.[35]

Central American labor organizations faced a similar situation after the civil wars ended, human rights violations declined, and "democracy" returned. They technically had greater "freedom" than they had under authoritarian rule, but unions and confederations faced new structural constraints—namely skyrocketing unemployment and poverty rates generated (partially) as a result of the IMF and World Bank's "structural adjustment policies."[36] Economists have long noted that high unemployment inhibits unionization because employers can selectively choose from a larger, ever-expanding labor market. Institutionally, labor confederations in all four countries were extremely weak and ideologically divided after state repression subsided.[37] This factor has severely hampered new organizing campaigns and initiatives. Finally, despite the legalization of guerrilla organizations and the re-emergence of social-democratic and leftist political parties, political constraints ("neoliberal polyarchy") make labor organizing difficult. These center-left political forces currently do not have enough power to adopt new economic programs and pass labor laws that might facilitate unionization and generate widespread social and economic benefits.[38]

Based on Robinson and Drake's work, the structural, institutional, and political conditions for *maquila* labor organizing were generally not favorable in any of the four countries in the 1990s. Despite overwhelming odds, *maquila* workers from four separate factories (Camisas Modernas, Mandarin International, Kimi, and Chentex) organized themselves and pressed for better wages and working conditions within the context of their respective nation-states. These initial efforts were largely unsuccessful. Mass firings, violence, intimidation, and bureaucratic intransigence thwarted these campaigns before they gained substantial strength and momentum. Moreover, the relative absence of intra-elite divisions and powerful external allies also limited their effectiveness. Some *maquila* workers developed ties with domestically-based political parties as well as women's, human rights, labor, student, and community-based organizations, but those groups did not have sufficient resources for obtaining concessions.

Since these workers had very little leverage, they established links with transnational non-government organizations (NGOs), based mostly in the United States. These NGOs became the *maquila* workers' key "external allies," providing them with greater political opportunities than they had before. The NGOs eventually formed a "transnational activist network" (TAN) that helped generate positive "boomerang effects" through information, symbolic, leverage, and accountability politics.[39]

To illustrate this process, let us review one specific example. In the Gap campaign, the National Labor Committee (NLC) and UNITE (Union of Neddletrades, Industrial, and Textile Employees) flew two women *maquiladora* workers to the United States for a nationwide speaking tour in mid-1995. The NLC also produced a short documentary film called *Zoned For Slavery*, which focused on human rights violations and sweatshop labor practices in the Central American *maquiladora* industry. *Zoned For Slavery* was shown widely on college campuses throughout the United States. The NLC, moreover, held press conferences, posted campaign updates on its Web site, and coordinated leafleting actions against the Gap. These strategies sparked media coverage in major newspapers like the *New York Times* and the *Washington Post*.

This "repertoire of contentious activity" (to use Charles Tilly and Sidney Tarrow's language) highlights two crucial theoretical issues.[40] First, the NLC and UNITE acted as "mobilizing structures," disseminating information that spurred thousands of people to take collective action. McAdam, McCarthy, and Zald contend that political opportunities, mobilizing structures, and framing processes are crucial for understanding the trajectories and dynamics of social movements.[41] They define mobilizing structures as "those collective vehicles, informal as well as formal, through which people mobilize and engage in collective action."[42] Information politics (the workers' speaking tour, *Zoned For Slavery*, leaflets, flyers, e-mail campaign updates, etc.) were the cornerstone of this mobilizing process, producing a strong U.S.-based solidarity campaign on behalf of the Gap's Salvadoran workers.

The second issue revolves around what David Snow and his colleagues (following Erving Goffman's work) call "framing processes."[43] McAdam, McCarthy, and Zald define framing as "conscious, strategic efforts by groups of people to fashion shared understandings of the world and of themselves that legitimate and motivate collective action."[44] The NLC symbolically framed (using information politics) the Gap as the "enemy," smearing it with allegations of "sweatshop labor." NLC Executive Director Charles Kernaghan served as the campaign's key "moral entrepreneur."[45] He sharply criticized the Gap for paying its workers "starvation wages" and consistently called for independent monitoring. The NLC's savvy media-driven campaign punctured the Gap's trendy, socially conscious public image. The small, but highly influential New York-based labor rights organization effectively held the Gap accountable to its lofty rhetoric, essentially telling it, "don't just talk the talk, walk the walk."

This campaign demonstrates the efficacy of information, symbolic, and accountability politics, but how did these strategies translate into leverage or power? In this case, the NLC's multi-faceted campaign, focusing on the disjuncture between the company's image and its sweatshop labor practices, left the Gap reeling. The NLC gained "moral leverage" based on these withering criticisms which called on the company to "bridge the gap between image and reality." The Gap then leaned on its contractor, Mandarin International, using its "material leverage," to resolve the conflict. Since over 80 percent of Mandarin's production orders came from the Gap, the company had tremendous power. Mandarin risked major financial losses if it did not accept the Gap's demands. The contractor seemingly understood these risks, signing an historic independent monitoring agreement that improved working conditions, but left wages intact.

This outcome illustrates the explanatory power of the "boomerang effect" model. The Mandarin International workers initially had very little leverage—hundreds were fired for organizing several strikes and forming a union. This response made Mandarin the "primary target." Because the domestic political opportunity structure was relatively restricted, the Mandarin workers established ties with NGOs like the NLC and UNITE, creating a powerful TAN. The

TAN, through information, symbolic, and accountability politics, gained "moral leverage" over the Gap—the "secondary target." The Gap then placed enormous financial pressure, exercising its "material leverage," on Mandarin, sparking the "boomerang effect." This latter move proved to be the crucial moment of the campaign because it generated a crack within the political opportunity structure, opening up space for the partially successful result (independent monitoring).

The three other campaigns followed a similar path, but with one key exception. In the Gap case, the local union was fairly weak (after Mandarin fired hundreds of its members), but the TAN initially had a relatively high degree of unity. The "final" result was an independent monitoring agreement that improved working conditions, but wages remained low. Internal conflicts within the TAN eventually became more pronounced, making progress on this latter issue nearly impossible.

The PVH, Kimi, and Chentex cases, in contrast, all involved strong local unions. In fact, STECAMOSA (the PVH Workers Union) and SITRAKIMIH (the Kimi Workers Union) expanded their membership base with financial and technical assistance from UNITE and the international garment workers' secretariat (the Chentex union was established without support from these two organizations). This process exemplifies what I call organization-building politics. Keck and Sikkink (1998) ignore this strategy because they position (or overdetermine) the TAN as the "key" agent of social change.[46] Within their model, TANs provide domestic non-state actors (e.g., unions) with greater political opportunities, generating leverage and space for potentially successful short-term gains. The Gap campaign largely followed this pattern.

While those results were remarkable, slightly more far-reaching change took place in the PVH and Kimi campaigns—wages *and* working conditions improved. How did this happen? In both cases, NGOs like the United States/Guatemala Labor Education Project (U.S./GLEP) and UNITE were deeply involved. These two organizations used trade pressure (the Generalized System of Preferences [GSP] labor rights petition process) to obtain "material leverage" over the Guatemalan and Honduran governments (which feared losing hundreds of millions of dollars in trading benefits) to help secure legal recognition for STECAMOSA and SITRAKIMIH. This strategy expanded or cracked open the political opportunity structure. The TAN (including U.S./GLEP, UNITE, and several other NGOs) could not put direct, shop floor pressure on the employer, however. The PVH and Kimi workers carried out that task. They organized themselves (with support from UNITE and the international garment workers' secretariat) into viable, sustainable organizations, despite great risk.

Through clandestine organizing, these unions expanded their membership base and became stronger. In these two cases, the TAN squeezed, using information, symbolic, leverage, and accountability politics, the "secondary targets" (manufacturers, nation-states, free trade zone officials, etc.), while the local unions pressured the "primary targets" (contractors) through strikes, rallies, and demonstrations. In the PVH campaign, for instance, the TAN began distributing information (passing out leaflets and posting updates on NGO Web sites) about the company's unfair labor practices on the same exact day that STECAMOSA filed for legal recognition in September 1996. The TAN also highlighted the contradiction between PVH CEO Bruce Klatsky's ties with Human Rights Watch and the company's human rights violations in Guatemala City. Through these strategies, the TAN acted as a mobilizing structure (spurring consumers, students, and other concerned individuals into taking collective action) by framing PVH as the "main target." In the Kimi campaign, the TAN mobilized activists using information politics (flyers, leaflets, e-mail updates), framed J.C. Penney (one of Kimi's main buyers) as a "key target," and raised the possibility of trade pressure, while the union held actions inside the factory in March 1999. This two-pronged approach (combining pressure from above and below) produced two-year contracts that improved wages and working conditions within both factories.

These results highlight two key issues. First, TANs can independently generate positive results (e.g., union recognition, better working conditions) without the active participation of local *maquila* unions. Second, the prospects for more "substantive" change (better wages *and* working conditions) improve when unions and TANs with a high degree of strength and unity are involved. TANs can only do so much—the PVH and Kimi cases indicate that far-reaching goals were obtained based on the dialectical relationship between the TAN and the local union. Keck and Sikkink's model downplays this possibility, marginalizing the role of domestic non-state actors. These two cases illustrate that collaboration between the TAN *and* the local union were both crucial, but do they constitute "necessary and sufficient" conditions for achieving successful results?

The Chentex campaign demonstrates that they are not. In that case, the local union was extremely strong and the TAN was broad-based (including NGOs from Asia, Africa, and the Americas). The TAN mobilized social justice activists from three different continents and framed Target and Kohl's as the "main targets." This was a very well-organized campaign that expanded the political opportunity structure through information, symbolic, leverage and accountability politics (leafleting actions, a video exposé, trade pressure, worker speaking tours, etc.) and a series of on-the-ground strikes and demonstrations. The end result was a two-year contract that improved working conditions, but left wages intact. This outcome closely resembles the Gap campaign. Comparing both cases, one might assume that relatively strong local unions are not necessary because working conditions improved with or without them.

These viewpoints seem plausible, but let us look at the larger picture (see Table 6.1). In the PVH case, the union's degree of strength was high as was the TAN's degree of unity. These two actors—the local union and TAN—worked closely with each other and obtained better wages and working conditions. In the Kimi campaign, the local union's strength was high, but some NGOs (NLC and UNITE) within the TAN disagreed, sometimes rather vehemently, with each other. The result (better wages and working conditions) was the same, however, indicating that the degree of unity within the TAN may not make that much difference. In the Chentex case, the local union's strength was high and the TAN had a high degree of unity, but the outcome did not match the PVH campaign. These findings indicate that the presence of these two factors—high union strength and high TAN unity—are important, but they are not "necessary and sufficient" conditions for achieving better wages *and* working conditions. High union strength and high TAN unity were effective in one campaign (PVH), but not the other (Chentex).

How can we understand these seemingly paradoxical results? Following Naomi Klein's notion of the "brand boomerang," I contend that the degree of corporate vulnerability often plays a vital role in cross-border labor solidarity campaigns.[47] In the PVH case, the company owned its Guatemala City-based subsidiary (Camisas Modernas). This factor, combined PVH's socially responsible image and close links with Human Rights Watch, made it highly susceptible to brand-based attacks. In the Kimi campaign, the main target—J.C. Penney—did not have a high public profile like PVH, but the company was moderately concerned about "sweatshop" allegations. In the Gap case, the manufacturer was extremely concerned about its chic public image. It had tremendous leverage over Mandarin, yet the union's strength was quite low. In the Chentex campaign, corporate vulnerability was complicated. Target and Kohl's were susceptible, but Nien Hsing—Chentex's owner—was virtually untouchable. This factor partially explains why wages were not increased. The company simply brushed off nearly all forms of public criticism. Had Nien Hsing been more vulnerable, the Chentex campaign might have closely mirrored the PVH case. The same goes for the Gap case—had the union been stronger, wages would have probably risen.

These results indicate that levels of local union strength and corporate vulnerability matter. Looking across the cases (see Table 6.1), one can see that if the

Table 6.1 Explanatory Factors and Outcomes

Campaign	Degree of Union Strength	Degree of TAN Unity	Degree of Corporate Vulnerability	Better Wages	Better Working Conditions
PVH (Guatemala)	High	High	High	Yes	Yes
Kimi (Honduras)	High	Moderate	Moderate	Yes	Yes
Gap (El Salvador)	Low	Moderate	High	No	Yes
Chentex (Nicaragua)	High	High	Low	No	Yes

local union's strength was higher in the Gap campaign and if Nien Hsing was at least moderately vulnerable in the Chentex campaign, the results could have probably matched the PVH and Kimi cases. What does all this mean? No one single factor or series of factors explain why these cross-border labor solidarity campaigns produced positive short-term results. Each campaign had its own complexities and nuances. These dynamics limit us from making broad generalizations. Nevertheless, some key issues can be highlighted:

- *Maquila* unions and TANs with a high degree of strength and unity are important, but they do not constitute "necessary and sufficient" conditions for generating short-term gains. Sweatshop labor practices can be challenged without one or the other, but the potential for more far-reaching change is higher with both.
- TANs are essential because they can provide greater political opportunities for *maquila* unions. High levels of TAN unity are not critical. Internal conflicts within and between network actors are inevitable. Healthy debate and dialogue can be useful and productive, but too much dissension can undermine campaign effectiveness. The Gap and Kimi cases illustrate these points.
- Organization-building politics are crucial. TANs can independently produce meaningful results, but more "substantive" outcomes depend on the strength of the local union. The PVH and Kimi campaigns support that argument (but the Chentex case does not).
- Corporate vulnerability is also vital. TANs can exploit corporate weaknesses through speaking tours, videos, leaflets, press conferences, rallies, and "alternative fashion shows." Companies with a "socially responsible image" are especially susceptible to these attacks. These strategies and tactics are not fool-proof, however (e.g., Nien Hsing/Chentex)
- "Morally-leveraged" manufacturers and retailers are more likely to use their "material leverage" over their contractors to address or resolve "sweatshop allegations" and/or labor conflicts. Factories that are wholly-owned subsidiaries (e.g., Camisas Modernas) or are highly "dependent" on one or two suppliers (e.g., Mandarin International) are more likely to make concessions.
- Material leverage can also be obtained through trade pressure. In the PVH, Kimi, and Chentex cases, the Guatemalan, Honduran, and Nicaraguan governments either made concessions or took neutral or pro-union positions after they were threatened with the potential loss of trading benefits.
- The most optimal scenario for raising wages and improving working conditions involves moderate/high corporate vulnerability, high local union strength, and moderate/high TAN unity. These three factors were present in two cases (PVH and Kimi) and absent in the other two (Gap and Chentex).

These points should be seen as "general guidelines" that may or may not generate positive, short-term campaign victories. There are no ready-made formulas for producing and sustaining such an outcome. There is much wisdom in the old saying, "what is given can always be taken away." The *maquiladora* workers from all four factories learned that lesson the hard way.

Naming the Enemies: Breaking Down the Defeats

The four campaigns examined in this study were all "successful," but the gains that they made were not sustained over time. What theoretical frameworks and concepts help us understand why these victories turned into "defeats?" Following McAdam, McCarthy, and Zald's three-part model (political opportunities, mobilizing structures, and framing processes), we can examine each specific campaign's trajectory and identify the key obstacle or "enemy" (to use Amory Starr's terminology) that sparked its decline or limited its impact.[48]

Capital mobility was the main culprit in two of the four campaigns. In the PVH campaign, trade pressure and attacks on the company's socially responsible image expanded the political opportunity structure, opening up space for STECAMOSA to expand its membership (through organization-building politics) and negotiate a two-year contract guaranteeing better wages and working conditions. The U.S. government eventually lifted the GSP "review" (after several more *maquila* unions were recognized) of Guatemala's trading benefits and PVH became less concerned about negative publicity. These two factors narrowed the political opportunity structure, paving the way for the factory to shut down. STECAMOSA (along with the TAN) tried to reopen it, but corruption and economic hardship limited the "mobilizing structure's" effectiveness. Despite these factors, PVH bears ultimate responsibility for closing down the factory and establishing ties with non-union contractors. The company's ability to shift and relocate production generated the final negative outcome.

The Kimi campaign followed a similar pattern. Trade pressure and image-based attacks on J.C. Penney opened up a "window of opportunity" that SITRAKIMIH climbed through. After numerous delays and internal conflicts within the TAN (between UNITE and the NLC), the union signed a two-year contract that improved wages and working conditions inside the factory. Political opportunities became more restricted over time, however. Kimi's management and the free trade zone owner began making threats to shut down the factory and/or pull its lease. Trade, shop floor, and image-related pressure kept it open, but after J.C. Penney pulled out, SITRAKIMIH and the TAN lost a key source of material leverage over Kimi. Kimi eventually shut down and moved to Guatemala. More unity within the TAN might have made a difference in the short-run, but that probably would not have affected the ultimate result. Capital mobility was the key factor that generated this outcome.

In the Chentex campaign, the *Hard Copy* television series symbolically framed Wal-Mart, Kmart, and J.C. Penney as the "corporate villains." The NLC's "smear campaign" created a more permeable political opportunity structure, giving the Chentex Workers Union room to ratify a two-year contract that improved working conditions, but left wages unchanged. Despite frequent assurances from the company, negotiations for a salary increase never took place. The union then held two strikes, sparking massive firings. The union and TAN responded, using trade pressure, delegations, demonstrations, leafleting actions, lawsuits, civil disobedience, and image-based attacks. They also lobbied the United States, Taiwanese, and Nicaraguan governments and gained support from garment workers and NGOs from three continents. These strategies produced a notable short-term victory—some union leaders and members were rehired, but they faced relentless pressure from Chentex. They eventually quit and the union collapsed. In this case, corporate intransigence and repression were the enemies that sparked this result.

The Gap campaign differed from the previous three cases in one important way. The NLC's media-driven campaign generated greater political opportunities for the Mandarin workers and the TAN, paving the road for the independent monitoring agreement. That pact, while largely successful, did not raise wages inside the factory, however. For this reason, I contend that this campaign should be seen as a "partial defeat" because more progress could have been made on this issue. Strategic, ideological, and historical conflicts between the two "mobilizing structures" (NLC and UNITE) within the TAN stopped this from happening. These organizations could have worked more closely together to strengthen the Mandarin International Workers Union so that it could demand higher wages, but they did not. In this case, internal divisions within the anti-sweatshop movement helped create this outcome.

These four cases illustrate that there are several different factors that blocked them from achieving long-term success. Table 6.2 highlights the specific obstacle

Table 6.2 Campaign Outcomes and Obstacles

Campaign	Positive Outcome	Negative Outcome	Obstacle/Enemy
PVH (Guatemala)	Two-Year Contract (1997)	Factory Closed (1998)	Capital Mobility
Kimi (Honduras)	Two-Year Contract (1999)	Factory Closed (2000)	Capital Mobility
Chentex (Nicaragua)	Two-Year Contract (with no wage increase) (1998)	Low Wages; Union Destroyed (over time) (2001)	Corporate Intransigence/ Repression
Gap (El Salvador)	Independent Monitoring Agreement (1996)	Low Wages (factory still open; monitoring continues)	Divisions within the Anti-Sweatshop Movement

Note: The years refer to the dates of the outcomes.

that affected each campaign, along with their positive and negative outcomes. These results indicate that the short-term gains that these four campaigns made were either rolled back or not expanded over time. Given these mixed results, what lessons can be learned from these case studies? Where does the anti-sweatshop movement go from here?

What Is To Be Done? Short, Medium, and Long-Term Strategies

Based on these four case studies, the anti-sweatshop movement faces three significant obstacles—internal divisions within the movement, corporate intransigence/repression, and capital mobility. How might activists and academics confront and, even potentially, overcome these enemies? From my perspective, internal conflicts within the anti-sweatshop movement should be addressed first because corporate inflexibility, capital mobility, and any other obstacle (e.g., linguistic, cultural, gender, racial, or national differences) cannot be effectively addressed until activists and NGOs discuss their ideological, strategic, and historical differences.

The United Students Against Sweatshops (USAS) has been seen as the most vibrant cutting edge organization within the anti-sweatshop movement.[49] One might compare USAS to the Student Nonviolent Coordinating Committee (SNCC), one of the leading groups within the civil rights movement in the 1960s, due to its youthful membership, militancy, and willingness to engage in direct action. SNCC periodically organized retreats to discuss its strengths and weaknesses, as well as the overall direction of the civil rights movement.[50] USAS has held similar conferences on these issues over the past few years, but those meetings have not included a broad range of organizations and actors.[51] It is not USAS' responsibility to call such a meeting, but in order to deepen the movement's impact, future conferences should include a diverse array of groups from all over the world.[52]

Maquila workers should also be more deeply involved in conversations regarding the movement's future direction.[53] Some activists, scholars, and writers have observed that the U.S.-based student anti-sweatshop movement generally includes white, middle-class men and women.[54] In 2002, for instance, nearly all USAS staff members were white women.[55] People of color—especially women of color—were largely absent from the organization's leadership and membership (although this situation has gradually changed over the past two years).[56] Other leading U.S.-based anti-sweatshop organizations—NLC, U.S./LEAP, Campaign for Labor Rights, Witness for Peace, UNITE, and so on—also include mostly white men and women.

Most *maquila* workers, in contrast, are typically seen (in the U.S. context) as "women of color" whose bodies, faces, stories, and voices have been widely disseminated inside and outside the anti-sweatshop movement. Ethel Brooks argues that these women *maquiladora* workers have often been framed as "victims" while U.S.-based consumers and activists are seen as "saviors."[57] She contends that this "victim-savior" trope is one the anti-sweatshop movement's biggest stumbling blocks. Brooks claims that U.S. NGOs sometimes make decisions without fully consulting with *maquila* workers or considering what the long-term consequences might be. In the Gap campaign, the NLC, for instance, pushed for independent monitoring, which improved working conditions, but over three hundred workers were not re-hired after the agreement was signed.[58] Brooks alleges that this case and others like it show that anti-sweatshop organizations have sometimes manipulated, rather than fully empowered, "third world women" for their own benefit.[59]

This is a stinging and perhaps overstated critique, but it has some merit. Strategic conflicts over the efficacy of independent monitoring versus collective bargaining impacted the Gap campaign, negatively affecting the very workers that the NLC and UNITE were focused on empowering. This same debate also influenced and momentarily slowed down the Kimi campaign. Generally speaking, the NLC has unintentionally framed women *maquila* workers as "victims" more than UNITE has, but both groups have employed this "colonialist" practice. This framing process can be viewed dialectically. Worker *testimonios* and videos have mobilized consumers and activists in the United States who, in turn, unconsciously see themselves as the protectors/saviors of the "wretched of the earth."

Brooks' analysis highlights some key dilemmas that the anti-sweatshop movement currently faces. When the movement first emerged nearly ten years ago, white women and women of color like Kathie Lee Gifford, Wendy Diaz (Honduran *maquila* worker), Judith Viera (Mandarin International worker), and the El Monte Thai "slave-shop" workers became its symbolic public face.[60] Their *testimonios* helped facilitate the movement's emergence in the mid-1990s. Over time, some important victories were achieved. Brooks suggests that the most visible, shocking, and egregious sweatshop labor practices (child labor, firing pregnant workers, forcing women workers to take birth-control pills) were occasionally ameliorated, but widespread labor rights violations that cannot be easily (visually) represented, continue unabated.[61]

Many organizations within the anti-sweatshop movement understand this latter problem all too well. Garment workers, NGOs, and social justice activists also realize that time is a key factor for the overall movement. Nelson Lichtenstein, analyzing the changes made within the AFL-CIO since 1995, emphasized this point:

> In a speech at Berkeley, the British historian E. P. Thompson once asserted that a mass movement has approximately six years in which to make its mark, to change popular consciousness, to institutionalize some of its enthusiastic expectations in law and politics. Otherwise, it faces a long,

hard, frustrating road. Its ideas and adherents do not vanish, but they become a more normalized part of the social and political landscape. The capacity to shock, inspire, and motivate a genuine social movement is lost.[62]

Despite recent campaign victories in Mexico, Central America, and Asia and involvement with farm worker struggles, the California grocery workers strike, and the anti-war movement, the anti-sweatshop movement's "capacity to shock, inspire, and motivate" the public has declined over the past few years.[63] The NLC's recent campaign targeting Sean ("P-Diddy") Combs for sweatshop labor practices has not generated the same publicity as the Kathie Lee Gifford exposé did.[64]

To re-energize and re-define the movement's "imagined community," NGOs like USAS, the NLC, U.S./LEAP, UNITE, the International Textile, Garment, and Leather Workers Federation (ITGLWF), the American Center for International Labor Solidarity (ACILS), the Campaign for Labor Rights, and Witness for Peace should meet with Central American *maquila* workers and NGOs to discuss the movement's future direction. Questions regarding diversity and power within the movement should be raised and debated and historical disputes between organizations should be swept aside.

Greater unity, diversity, and power-sharing within the anti-sweatshop movement are crucial, but much more is needed. Most corporations remain intransigent and resistant when confronted a labor organizing drive. Company executives typically claim that they are not responsible for anti-union responses, such as mass firings.

To address this issue, *maquila* workers and activists should focus on corporations claiming to be "socially conscious," or who have an extensively branded label. The Gap and PVH fall into these two categories. Image was the Achilles heel of both companies. When activists confronted them within the United States, officials exercised their material leverage over highly dependent contractors and subsidiaries. This strategy can be quite useful, but it might not be as useful in all cases. Activists should carefully examine which companies have greater vulnerabilities before acting and relying on brand-based politics.

Movement cohesion and strategic corporate targeting are essential, but long-term success depends on confronting capital mobility. If movement actors resolved their differences, if women *maquila* workers moved "from the margins to center" (to use bell hooks's famous words), and if more corporations were susceptible to image-based attacks, company supervisors could still "cut and run."[65]

To address this latter possibility, workers and activists have mentioned two strategies—region-wide organizing and production-chain organizing. The former would involve organizing workers regionally, rather than on a factory-by-factory basis. This model, hypothetically speaking, would limit companies like PVH and Kimi from closing down and shifting production to non-unionized sites in Central America because all the *maquila* workers in the region would be organized and unionized.

The prospects for implementing this sorely needed strategy are extremely remote, however. Structural, institutional, and political constraints make it highly unlikely. High unemployment rates, the privatization of state-owned enterprises, pro-corporate labor reforms, extensive incentives for foreign investors, feeble labor confederations, and ineffectual progressive/left political parties all limit the possibility of region-wide organizing. Henry Frundt summarized this situation, "the prospects for significant unionization in Central America remain bleak."[66] Neoliberal polyarchic regimes thus make this proposal look like a distant, far-off dream.

Region-wide organizing also depends on the politics of the U.S. labor movement. Over the past decade, the AFL-CIO has made some major strides internationally, closing down the long-discredited American Institute for Free Labor Development (AIFLD) and opening up the new American Center for International Labor Solidarity. The federation has also filed labor rights petitions and vigorously backed "fair trade" legislation. Some AFL-CIO linked unions like UNITE have also worked directly with Central America garment workers.

Despite these taking these positive steps, UNITE essentially abandoned garment worker organizing after the Guess campaign fell apart in the middle and late 1990s.[67] Capital mobility definitely limits the union's options, but its unwillingness to organize nationally calls into question its desire and potential to organize internationally. Ten years into the John Sweeney-led AFL-CIO, labor remains feeble, falling to its lowest membership rates in twenty years in 2003.[68] Given the weaknesses of the U.S. and Central American labor movements, region-wide organizing makes great strategic sense, but it is years away from being actually implemented and even if it was, the industry still might move to "safer" [nonunion] locations like China. The scheduled phase out of the Multi-Fiber Agreement (MFA) on December 31, 2004 increases that possibility.[69]

Given these problems, production-chain organizing seems like a more realistic option for countering capital mobility. This strategy would focus on organizing the entire "production chain" of one specific transnational corporation like the Gap, for instance. The Gap has ties with contractors in over forty countries. Based on this plan, the workers from all these countries would be organized into unions. Collective bargaining would take place on a transnational basis, thereby providing all Gap workers with some degree of power.

Production-chain organizing closely resembles the old "world company council" strategy that emerged in the automobile industry in the 1950s.[70] To be successful, major financial resources, deep organizational commitment, and the negotiation of a dizzying array of racial, gender, and linguistic differences would be necessary. Organizing workers from forty different countries would be a complicated and possibly futile endeavor, but under the auspices of the international garment workers secretariat, which would oversee and coordinate the plan, it just might work—in the very long run.

Region-wide and production-chain organizing could limit, but not eliminate, capital mobility. There may be no strategy that can remove that threat. Unless global policies and regulatory bodies are reformed and/or introduced, corporations may always have the option to cut and run. Notwithstanding that fact, let us imagine for a moment that all Central American *maquila* workers were unionized and capital mobility was limited. These conditions would be highly favorable for challenging sweatshop labor practices, but one might rhetorically ask, "what about the millions of people who do not work inside these garment factories?" How would their lives change? What would they gain?

They would, frankly speaking, achieve very little. Poverty, hunger, malnutrition, misery, and the wide gap between the rich and the poor would still exist. Cross-border labor solidarity cannot substantially affect these issues because this strategy ultimately privileges the "point of production" rather than the broader political economy. In the short, medium, and long-run, it can bring about much-needed relief (better wages and working conditions) for potentially hundreds of thousands of *maquila* workers. For that reason alone, all forms of cross-border labor solidarity should be embraced, but they are not a panacea for resolving the capitalist world-system's deep inequities.

No one within the anti-sweatshop movement has ever stated that cross-border labor solidarity is a magic "cure-all" for the world's ills, but some have questioned its limited focus. The anti-sweatshop movement's main objective is to eliminate sweatshop labor practices. Most Central American *maquila* workers, social justice activists, and consumers support that goal. All agree low wages and poor working conditions are the problem, not the jobs themselves. I share these viewpoints, but contend that the movement's gains will remain ephemeral until neoliberal capitalism, which explicitly encourages capital mobility and the attendant "race to the bottom," is challenged and ultimately replaced.

This position closely follows Drake's emphasis on structural, institutional, and political factors. The four campaigns studied here and others like them probably would have been more successful over time in a global economy that was based on full employment, sustainable development, enforceable labor rights standards, income and wealth redistribution, extensive citizenship rights for women, people of color, and all marginalized groups, and popular democracy.[71] These conditions currently do not exist. To achieve them would require systemic change.

Between Hope and Despair: The Anti-Sweatshop and Global Justice Movements Post-September 11

In a post-September 11 world, systemic change is off the radar screen, however. Civil liberties have been curtailed under the so-called "Patriot Act."[72] The U.S.

economy is stagnant. Manufacturing and white-collar jobs are leaving the country, companies are demanding concessions from workers and labor unions, and the number of uninsured and poor people has risen over the past three years (2000–2003).[73] Tax cuts and the war on terrorism have generated record budget deficits surpassing $500 billion.[74] Meanwhile, in Central America, conservative government officials continue supporting neoliberal policies (the "Washington Consensus") that have exacerbated poverty and unemployment levels.[75] The latter will surely rise with the scheduled MFA phase out.

From this perspective, another world looks far from being possible. And yet, amid despair, fear, and paranoia, there are signs of hope and resistance. Ten million people all over the world demonstrated against the war in Iraq in February 2003 before hostilities actually began.[76] Most U.S. unions (including an initially reluctant AFL-CIO) and unions from across the globe opposed the war. [77] More recently activists marched against the proposed Free Trade of the Americas (FTAA, November 2003) in Miami, Florida and met for the 4th Annual World Social Forum in Mumbai, India in January 2004.

These actions—combined with garment worker struggles for respect and dignity in Central America, Mexico, the Caribbean, the United States, Canada, Europe, Asia, and Africa—inspire many and give one hope that another world *may be* possible. The *maquila* workers that led these four campaigns—sweatshop warriors like Mónica Felipe Alvarez, Yesenia Bonilla, Sara Aguillón, and Gladys Manzanares—had visions of that other world. They wanted a world where they could work without fear, intimidation, and terror; a world where they could provide food, clothing, and shelter for their families and loved ones; a world where they treated justly and humanely. Is that other world possible?

The garment workers and social justice activists from these four campaigns showed that it is. The challenge that lies ahead is to widen and sustain the gains that they made. This will be no easy task. Formidable obstacles will emerge along the way. How well garment workers and activists confront them remains an open question. One can only hope that their efforts will be fruitful.

Appendix A
Glossary of Organizations

Acronym	Organization
ACILS	American Center for International Labor Solidarity (United States)
ACTWU	Amalgamated Clothing and Textile Workers Union (United States)
AID	Agency for International Development (United States)
AIFLD	American Institute for Free Labor Development (United States)
AIP	Apparel Industry Partnership (United States)
AFL-CIO	American Federation of Labor-Congress of Industrial Organization (United States)
ARENA	Nationalist Republican Alliance (El Salvador)
ATC	Rural Workers Association (Nicaragua)
AUCCTU	All-Union Central Council of Soviet Trade Unions
ATEMISA	Mandarin International Workers Association (El Salvador)
BSR	Business for Social Responsibility (United States)
CAUS	Union Action and Unity Central (Nicaragua)
CENDIH	Nicaraguan Center for Human Rights
CENTRA	Center for Labor Studies (El Salvador)
CFO	Border Women Workers Committee (Mexico)
CGT	General Confederation of Workers (Nicaragua)
CGT-I	General Confederation of Workers-Independent (Nicaragua)
CGTG	General Confederation of Guatemalan Workers
CIA	Central Intelligence Agency (United States)
CJM	Coalition for Justice in the Maquiladoras (United States)
CLR	Campaign for Labor Rights (United States)

Acronym	Organization
CLAT	Latin American Confederation of Workers
CODEH	Committee for the Defense of Human Rights in Honduras
CODEMUH	Collective of Honduran Women
COVERCO	Guatemalan Commission for the Monitoring of Codes of Conduct
CPT	Permanent Congress of Workers (Nicaragua)
CROC	Revolutionary Confederation of Workers and Peasants (Mexico)
CST	Sandinista Workers Central (Nicaragua)
CTD	Democratic Workers Central (El Salvador)
CTH	Confederation of Honduran Workers
CTN	Nicaraguan Workers Confederation
CTN-A	Nicaraguan Workers Confederation-Autonomous
CTS	Salvadoran Workers Central
CUS	Confederation of Union Unification (Nicaragua)
CUSG	Guatemalan Confederation of Trade Union Unity
CUTH	United Confederation of Honduran Workers
CWA	Communication Workers of America
EMI	Independent Monitoring Team (Honduras)
ERIC	Reflection, Research, and Communication Team (Honduras)
FAT	Authentic Workers Front (Mexico)
FEASIES	Federation of Associations and Independent Unions of El Salvador
FECESITLIH	Central Federation of Free Trade Unions of Honduras
FENASTRAS	National Federation of Salvadoran Workers
FESITRANH	Federation of Northern Workers of Honduras
FESITRAINCOH	Union Federation of Honduran Textile Workers
FESTES	Union Federation of El Salvador
FITH	Independent Federation of Honduran Workers
FITTIV	Inter-American Textile and Garment Workers Federation
FLA	Fair Labor Association (United States)
FMLN	Farabundo Martí National Liberation Front (El Salvador)
FNT	National Workers Front (Nicaragua)
FO	Workers Front (Nicaragua)
FPL	Popular Liberation Forces (El Salvador)
FRTS	Regional Federation of Salvadoran Workers
FSLN	Sandinista National Liberation Front (Nicaragua)
FSR	Revolutionary Trade Union Federation (El Salvador)
FSH	Honduran Syndical Federation

Acronym	Organization
FUGTS	Construction Workers Union (El Salvador)
FUSS	Unitary Trade Union Federation of El Salvador
GMIES	Independent Monitoring Group of El Salvador
HAMA	Honduran Apparel Manufacturers Association
HRW	Human Rights Watch (United States)
ICCR	Inter-faith Center for Corporate Responsibility (United States)
ICFTU	International Confederation of Free Trade Unions
ILRF	International Labor Rights Fund (United States)
IMF	International Monetary Fund
ILGWU	International Ladies Garment Workers Union (United States)
ILO	International Labor Organization
ITGLWF	International Textile, Garment, and Leather Workers Federation
ITS	International Trade Secretariat
IUF	International Union of Food Workers
IWW	Industrial Workers of the World
MOSAN	Nicaraguan Autonomous Union Movement
NISGUA	Network in Solidarity with the Guatemalan People (United States)
NLC	National Labor Committee (United States)
PCN	Party of National Conciliation (El Salvador)
PCS	Salvadoran Communist Party
PDC	Christian Democratic Party (El Salvador)
PDDH	Ombudsperson for the Defense of Human Rights (El Salvador)
PVH	Phillips Van-Heusen
RN	National Resistance (El Salvador)
SETMI	Mandarin International Workers Union (El Salvador)
SITRAKIMIH	Kimi Workers Union (Honduras)
STECAMOSA	Camisas Modernas (PVH) Workers Union
STITCH	Support Team International for Textileras (United States)
TUC	Trade Union Congress (England)
UAW	United Auto Workers (United States)
UE	United Electrical Workers Union (United States)
UCFO	United Fruit Company
UFCW	United Food and Commercial Workers (United States)
UNITE	Union of Needletrades, Industrial, and Textile Employees (United States)

Acronym	Organization
UNSITRAGUA	Union-Unity of Guatemalan Workers
UNO	United National Opposition (Nicaragua)
UNOC	National Union of Workers and Campesinos (El Salvador)
UNTS	National Unity of Salvadoran Workers
UPD	Democratic Popular Unity (El Salvador)
USAS	United Students Against Sweatshops
U.S./GLEP	United States/Guatemala Labor Education Project
U.S./LEAP	United States/Labor Education in the Americas Project
USTR	United States Trade Representative
USWA	United Steelworkers of America
WFP	Witness for Peace (United States)
WFTU	World Federation of Trade Unions
WRC	Worker Rights Consortium (United States)
WTO	World Trade Organization

Notes

Chapter 1

1. William Blake coined this phrase in the novel *Milton* (1808). Devon Peña's *Terror of the Machine: Technology, Work, Gender, and Ecology on the U.S.-Mexico Border* (Center for Mexican-American Studies: University of Texas Press, 1997), 25–26 discusses how Marx used Blake's metaphor in *Capital* (1867 [1977]) to critique the widespread exploitation that existed within English textile factories. Marx's collaborator, Friedrich Engels, incidentally, examined these abysmal conditions twenty years before *Capital* in *The Condition of the English Working Class* (1845 [1958]).

2. This "historical background" is based on the following sources—Daniel Bender, *Sweated Work, Weak Bodies: Anti-Sweatshop Campaigns and Languages of Labor* (New Brunswick, NJ: Rutgers University Press, 2004); Daniel Bender and Richard Greenwald, *Sweatshop USA: The American Sweatshop in Historical and Global Perspective* (New York: Routledge, 2003); Miriam Ching Yoon Louie. *Sweatshop Warriors: Immigrant Women Workers Take on the Global Factory* (Boston: South End Press, 2001); Peter Liebhold and Harry R. Rubenstein, *Between a Rock and a Hard Place: A History of American Sweatshops, 1820–Present* (Los Angeles: UCLA Asian American Studies Center and Simon Wiesenthal Center Museum of Tolerance, 1999); Sweatshop Watch, "Frequently Asked Questions" (www.sweatshopwatch.org). I should point out here that there is no one single, commonly accepted definition for what constitutes a "sweatshop" today. In *Behind the Label: Inequality in the Los Angeles Apparel Industry* (Berkeley: University of California Press, 2000) 3, Edna Bonacich and Richard Appelbaum define a sweatshop as a "factory or a homework operation that engages in multiple violations of the law, typically the non-payment of minimum or overtime wages and various violations of health and safety regulations." Sweatshop Watch, moreover, claims "a sweatshop is a workplace where workers are subject to extreme exploitation, including the absence of a living wage or benefits, poor working conditions, and arbitrary discipline, such as verbal and physical abuse." Based on these two definitions, the word "sweatshop" will loosely mean "garment factories with very low wages and poor working conditions" for the purposes of this study.

3. Homework was a common feature in the garment and needle-trade industries in the late nineteenth and early twentieth centuries. For more a detailed analysis of this issue, see Eileen Boris, *Home To Work: Motherhood and the Politics of Industrial Homework in the United States* (Cambridge: Cambridge University Press, 1994).

4. For more on the history of sweatshops within the United States, as well as strikes and organizing campaigns against them, see Bender (2004); Nancy Dye, *As Equals and As Sisters: Feminism, the Labor Movement, and the Women's Trade Union League of New York* (Columbia: University of Missouri Press, 1980); Alan Howard, "Labor, History, and Sweatshops in the New Global Economy," in *No Sweat: Fashion, Free Trade, and the Rights of*

Garment Workers (New York: Verso, 1997), Andrew Ross (ed.), 151–72; Joan Jensen and Sue Davidson (eds.), *A Needle, A Bobbin, and A Strike: Women Needleworkers in America* (Philadelphia: Temple University Press), 1984; Liebhold and Rubenstein (1999); Stein (1977); Gus Tyler. *Look For the Union Label: A History of the International Ladies Garment Workers' Union* (Armonk, NY: M.E. Sharpe, 1995).

5. For more on the Triangle Shirtwaist fire, see Leon Stein, *The Triangle Fire* (New York: Carroll and Graf, 1962); David Von Drehle, *Triangle: The Fire That Changed America* (New York: Atlantic Monthly Press, 2003). The Kheel Center at the Cornell University School of Industrial and Labor Relations also has an excellent Web site (www.ilr.cornell.edu/trianglefire) on the fire and its aftermath.

6. For more on these organizing efforts see Bender (2004); Boris (1994); Dye (1980); Landon R.Y. Storrs, *Civilizing Capitalism: The National Consumers League, Women's Activism, and Labor Standards in the New Deal Era* (Chapel Hill: University of North Carolina Press, 2000); Tyler (1995).

7. Garment sweatshops never completely disappeared between the New Deal and the 1970s. Despite *Time*'s sanguine claim that sweatshops were "virtually gone" in 1938, they remained alive and well in the South and began emerging overseas, in Southeast Asia, in the late 1950s and early 1960s. See Ellen Israel Rosen, *Making Sweatshops: The Globalization of the U.S. Apparel Industry* (Berkeley: University of California Press, 2002) and Bender and Greenwald (2003) for more on the persistence and spatial dispersion of the garment industry.

8. For more on the resurgence/expansion of sweatshops since the 1970s, see Bonacich and Appelbaum (2000); Jane L. Collins, *Threads: Gender, Labor, and Power in the Global Apparel Industry* (Chicago: University of Chicago Press, 2003); Rosen (2002).

9. The globalization of garment production and the rise of apparel imports made major news headlines within the United States in the 1970s and 1980s. For a fuller analysis of this issue, see Dana Frank, *Buy American: The Politics of Economic Nationalism* (Boston: Beacon Press, 1999), 131–59. Those reports, while substantial, seem relatively minor, however, when compared to the extensive coverage that occurred in the mid-1990s and afterwards.

10. Liebhold and Rubenstein (1999), 64. Some workers, incidentally, toiled twenty hours a day. See Ching Yoon Louie (2001), 236.

11. For more on the Thai slavery case, see Liebhold and Rubenstein (1999), 62–66; Julie Su, "El Monte Thai Garment Workers: Slave Sweatshops," in *No Sweat: Fashion, Free Trade, and The Rights of Garment Workers* (New York: Verso, 1997), Andrew Ross (ed.), 143–149.

12. For more on the Kathie Lee Gifford case, see Kitty Krupat, "From War Zone To Free Trade Zone: A History of the National Labor Committee," in *No Sweat*, 51–77.

13. See Liza Featherstone and United Students Against Sweatshops (USAS). *Students Against Sweatshops* (London: Verso, 2002) for some of these pop culture citations. Bonacich and Appelbaum (2000) make use of the *Doonesbury* Nike strips.

14. For more on the globalization of the garment industry, see Edna Bonacich, Lucie Cheng, Norma Chinchilla, Nora Hamilton, and Paul Ong (eds.), *Global Production: The Apparel Industry in the Pacific Rim* (Philadelphia: Temple University Press, 1994); Collins (2003); International Labor Organization (ILO). *Globalization of the Footwear, Textiles, and Clothing Industries* (Geneva: ILO, 1996); Rosen (2002).

15. Edward Graham, *Fighting the Wrong Enemy: Antiglobal Activists and Multinational Enterprises* (Washington D.C.: Institute for International Economics, 2000); Nicholas Kristoff and Sheryl WuDunn, "Two Cheers for Sweatshops," *New York Times Magazine* (September 24, 2000).

16. See, for instance, Charles Bowden's piece, "Keeper of the Fire," *Mother Jones* (July/August 2003: 68–73) on National Labor Committee Executive Director Charles Kernaghan for a strong viewpoint representing this perspective.

17. Mark Anner, "Defending Labor Rights Across Borders: Central American Export Processing Plants," in *Struggles for Social Rights in Latin America* (New York: Routledge, 2003), Susan Eva Eckstein and Timothy Wickham-Crowley (eds.), 147–66; Joe Bandy and Jennifer Bickham Mendez, "A Place of Their Own? Women Organizers in the Maquilas of Nicaragua and Mexico." *Mobilization* (June 2003): 173–88; Jennifer Bickham Mendez, "Creating Alternatives from a Gender Perspective: Central America Women's Transnational Organizing for Maquila Workers' Rights," in *Women's Activism and Globalization: Linking Local*

Struggles and Transnational Politics (New York: Routledge, 2002), Nancy Naples and Manisha Desai (eds.), 121–41.

18. These claims are based on interviews with dozens of interviews with labor activists and organizers in Central America.

19. The literature on the contemporary anti-sweatshop movement is growing. See Anner (2003); Xiaolan Bao, *Holding Up More Than Half the Sky: Chinese Women Garment Workers in New York City, 1948–1992* (Urbana: University of Illinois Press, 2001); Bender and Greewald (2003); Ethel Brooks, "The Ideal Sweatshop? Gender and Transnational Protest," *International Labor and Working Class History* (Spring 2002): 91–111; Ching Yoon Louie (2001); Jill Esbenshade, *Monitoring Sweatshops: Workers, Consumers, and Global Apparel Industry* (Philadelphia: Temple University Press, 2004); Featherstone and USAS (2002); Ross (1997); Andrew Ross, *Low Pay, High Profile: The Global Push for Fair Labor* (New York: Free Press, 2004); Randy Shaw, *Reclaiming America: Nike, Clean Air, and the New National Activism* (Berkeley: University of California Press, 1999). Magazines such as the *Nation, In These Times, Dollars and Sense, The Progressive, Against the Current,* and *Mother Jones* have all published numerous articles on the movement as well.

I should emphasize here that the anti-sweatshop movement is one of the many social movements that are involved within the broader "global justice" (mistakenly called "anti-globalization") movement. For more on the global justice movement, see Jeremy Brecher, Tim Costello, and Brendan Smith, *Globalization From Below: The Power of Solidarity* (Boston: South End Press, 2000); Alexander Cockburn and Jeffrey St. Clair, *Five Days That Shook the World: Seattle and Beyond* (London: Verso, 2000); Kevin Danaher (ed.), *Democratizing the Global Economy: The Battle Against the IMF and World Bank* (Monroe, ME: Common Courage Press, 2000); Barbara Epstein, "Anarchism and Anti-Globalization," *Monthly Review,* September 2001: 1–14; David Graeber, "For A New Anarchism," *New Left Review,* January–February 2002: 61–73; Naomi Klein, *No Logo: Taking on the Brand Bullies* (New York: Picador, 2002); Naomi Klein, "Reclaiming the Commons," *New Left Review* (May–June 2001): 81–89; Rachel Neumann (ed.), *Anti-Capitalism: A Field Guide to the Global Justice Movement* (New York: New Press, 2004); Mike Prokosch and Laura Raymond (United for a Fair Economy) (eds.), *The Global Activists Manual: Local Ways to Change the World* (New York: Thunder Mouth/Nation Books, 2002); *Monthly Review,* "After Seattle: A New Internationalism?" July/August 2000; *New Labor Forum,* "Let There Be One, Two, Many Seattles: Observations and Reflections," Spring/Summer 2000; Anita Roddick, *Take it Personally: How to Make Conscious Choices to Change the World* (Berkeley: Conari Press, 2001); Jackie Smith, "Globalizing Resistance: The Battle of Seattle and the Future of Social Movements," *Mobilization* (Spring 2001): 1–20; Amory Starr, *Naming the Enemy: Anti-Corporate Movements Confront Globalization* (London: Zed Press, 2000); Janet Thomas, *The Battle in Seattle: The Story Behind and Beyond the WTO Demonstrations* (Golden, CO: Fulcrum, 2000); Neva Welton and Linda Wolf (eds.), *Global Uprising: Confronting the Tyrannies of the 21st Century* (Gabriola Island, British Columbia: New Society Publishers, 2001); Mathew Williams, "Towards More Democracy or More Bureaucracy: Civil Society, NGOs, and the Global Justice Movement," *Social Anarchism,* #30 (2001): 5–26; Eddie Yuen, George Katsiaficas, and Daniel Burton Rose (eds.), *The Battle of Seattle: The New Challenge To Capitalist Globalization* (New York: Soft Skull Press, 2001). For more on the relationship between the anti-sweatshop and global justice movements, see chapter six.

20. I should mention here that many analysts assume that student anti-sweatshop activism first emerged in the late 1990s. David Von Drehle (2003: 74–75) new book on the Triangle Shirtwaist Fire, however, indicates women college students from elite East Coast campuses actively supported the "Uprising of the 20,000" in 1909.

21. The anti-sweatshop movement includes many other organizations. For a more more thorough listing of groups mentioned in this study, see Appendix A.

22. Chapters two through five in this volume document these activities.

23. See, for instance, Mark Anner, 1998, "Transnational Campaigns to Defend Labor Rights in Export Processing Plants in El Salvador, Honduras, Guatemala, and Haiti." Paper Presented at the Latin American Studies Association 21st International Congress. Anner (2003); Ralph Armbruster-Sandoval, 1999, "Globalization and Cross-Border Labor Organizing: The Guatemalan Maquiladora Industry and the Phillips-Van Heusen Case," *Latin American*

Perspectives 26(2): 108–128; Ralph Armbruster-Sandoval, 2003, "Globalization and Transnational Labor Organizing: The Honduran Maquiladora Industry and the Kimi Campaign," *Social Science History* 27(4); Bandy and Bickham Mendez (2003); Bender and Greenwald (2003); Brooks (2002); Esbenshade (2004); Featherstone and USAS (2002); Henry Frundt. 1999. "Cross-Border Organizing in Apparel: Lessons from the Caribbean and Central America," *Labor Studies Journal* 24(1): 89–106; Henry Frundt, 2002, "Four Models of Cross-Border Maquila Organizing," in *Unions in a Globalized Environment* (Armonk, NY: M.E. Sharpe), Bruce Nissen (ed.), 45–75; David Moberg, 1998, "Lessons from the Victory at Phillips Van-Heusen," *Working USA* (May–June): 39–50; Tom Ricker and Dale Wimberley, 2003, "Global Networking in the 21st Century: Labor Rights Movements and Nicaragua's Maquilas," in *Crises and Resistance in the 21st Century World System* (Westport, CT: Greenwood Press); Shaw (1999). These studies have focused on the garment industry specifically. There are many more that have examined cross-border labor solidarity campaigns in a variety of other industries. See the *Social Science History* Winter 2003 special issue on labor internationalism for more on these non-garment industry cases.

24. This is the title of Charles Derber's book, *People Before Profit: The New Globalization in the Age of Terror, Big Money, and Economic Crisis* (New York: St. Martin's Press, 2002).
25. See Bonacich et al. (1994) for a fuller discussion of this trend.
26. The term "transnational activist network" is developed in Margaret Keck and Kathryn Sikkink's *Activists Beyond Borders* (Ithaca, NY: Cornell University Press, 1998), 1–10.
27. Two points are relevant here—one, the battle against Nike (Shaw 1999) mostly took place in Southeast Asia and generated as much press, if not more, than these four Central American cases, and two, the literature that I am referring to here includes Keck and Sikkink's (1998) book and those studies (see pages 15–18 for an extended analysis of this point) that have claimed that capital mobility has dramatically undermined the possibility of resistance and social change.
28. Keck and Sikkink (1998: 12–14) position the TAN as possessing far more agency than the "domestic non-state actor" (local union).
29. Some studies have examined these cases separately. See Armbruster-Sandoval (1999); Frundt (1999); Moberg (1998), for instance, on Phillips Van-Heusen; Anner (1998, 2003); Brooks (2002); Esbenshade (2004) on Mandarin International; Anner (1998); Frundt (1999) on Kimi; and Ricker and Wimberley (2003) on Chentex. Frundt (2002) analyzed all four cases, but his excellent chapter-long piece was not as thorough or theoretical as the work presented here.
30. NGOs like Sweatshop Watch and UNITE have used this metaphor for years. In training sessions and workshops, activists illustrate the industry's structure by outlining a four-tiered pyramid. Retailers occupy the top rung, manufacturers come next, contractors after that, and workers are on the bottom. Scholars like Edna Bonacich and Richard Appelbaum describe the industry in a similar manner. See *Behind the Label*, *Sweatshop Warriors*, and Sweatshop Watch's website (www.sweatshopwatch.org) for more details on the structure of the industry.
31. Bonacich and Appelbaum (2000), 80–89.
32. Abigail Goldman and Nancy Cleeland, "An Empire Built on Bargains Remakes the Working World," *Los Angeles Times* (November 23, 2003): A1.
33. These figures are drawn from the 2002 Annual Reports of Sears, Dayton-Hudson, and Kmart. In January 2002 Kmart filed for bankruptcy. Many analysts believe that Wal-Mart's huge market share and competitive prices helped spark this decision. I should mention here that Kmart has certainly not gone "out of business." Nearly three hundred Kmart stores have been shut down, but many will remain open as the troubled retailer restructures its operations.
34. The information (particularly the quoted material) included within this paragraph comes from Nancy Cleeland, Evelyn Iritani, and Tyler Marshall, "Scouring the Globe to Give Shoppers an $8.63 Polo Shirt," *Los Angeles Times* (November 24, 2003): A1.
35. Cleeland, Iritani, and Marshall (2003).
36. See Bonacich and Appelbaum (2000), 89–96 for more on these dynamics.
37. Bonacich and Appelbaum (2000), 99.
38. Bonacich and Appelbaum (2000), 101-103.

39. Bonacich and Appelbaum (2000), 89–96.

40. Some scholars like Paul Hirst and Grahame Thompson (*Globalization in Question*. Cambridge: Polity Press, 1996) and Kim Moody (*Workers in a Lean World*. London: Verso, 1997) contend that globalization is a "myth" because most foreign direct investment (DFI) occurs between and within developed countries. Others like William Tabb (*Amoral Elephant: Globalization and the Struggle for Justice in the 21st Century*. New York: Monthly Review, 2001) suggest that globalization is not "new." Companies have been moving in search of cheaper labor for decades, if not centuries. Jefferson Cowie's excellent study, *Capital Moves: RCA's Seventy-Year Quest for Cheap Labor* (New York: New Press, 2000) clearly illustrates this point.

    I understand and agree with some of these arguments. "Globalization" began over five hundred years ago when Columbus "discovered" the Americas. All DFI and manufacturing production has not, moreover, moved overseas. These two factors do not mean, however, that "globalization" is nothing more than "globaloney." Over the past thirty years transnational corporations within the garment industry have moved their production facilities and factories all over the world. This process started in the 1950s, but it has dramatically expanded since the 1970s. The literature on this subject is broad and deep (see Bonacich et al., 1994; ILO 1996; Rosen 2002). For direct empirical evidence all one has to do is turn over the label of any clothing or apparel product. I recognize caution regarding the origins, extent, and impact of "globalization" is necessary, but I feel that one cannot deny that off-shore garment production exists. A significant portion of garment production remains in cities like Los Angeles and New York, but again, most clothing and apparel factories have moved off-shore.

41. For more on these factors, see Bonacich et al. (1994); Bonacich and Appelbaum (2000), 4–25; Collins (2003); Rosen (2002).

42. For more on the IMF, World Bank, WTO, and globalization, see Sarah Anderson and John Cavanagh (with Thea Lee), *Field Guide to the Global Economy* (New York: New Press, 2000); Joaquín Arriola and José Víctor Aguilar, *Globalización de la Economía* (Equipo Maíz: San Salvador, 1999); Walden Bello, *Dark Victory* (San Francisco: Food First Books, 1999); Jeremy Brecher and Tim Costello, *Global Village or Global Pillage? Economic Reconstruction From the Bottom Up* (Boston: South End Press, 1998); Kevin Danaher (ed.), *Fifty Years is Enough: The Case Against the World Bank and the International Monetary Fund* (Boston: South End Press, 1994); Ankie Hoogvelt, *Globalization and The Postcolonial World* (Baltimore: Johns Hopkins University Press, 1997); International Forum on Globalization, *Does Globalization Help the Poor?* (San Francisco: IFG, 2001); Eric Pooley, "The IMF: Dr. Death? A Case Study of How the Global Banker's Shock Therapy Helps Economies but Hammers the Poor," *Time* (April 24, 2000); Joseph Stiglitz, "What I Learned at the World Economic Crisis: An Insider's Perspective," *New Republic* (April 17, 2000); Lori Wallach and Michelle Sforza, *Who's Trade Organization? Corporate Globalization and the Erosion of Democracy* (Washington DC: Public Citizen, 1999).

43. Bonacich and Appelbaum (2000), 8–9, 14, 56, 144.

44. Brecher and Costello (1998).

45. All three countries show equal disdain for labor organizing. Mexico and Haiti are slightly more "attractive," from an economic standpoint, than El Salvador because they have lower wages *and* weak labor movements.

46. Despite these limitations, workers within both countries have struggled for social change, organizing strikes and independent labor unions over the past twenty years. For more on these activities, see Dan La Botz, *Made in Indonesia: Indonesian Workers Since Suharto* (Boston: South End Press, 2001); Trini Wing-yue, Leung, *Smashing the Iron Rice Pot: Workers and Unions in China's Market Socialism* (Hong Kong: Asia Resource Monitor Center, 1988)

47. The wages cited here are based on the National Labor Committee's report, *Help End the Race to the Bottom* (New York, NLC, 1999). For more on apparel industry wages, see International Labor Organization, *Labor Practices in the Footwear, Leather, Textiles, and Clothing Industries* (Geneva: ILO, 2000), 37–47.

48. Andrew Herod, *Labor Geographies: Workers and the Landscape of Capitalism* (New York: Guilford Press, 2001); J. K. Gibson-Graham, *The End of Capitalism (As We Knew It): A Feminist Critique of Political Economy* (Cambridge: Blackwell, 1996).

49. Richard Barnet and John Cavanagh, *Global Dreams: Imperial Corporations and the New World Order* (New York: Touchstone, 1994); Brecher and Costello (1998); Kevin Danaher (ed.), *Corporations Are Gonna Get Your Mama* (Monroe, ME: Common Courage Press, 1996); David Korten, *When Corporations Rule the World* (West Hartford, CT: Kumarian Press, 1995); Wallace and Sforza (1999), I am not suggesting that these books make these specific arguments. They do not claim that social change is impossible; indeed, the authors explore a wide variety of social movements and strategies of resistance. Nevertheless, they exaggerate or "over-determine" the power of TNCs and multi-lateral institutions, making them seem "unbeatable." This debate between structure and agency is a delicate one. I think that some critically-minded globalization scholars have unwittingly committed the error of "structural-determinism," while others have fallen into the trap of "proletarian messianism." (Cohen, 1991.) The former viewpoint prevailed until the Battle in Seattle exposed its flaws. Seattle raised revolutionary expectations and ideals, but police violence against global justice movement activists during the Group of Eight (G8) meeting in Genoa in July 2001 and the "war on terrorism" temporarily short-circuited those notions. The dialectic between these two positions continues.

50. David Harvey, *The Limits To Capital* (London: Verso, 1982); *Spaces of Hope* (Berkeley: University of California Press, 2000).

51. Herod (2001: 29), incidentally, critiques *The Limits To Capital* for minimizing the ability of workers to shape the spatial landscape of capitalism. For his critique of neo-classical and Marxist theories of geography, as well as his own position, see 13–49.

52. These categories are borrowed from Edna Bonacich, "The Past, Present, and Future of Split-Labor Market Theory," *Research in Race and Ethnic Relations* (Volume One), (1979): 17–64.

53. Edna Bonacich, "A Theory of Ethnic Antagonism: The Split Labor Market," *American Sociological Review* (October 1972): 547–59; "Advanced Capitalism and Black/White Relations in the United States: A Split Labor Market Interpretation," *American Sociological Review* (February 1976): 34–51; "The Past, Present, and Future of Split-Market Theory," (1979).

54. The following scholars have made this argument: Arrighi Emmanuel. "The Delusions of Internationalism," *Monthly Review* (June 1970): 13–18; Nigel Haworth and Harvie Ramsay, "Grasping the Nettle: Problems in the Theory of International Labor Solidarity," in *For a New Labour Internationalism* (The Hague: International Labour Education Research and Information Foundation, 1984); Peter Waterman (ed.), 60–85; Nigel Haworth and Harvey Ramsay, "Workers of the World Undermined: International Capital and Some Dilemmas in Industrial Democracy," in *Trade Unions and the New Industrialization of the Third World* (London: Zed Books, 1987), Roger Southall (ed.), 306–31; John Logue. *Toward a Theory of Trade Union Internationalism* (University of Gothenburg, Sweden: Research Section on Post-War History, 1980); Werner Olle and Wolfgang Schoeller, "World Market Competition and Restrictions Upon International Trade Union Policies," *Capital and Class* #2 (1977): 56–75. This literature is not homogeneous, but there is a deep skepticism regarding the possibility of cross-border labor solidarity underlying these works.

55. Bonacich (1979), 32–35.

56. For more on the ILGWU's international labor politics in the 1970s and 1980s, see Frank (1999), 131–159.

57. Jensen and Davidson (1984); Stein (1977); Tyler (1995); Kenneth C. Wolensky, Nichole H. Wolensky, and Robert P. Wolensky, *Fighting For the Union Label: The Women's Garment Industry and the ILGWU* (University Park: Pennsylvania State University Press, 2002).

58. Marx and Engels did not actually coin this phrase. Flora Tristan, a French feminist activist, used it several years before they did in the *Communist Manifesto*.

59. These strategies are discussed more fully in Ralph Armbruster, "Cross-National Organizing Strategies," *Critical Sociology* (1995), 21(2): 75–89. See also Ralph Armbruster, "Globalization and Cross-Border Labor Organizing in the Automobile and Garment Industries" (PhD Dissertation: UC Riverside, 1998).

60. See Pamela Varley (ed.), *The Sweatshop Quandary: Corporate Responsibility on the Global Frontier* (Washington, DC: Investor Responsibility Research Center, 1998) for more on the relationship between the reemergence of sweatshops and corporate codes of conduct in the garment industry in the 1990s. See also Karl Schoenberger, *Levi's Children: Coming*

to Terms with Human Rights in the Global Marketplace (New York: Atlantic Monthly, 2000) for a specific case study of the politics and challenges surrounding Levi's code of conduct.

61. See Varley (1998),401–594 for more specific information on the provisions included within most codes of conduct. Appendix 2 (pp. 505–594) includes codes of conduct from 46 different companies, some of whom are not garment industry-based.

62. Several excellent critiques of corporate-backed "independent monitoring" include: Jill Esbenshade and Edna Bonacich, "Can Codes of Conduct and Monitoring Combat America's Sweatshops?" *WorkingUSA* (July/August 1999): 21–33; Esbenshade (2004); Bob Jeffcoat and Lynda Yanz, "Voluntary Codes of Conduct: Do They Strengthen or Undermine Government Regulations and Worker Organizing?" (Toronto: Maquila Solidarity Network, October 1999); Dara O'Rourke, "Monitoring the Monitors: A Critique of PricewaterhouseCoopers Labor Monitoring." (http://web.mit.edu/dorourke/www/).

63. Medea Benjamin, "What's Fair About the Fair Labor Association?" *Against the Current* (March–April 1999): 8–9. Many other activists have used this phrase as well.

64. Bonacich and Appelbaum (2000), 303–05.

65. For more on the establishment of the AIP, see Varley (1998), 7–26, 464–67.

66. The initial members of the AIP included: Karen Kane, Liz Claiborne, L.L. Bean, Nicole Miller, Nike, Patagonia, Phillips Van-Heusen, Reebok, Tweeds, Warnaco, Kathie Lee Gifford, Business for Social Responsibility, the Interfaith Center for Corporate Responsibility, the International Labor Rights Fund, the Lawyers Committee for Human Rights, the National Consumers League, the Retail, Wholesale, and Department Store Union of the AFL-CIO, the Robert F. Kennedy Memorial Center for Human Rights, and UNITE. See Varley (1998), 476.

67. Varley (1998), 470–75.

68. This point was never actually agreed upon, but it could be implemented in the future under the auspices of the AIP's successor, the Fair Labor Association (FLA).

69. Varley (1998), 470–75.

70. *Working Together*, "Sweatshop Task Force Fuels Controversy." (May–June 1997).

71. For UNITE's objections surrounding the AIP, see Alan Howard, "Why Unions Can't Support the Apparel Industry Sweatshop Code." *WorkingUSA* (May–June 1999): 34–50.

72. The International Labor Rights Fund (ILRF) was one key NGO that did not pull out from the AIP. In fact, it later joined the FLA. This decision prompted all labor representatives to resign from the organization's board of directors. The ILRF eventually resigned from the FLA Board in 2002. I should briefly mention here that some companies—like Warnaco—also left the AIP, but not because its provisions were "too weak." Warnaco claimed that it already had established its own independent monitoring program and thus the AIP's efforts were unnecessary. Karen Kane also withdrew from the AIP at the same time that Warnaco did. See Varley (1998), 466, 475 for more on these two companies and their relationship with the AIP.

73. For more on the FLA's code of conduct, check its website (www.fairlabor.org). See Esbenshade and Bonacich (1999) and Howard (1999) for a critique of its provisions.

74. For more on the WRC code of conduct, see (www.workerrights.org).

75. Medea Benjamin. "Foreword," in *Can We Put An End To Sweatshops?* Archon Fung, Dara O'Rourke, and Charles Sabel. (Boston: Beacon Press, 2001), x.

76. Interview with Gilberto García. CENTRA Director. San Salvador, El Salvador. August 24, 1999.

77. Tom Juravich and Kate Bronfenbrenner. *Ravenswood: The Steelworkers Victory and the Revival of American Labor* (Ithaca: Cornell University Press, 1999), 69–72.

78. For more on comprehensive campaigns, see Kate Bronfenbrenner and Tom Juravich, "The Evolution of Strategic and Coordinated Bargaining Campaigns in the 1990s: The Steelworkers' Experience," in *Rekindling the Movement: Labor's Quest for Relevance in the 21st Century* (Ithaca: Cornell University Press, 2001). Lowell Turner, Harry Katz, and Richard Hurd (eds.), 211–37; Robert Hickey, "Preserving the Pattern: PACE's Five-Year Comprehensive Campaign at Crown Central Petroleum," unpublished paper on file with author; Midwest Center for Labor Research, *No More Business As Usual*: "Taking a Comprehensive Approach," (Issue 21, 1993): 9–27. Bronfenbrenner and Juravich's (2001: 218) chapter examines how Roy Rogers-style "corporate campaigns," which emerged in the late 1970s

and mostly focused on pressuring corporate boards of directors, evolved into more sophisticated comprehensive campaigns that depended on "extensive research, constant escalation of strategically targeted tactics, and the involvement of rank-and-file workers in all aspects of the campaign."

79. Juravich and Bronfenbrenner (1999).
80. Hickey, 57.
81. Hickey, 58.
82. Lance Compa and Stephen Diamond (eds.), *Human Rights, Labor Standards, and International Trade: Law and Policy* (Philadelphia: University of Pennsylvania Press, 1995); Peter Dorman, "Worker Rights and U.S. Trade Policy: An Evaluation of Worker Rights Conditionality Under the Generalized System of Preferences." (Washington DC: Department of Labor, 1989); Mike Witt, "The Real Trade Wars: Solidarity and Worker Rights," *Labor Research Review* (Issue 17, 1989): 93–98.
83. For more on these standards, see Dorman (1989).
84. Henry Frundt, "Trade and Cross-Border Labor Organizing Strategies in the Americas," *Economic and Industrial Democracy* (Issue 21, 1996): 387–417. See also Chapter two for more on the use of worker rights petitions and the PVH case.
85. See Chapter two for more details on these two unions—especially the one at PVH.
86. Henry Frundt, *Trade Conditions and Labor Rights: U.S. Initiatives and Dominican and Central American Responses* (Gainesville: University Press of Florida, 1999), 354–92.
87. Martin Khor, "The World Trade Organization, Labor Standards, and Trade Protectionism," *Third World Resurgence* (May 1994): 30–34.
88. Dorman (1989).
89. Phone Interview with Leslie Gates, CFO Representative, April 5, 1994.
90. Interview with Leslie Gates (1994).
91. Interview with Flor de María Salguero, Mujeres en Solidaridad, Guatemala City, Guatemala, January 30, 1997.
92. Interview with Maritza Paredes, Director, Collective of Honduran Women (CODEMUH). San Pedro Sula, Honduras. September 28, 1999
93. Interview with Teresa Casertano, Inter-American Textile and Garment Workers Federation (FITTIV) Representative, Guatemala City, Guatemala, January 18, 1997.
94. Dale Hathaway, *Allies Across the Border: Mexico's Authentic Labor Front and Global Solidarity* (Boston: South End Press, 2001), 175–83.
95. Terry Davis, "Cross-Border Organizing Comes Home," *Labor Research Review* (Issue 23, 1995): 23–29.
96. Phone Interview with Bruce Fieldman, UNITE Representative, March 1997.
97. Phone Interview with Jeff Hermanson (1997).
98. For more on the cross-border organizing activities of these unions, see Armbruster (1998); Steve Dubb, *Logics of Resistance: Globalization and Telephone Unionism in Mexico and British Columbia* (New York: Garland, 1999); Hathaway (2000); Moody (1997); Jon Pattee, "Sprint and the Shutdown of *La Conexión Familiar*," *Labor Research Review* (Issue 23, 1995): 13–21; *Working Together*, "Hired Thugs Disrupt Union Election," (September-October), 8.
99. I have heard various anti-sweatshop activists loosely discuss the possibility of both strategies. See also Stephen Coats, "Central American Labor Solidarity: Lessons for Activists?" in *The Global Activist's Manual*. Mike Prokosch and Laura Raymond (eds.) (New York: Thunder Mouth/Nation Books, 2002), 199–208; Jeffecoat and Yanz (1999), The labor rights newsletter, *Working Together*, also reported (May–June 1998) that the international garment workers secretariat was developing strategies for undertaking a region-wide organizing project. I also heard this from other Central American labor activists who mentioned that some European (particularly Dutch) unions were also interested in this plan.
100. The literature on the history of labor internationalism (called "cross-border" or "transnational" labor organizing" for the purposes of this study) is broad and deep. Several excellent sources include Henry Collins and Chimen Abramsky, *Karl Marx and the British Working Class Movement: Years of the First International* (New York: Macmillan, 1965); David Fernbach, *Karl Marx: The First International and After* (New York: Penguin, 1992); Frits Holthoon and Marcel Van der Linden (eds.), *Internationalism in the Labor Movement* (London: E.J. Brill, 1988); James Joll, *The Second International, 1889–1914* (New

York: Praeger, 1956); Lewis Lorwin, *Labor and Internationalism* (New York: Macmillan, 1929); Timothy Messer-Kruse, *The Yankee International, 1848–1872* (Chapel Hill: University of North Carolina Press, 1998); Peter Waterman, *Globalization, Social Movements, and the New Internationalisms* (London: Continuum, 2001). For a solid, although largely non-theoretical, discussion of contemporary labor internationalism, see Michael E. Gordon and Lowell Turner (eds.), *Transnational Cooperation among Labor Unions* (Ithaca, NY: ILR Press, 2000).

101. For the AFL and the AFL-CIO's model of business unionism and internationalism, as well as its twentieth century activities within Latin America, see Gregg Andrews, *Shoulder To Shoulder? The American Federation of Labor, the United States, and Mexico* (Berkeley: University of California Press, 1992); Paul Buhle, *Taking Care of Business: Samuel Gompers, George Meany, Lane Kirkland, and the Tragedy of American Labor* (New York: Monthly Review, 1999); Phillip Foner, *U.S. Labor and Latin America: A History of Workers' Responses to Intervention (Volume I: 1848–1919)* (South Hadley, MA: Bergin and Garvey, 1988); Herod (2001); Ted Morgan, *Jay Lovestone: Communist, Anti-Communist, and Spymaster* (New York: Random House, 1999); George Morris, *CIA and American Labor: The Subversion of the AFL-CIO's Foreign Policy* (New York: International Publishers, 1967); Ronald Radosh, *American Labor and U.S. Foreign Policy* (New York: Random House, 1969); Serafino Romualdi. *Presidents and Peons* (New York: Funk and Wagnalls, 1967); Jack Scott, *Yankee Unions Go Home: How the AFL Helped the U.S. Build An Empire in Latin America* (Vancouver: New Star, 1978); Beth Sims, *Workers of the World Undermined* (Boston: South End Press, 1992).

102. For more on the history of the Wobblies, see Melvyn Dubofsky, *We Shall Be All* (New York: Quadrangle, 1969); Joyce Kornbluh (ed.), *Rebel Voices: An IWW Anthology* (Chicago: Charles Kerr, 1988); Patrick Renshaw, *The Wobblies: The Story of the IWW and Syndicalism in the United States* (Chicago: Ivan R. Dee, 1967). For more on the IWW's ties with Latin American radicals like the Flores Magón brothers in Mexico, see John Hart, *Anarchism and the Mexican Working Class, 1860–1931* (Austin: University of Texas Press, 1978); Dirk Raat, *Revoltosos: Mexican's Rebels in the United States, 1903-1923* (College Station, TX: Texas A & M Press, 1981).

103. For more on the CIO, see Walter Galenson, *The CIO Challenge to the AFL* (Cambridge: Harvard University Press, 1960); Steve Rosswurm (ed.), *The CIO's Left-Led Unions* (New Brunswick, NJ: Rutgers University Press, 1992); Robert Zieger, *The CIO, 1935–1955* (Chapel Hill: University of North Carolina Press, 1995). For more on the CIO's ties with the AUCCTU and TUC and its role within the WFTU, see Victor Silverman, *Imagining Internationalism in American and British Labor, 1939–1949* (Urbana: University of Illinois Press, 2000).

104. For more on the politics surrounding the WFTU, CIO, and AFL, see Denis MacShane, *International Labor and the Origins of the Cold War* (Oxford: Clarendon Press, 1992); Silverman (2000); John Windmuller, *American Labor and the International Labor Movement, 1940–1953* (Ithaca, NY: Cornell University Press, 1954).

105. Rosswurm (1992); Silverman (2000); Windmuller (1954).

106. For more on the ICFTU-WFTU split, see MacShane (1992); Silverman (2000); and Windmuller (1954).

107. It should be emphasized here that long before the AFL and CIO merged, the former was deeply involved for decades in Latin America. The AFL established, for instance, the Pan-American Federation of Labor (PAFL) in 1918. After Gompers' death in 1924, the PAFL fell apart. The AFL, based on its anti-communist orientation, did not join the short-lived communist Latin American Union Confederation (CSLA) or the militant Confederation of Latin American Workers (CTAL), which the CIO maintained ties with, in the 1920s and 1930s. During World War II, the AFL worked with the State Department's Office of Inter-American Affairs (OIAA) headed by Nelson Rockefeller. The OIAA initially formed an alliance with CTAL, but as the war wound down, Serafino Romualdi, a former ILGWU official and member of the Office of Strategic Services (OSS—the CIA's precursor), engineered its demise. After World War II, the AFL created the Inter-American Federation of Labor (CIT) and the Inter-American Regional Organization of Workers (ORIT). In 1954, ORIT, the CIA, the State Department, and the United Fruit Company worked together to overthrow the democratically elected government of Jacobo Arbenz in Guatemala. AFL

President George Meany praised the coup, claiming that it would be "hailed by the free world." This long list of activities indicates that the AFL's Latin American activities typically favored U.S. economic and foreign policy interests in the region before AIFLD was established. For more on the activities mentioned above see Andrews (1992); Buhle (1999); Herod (2001); Jon Kofas, *The Struggle for Legitimacy: Latin American Labor and the United States, 1930–1960* (Center for Latin American Studies, Arizona State University: Tempe, 1992); Radosh (1969); Romualdi (1967); Scott (1978); Sims (1992).

108. For more on the origins and trajectory of AIFLD, see Robert Armstrong, Henry Frundt, Hobart Spalding, and Sean Sweeney. *Working Against Us: AIFLD and the International Policy of the AFL-CIO* (New York: North American Congress on Latin America. 1987); Tom Barry and Deb Preusch, *AIFLD in Latin America: Agents as Organizers* (2nd ed.) (Albuquerque: Resource Center, 1990); Buhle (1999); Herod (2001); Morris (1967); Radosh (1969); Romualdi (1967); Sims (1992); Hobart Spalding, *Organized Labor in Latin America* (New York: NYU Press, 1977).

109. Buhle (1999), 152–53.

110. For more on these activities, see Barry and Preusch (1990).

111. For more on AIFLD's role in El Salvador, see Armstrong et al. (1987); Barry and Preusch (1990); Daniel Cantor and Juliet Schor, *Tunnel Vision: Labor, the World Economy, and Central America* (Boston: South End Press, 1992); Sims (1992); Hobart Spalding, "The Two Latin American Foreign Policies of the U.S. Labor Movement: The AFL-CIO Versus the Rank-and-File," *Science and Society* (Winter 1992-93): 421–39.

112. See Nelson Lichtenstein, *The Most Dangerous Man in Detroit* (Urbana: University of Illinois Press, 1995), 406–09; Morris (1967), 7.

113. Barry and Preusch (1990); Cantor and Schor (1987); Spalding (1992–1993).

114. The National Labor Committee (NLC), *The Search for Peace in Central America* (New York: NLC, 1985).

115. Anderson and Cavanagh (2000); Chuck Collins and Felice Yeskel, *Economic Apartheid in America* (New York: New Press, 2000).

116. Moody (1997), 239–40.

117. John French, Jefferson Cowie, and Scott Littlehale, *Labor and NAFTA: A Briefing Book* (Prepared for National Trade Union Responses in a Transnational World Conference, Duke University, 1996); Interview with Jeff Hermanson, UNITE Organizing Director (1997).

118. Buhle (1999), 245.

119. Barbara Shailor, former Director of International Affairs for the International Association of Machinists (IAM) and long-time AIFLD critic, who often called the AFL-CIO "the AFL-CIA," became the ACILS Director in 1997. See Moody (1997), 239.

120. This statement is based on the author's personal observations, as well as conversations and interviews with a wide variety of workers, social justice activists, union officials, and ACILS representatives. The "old days" when AIFLD organizers posed as CIA agents are apparently over—many ACILS representatives are relatively young (20s–30s), committed people that have participated in a wide variety of progressive social movements like the Central American, peace, feminist, and anti-sweatshop movements.

121. See Coats (2002) as well as chapters two through five for more on these differences.

122. For more on the literature on social movement outcomes, see chapter six.

123. Harvey (2000); Herod (2001).

124. Worker Rights Consortium (WRC), *WRC Investigation: Complaint Against Kukdong (Mexico). Report and Recommendations* (Washington DC: WRC, June 20, 2001), 4–6. 31–32. This report can be obtained through the WRC's website (www. workerrights.org).

125. WRC (2001), 33–34. The CROC is one several "official" labor confederations within Mexico that had ties with the long-time ruling Institutional Revolutionary Party (PRI). Often times, "official" unions like the CROC sign what are called "protection contracts" or "sweetheart deals" with employers. These contracts are signed without the knowledge of the workers. They serve to "protect" the employer from the possibility of dealing with a legitimate union that might truly represent the workers' interests, bargaining on their behalf for better wages and working conditions. The June 2001 WRC Report provides ample evidence (pp. 24–30) that the CROC favored the company's interests more than the workers it supposedly represented. For more on Mexico's official unions and protection contracts, see Dan La Botz. *Mask of Democracy: Labor Suppression in Mexico Today* (Boston: South End Press, 1992).

126. WRC (2001), 32–40.
127. WRC, *Report by the WRC on the Kukdong Investigation* (Washington D.C.: WRC, January 24, 2001). For this report, see the WRC Web site (www.workerrights.org).
128. For the ILRF report, see "Opinion Presented by Arturo Alcalde Justiniani Regarding the Case of Kukdong International," (www.laborrights.org/projects/sweatshops/ kukdong). For the Verité report, see "Comprehensive Factory Evaluation Report on Kukdong International Mexico," March 2001. See also Tim Connor. *Still Waiting for Nike to do it* (San Francisco: Global Exchange, 2001) for more on the Kukdong case.
129. U.S./Labor Education in the Americas Project, "Independent Union Wins at Nike Supplier!" December 2001 Update, 1, 4.
130. U.S./LEAP December 2001 Update; Sweatshop Watch, "Mexican Workers Win Unprecedented Victory," December 2001 Newsletter, 2–3.
131. U.S./LEAP December 2001 Update.
132. U.S./LEAP December 2001 Update.
133. U.S./LEAP December 2001 Update.
134. U.S./LEAP December 2001 Update.
135. U.S./LEAP December 2001 Update.
136. U.S./LEAP, "Nike Workers Win Increase," April 2002 Update, 8.
137. U.S./LEAP December 2001 Update.
138. U.S./LEAP April 2002 Update.
139. For some of this literature, see John Guidry, Michael Kennedy, and Mayer Zald (eds.), *Globalizations and Social Movements: Culture, Power, and the Transnational Sphere* (Ann Arbor: University of Michigan Press, 2000); Margaret Keck and Kathryn Sikkink, *Activists Beyond Borders: Advocacy Networks in International Politics* (Ithaca: Cornell University Press, 1998); Sanjeev Khagram, James V. Riker, and Kathryn Sikkink (eds.), *Restructuring World Politics: Transnational Social Movements, Networks, and Norms* (Minneapolis: University of Minnesota Press, 2002); Gregory Maney, "Transnational Structures and Protest: Linking Theories and Assessing Evidence," *Mobilization* 6(1): 83–100; Robert O'Brien, Anne Marie Goetz, Jan Aard Scholte, and Marc Williams, *Contesting Global Governance: Multilateral Economic Institutions and Global Social Movements* (New York: Cambridge University Press, 2000); Donatella della Porter, Hanspeter Kriesi, and Dieter Rucht, *Social Movements in a Globalizing World* (London: Macmillan, 1999); Jackie Smith, Charles Chatfield, and Ron Pagnucco (eds.), *Transnational Social Movements and Global Politics: Solidarity Beyond the State* (Syracuse, NY: Syracuse University Press, 1997); Smith (2001); Sidney Tarrow, *Power in Movement* (2nd ed.) (Cambridge: Cambridge University Press, 1998); Waterman (2001).
140. Keck and Sikkink (1998), 12–13.
141. Keck and Sikkink (1998),13.
142. Keck and Sikkink (1998), 16–25.
143. Keck and Sikkink (1998: 15) contend that, "although labor internationalism has survived the decline of the left, it is based mainly on large membership organizations representing (however imperfectly) bounded constituencies. Where advocacy networks have formed around labor issues, they have been transitory, responding to the pressure of domestic labor movements (as in labor support networks formed around Brazil, South Africa, and Central America in the 1980s)." Margaret Keck also stated during the 2000 Latin American Studies Association (LASA) conference that the "boomerang model" did not apply to labor-related issues.

These claims are startling for several reasons. First, labor internationalism has been mostly expressed through large labor organizations such as the AFL-CIO. For nearly 100 years, the AFL and later the AFL-CIO did not actually in engage in "genuine" labor internationalism—they supported the interests of corporations, the state, and mostly white working-class men (see note 101). In 1995, the AFL-CIO underwent a fairly significant shift, however, and while it is still evolving, the federation is actively involved in several cross-border labor solidarity campaigns. Keck and Sikkink explicably ignore this issue. Second, they remarkably state that advocacy networks formed around labor issues are "transitory." In a footnote they discuss the formation of the National Labor Committee (NLC). The NLC was created in 1981. It still exists in 2004. This hardly sounds like a "transitory" organization. A number of other organizations, which began as Central American "solidarity" groups like Witness for Peace and the Committee in Solidarity with the People of El Salvador (CISPES), have switched gears and have been working on cross-border labor solidarity issues for over 10 years. Thus, Keck and Sikkink's claims regarding labor internationalism are puzzling.

144. Keck and Sikkink (1998), 23–24.
145. Brooks (2002).
146. Naomi Klein, *No Logo: Taking on the Brand Bullies* (New York: Picador, 2000).

Chapter 2

1. Interview with STECAMOSA union members. Guatemala City, Guatemala. September 26, 1996.
2. Interview with STECAMOSA union members. September 26, 1996.
3. For two "early" overviews of the PVH campaign, see Ralph Armbruster-Sandoval, "Globalization and Cross-Border Labor Organizing: The Guatemalan Maquiladora Industry and the Phillips Van-Heusen Workers Movement," *Latin American Perspectives* (1999), 26(2): 108–28; David Moberg, "Lessons From the Victory at Phillips Van-Heusen," *Working USA* (May–June 1998): 39–50. Both articles were written before PVH shut down *Camisas Modernas*. See also Marion Traub-Werner and Altha Cravey, 2002, "Spatiality Sweatshops, and Solidarity in Guatamala," *Social and Cultural Geography* 3(4): 383–400.
4. There were several mutual-aid societies (known as *mutualistas*) that were actually formed before the twentieth century. Some of these organizations later blossomed into the country's initial labor unions. For more on the incipient history of the Guatemalan labor movement, see Deborah Levenson-Estrada. *Trade Unionists Against Terror, 1954–1985* (Chapel Hill: University of North Carolina Press, 1994); Marc Christian McLeod, "Maintaining Unity: Railway Workers and the Guatemalan Revolution," in *Workers Control in Latin America, 1930–1979*, in Jonathan Brown (ed.). (Chapel Hill: North Carolina Press, 1997); Mario López Larrave, *Breve Historia del Movimiento Sindical Guatemalateco* (Guatemala City: Editorial Universitaria, 1979); Antonio Obando Sánchez, *Memorías: La Historia del Movimiento Obrero* (Guatemala City: Editorial Universitaria, 1978); Renate Witzel de Ciudad, *Más de 100 Años del Movimiento Obrero Urbano en Guatemala (Tomo I: Artesanos y Obreros en el Período Liberal, 1877–1944)* (Guatemala City: Asociación de Investigación y Estudios Sociales [ASIES], 1991).
5. See López Larrave (1979), Obando Sánchez (1978); Witzel de Ciudad (1991). For more on the activities of the United Fruit Company during this period, see Paul Dossal, *Doing Business with Dictators: A Political History of United Fruit, 1899–1944* (Wilmington: DE: Scholarly Books, 1993).
6. Levenson-Estrada (1994), 16.
7. For more on these events, see Piero Gleijeses, *Shattered Hope: The Guatemalan Revolution and the United States, 1944–1954* (Princeton: Princeton University Press, 1991).
8. See Edward Bishop, *The Guatemalan Labor Movement, 1944–1959* (University of Wisconsin: PhD Dissertation, 1959); Archer Bush, "Organized Labor in Guatemala, 1944–1949" (Colgate University: Master's Thesis, 1950); López Larrave (1979); Renate de Witzel Ciudad. *Más de 100 Años del Movimiento Obrero Urbano de Guatemala (Tomo II: El Protagonismo Sindical en la Construcción de la Democracia, 1944–1954)* (Guatemala City, ASIES: 1992).
9. See Gleijeses (1991).
10. See Paul Buhle, *Taking Care of Business: Samuel Gompers, George Meany, Lane Kirkland, and the Tragedy of American Labor* (New York: Monthly Review Press, 1999); Nick Cullather, *Secret History: The CIA's Classified Account of its Operations in Guatemala, 1952–1954* (Stanford: Stanford University Press, 1999); Gleijeses (1991); Richard Immerman, *The CIA in Guatemala* (Austin: University of Texas, 1982); Susanne Jonas, *The Battle for Guatemala: Rebels, Death Squads, and U.S. Power* (Boulder, CO: Westview Press, 1991); Stephen Kinzer and Stephen Schlesinger, *Bitter Fruit: The Untold Story of the American Coup in Guatemala* (New York: Doubleday, 1982). For more on the ties between Arbenz and the Guatemalan Communist Party, see Marco Antonio Flores, *Fortuny: Un Comunista Guatemalteco* (Guatemala City: Editorial Oscar de León Palacios, 1994).
11. Cullather (1999); Gleijeses (1991); Immerman (1982); Kinzer and Schlesinger (1982).
12. Levenson-Estrada (1994), 25.

13. Levenson-Estrada (1994); López Larrave (1979); Renate de Witzel Ciudad, *Más de 100 Años del Movimiento Obrero Urbano de Guatemala (Tomo III: Reorganización, Auge, y Desarticulación del Movimiento Sindical, 1954–1982)* (Guatemala City: ASIES, 1994).

14. See Jonas (1991), chapters 7–9. The definitive account on the Guatemalan popular movement in the 1970s has not yet been published.

15. See Levenson-Estrada (1994); López Larrave (1979); Witzel de Ciudad (1994).

16. For many years, popular movement organizations and labor unions denied that they had ties with revolutionary groups. Over the last few years, after the peace accords were signed, however, some organizations have admitted that there were some linkages between them and one of the four guerrilla groups. These ties may have been established rather loosely through specific individual activists. For a discussion of the links between left-leaning labor unions like the National Central of Workers (CNT), the National Committee on *Trade* Union Unity (CNUS) and the guerrilla movement, see Levenson-Estrada (1994), 132–35.

17. There are many studies that have documented these atrocities. Excellent sources include: Robert Carmack (ed.), *Harvest of Violence: The Maya Indians and the Guatemalan Crisis* (Norman: University of Oklahoma Press, 1988); Comisión para Esclarcimiento Histórico (CEH), *Guatemala: Memoria del Silencio* (Guatemala City: CEH, 1999); Ricardo Falla, *Massacres in the Jungle, 1975–1982* (Boulder, CO: Westview Press, 1994); Jim Handy, *The Gift of the Devil: A History of Guatemala* (Boston: South End Press, 1984). Jonas (1991); Beatriz Manz. *Refugees of a Hidden War: The Aftermath of Counterinsurgency in Guatemala* (Albany: SUNY Press, 1988); Michael McClintock, *The American Connection, Volume II: State Terror and Popular Resistance in Guatemala* (London: Zed Press, 1985); Rigoberta Menchú. *I, Rigoberta Menchú: An Indian Woman in Guatemala* (London: Verso, 1984); Victor Montejo, *Voices from Exile: Violence and Survival in Modern Maya History* (Norman: University of Oklahoma Press, 1999); Victor Perera, *Unfinished Conquest: The Guatemalan Tragedy* (Berkeley: University of California Press, 1993); Recovery of Historical Memory Project (REMHI), *Guatemala: Never Again* (Maryknoll, MY: Orbis Books, 1999); Jennifer Schirmer, *The Guatemala Military Project: A Violence Called Democracy* (Cambridge: Cambridge University Press, 1999).

18. See Carmack (ed.), (1988); Falla (1994); Manz (1989); Menchú (1984); Montejo (1999) for more information on human rights violations and the military's systematic campaign against indigenous people.

19. Interview with Rodolfo Robles, Former Secretary-General of the Coca-Cola Bottling Workers Union, Guatemala City, Guatemala. January 1997. See also Thomas Reed and Karen Brandow, *The Sky Never Changes: Testimonies from the Guatemalan Labor Movement* (Cornell: ILR Press, 1996); and Levenson-Estrada (1994).

20. For more on the Coca-Cola Workers Union, see Miguel Angel Albizures, *Tiempo de Sudor y Lucha* (Mexico City: Talleres de Praxis, 1987); Henry Frundt, *Refreshing Pauses: Coca-Cola and Human Rights in Guatemala* (New York: Praeger, 1987). Mike Gatehouse and Miguel Angel Reyes, *Soft Drink, Hard Labour: Guatemalan Workers Take on Coca-Cola* (London: Latin American Bureau, 1987); Levenson-Estrada (1994); Peter Waterman, "The New Internationalisms: A More Real Thing Than Big, Big Coke?" *Review* (1988), 11(3): 389-328; Witzel de Ciudad (1994).

21. Albizures (1987); Frundt (1987); Levenson-Estrada (1994).

22. Gatehouse and Reyes (1987); Frundt (1987); Levenson-Estrada (1994).

23. Albizures (1987); Frundt (1987); Levenson-Estrada (1994).

24. Albizures (1987); Frundt (1987); Levenson-Estrada (1994); Renate de Witzel Ciudad, *Más de 100 Años del Movimiento Obrero Urbano en Guatemala (Tomo IV: Recomposición y Busqueda de Unidad del Movimiento Sindical, 1982-1990)* (Guatemala City: ASIES, 1996).

25. Albizures (1987); Frundt (1987); Levenson-Estrada (1994).

26. See Deborah Levenson-Estrada and Henry Frundt, "Toward a New Internationalism," *NACLA: Report on the Americas* (1995), 28(5): 16–21. I should mention here that U.S./GLEP emerged from the Coca-Cola campaign (Phone Interview with U.S./GLEP Executive Director Stephen Coats, April 1994). For more on U.S./GLEP's history, see Peter Hogness, "One More Hole in the Wall: The Lunafil Strikers in Guatemala," *Labor Research Review* (#13): 1–13; Rebecca Johns, "Bridging the Gap Between Space and Class: U.S. Worker Solidarity with Guatemala," *Economic Geography* (July 1998): 252–71; U.S./GLEP, "Fighting

for Worker Justice in the Global Economy: 10 Years of Leadership by the U.S./Guatemala Labor Education Project" (December 1997).

27. See Jonas (1991) for a more in-depth analysis of the various forces that precipitated this crisis.

28. See Kurt Petersen, *The Maquiladora Revolution in Guatemala* (New Haven, CT: Schell Center for Human Rights, Yale Law School, 1992), chapter two, for more on Guatemala's shift towards economic diversification and export-led development.

29. Petersen (1992).

30. For more on the GSP review process, see Peter Dorman, "Worker Rights and U.S. Trade Policy," (Washington DC: U.S. Department of Labor, 1989).

31. See Henry Frundt, "AIFLD in Guatemala: End or Beginning of a New Regional Strategy?" *Interamerican Studies and World Affairs* (1995), 32(3): 287–317.

32. For more on CUSG's ties with Ríos Montt and AIFLD, see Frundt (1995); Jane Slaughter, "Which Side Are They On: The AFL-CIO Tames Guatemala's Unions," *The Progressive* (1987), 51: 32–36; Witzel de Ciudad (1994).

33. As Jonas (1991) notes, the Guatemalan military, despite democratic elections and procedures, never really relinquished power in the 1980s.

34. Interview with Julio Coj, UNSITRAGUA Secretary of International Relations. Guatemala City, Guatemala. July 27, 1999. See James Goldston. *Shattered Hope: Guatemalan Workers and the Promise of Democracy* (Boulder, CO: Westview Press, 1989) and Witzel de Ciudad (1996) for more on UNSITRAGUA and CGTG.

35. Coj (1999); Jonas (1991).

36. Goldston (1989); Jonas (1991); Witzel de Ciudad (1996).

37. I should mention here that CUSG is affiliated internationally with the International Confederation of Free Trade Unions (ICFTU) and regionally with its Latin American branch, the Inter-American Regional Organization of Workers (ORIT). The AFL-CIO is affiliated with both organizations as well. CUSG no longer receives funding from AIFLD since it no longer exists, however, the AFL-CIO's American Center for International Labor Solidarity (ACILS) still works with the federation. The CGTG is affiliated internationally with the World Confederation of Labor (WCL) and regionally with the Latin American Confederation of Workers (CLAT). UNSITRAGUA maintains no official ties with any international or regional labor organization.

38. For more on the background, signing, content, and on-going implementation of the peace accords, see Susanne Jonas, *Of Centaurs and Doves: Guatemala's Peace Process* (Boulder, CO: Westview Press, 2000).

39. See Instituto de Investigaciónes Económicos y Soicales, Universidad Rafael Landivar, "Empleo y Desarrollo Humano en Guatemala, 1980–1996," in *Guatemala: Las Particularidades de Desarrollo Humano, Vol. II: Sociedad, Medioambiente y Economía*, Edelberto Torres-Rivas and Juan Alberto Fuentes (eds.) (Guatemala City: PNUD, 1999).

40. See Asociación para el Avance de las Ciencias Sociales en Guatemala (AVANCSO), *El Significado de la Maquila en Guatemala* (Guatemala City: AVANCSO, 1994) and Petersen (1992) for a full, in-depth examination of the development and growth of the Guatemalan *maquiladora* industry.

41. See VESTEX. *Guatemala: Apparel and Textile Industry* (Guatemala City: VESTEX, 1999).

42. Petersen (1992), 1.

43. These figures are taken from AVANCSO (1994); Human Rights Watch, *From Household to the Factory: Sex Discrimination in the Guatemalan Labor Force* (Human Rights Watch: New York, 2002), 55; Petersen (1992); VESTEX (1999). It should be noted here that obtaining reliable information on the actual number of *maquila* factories and workers is very difficult. Many smaller factories are not registered. The statistical information presented here, therefore, is fairly conservative—the numbers could be higher, although the economic after-effects of the terrorist attacks on September 11, 2001 may have brought them down.

44. AVANCSO (1994), 19–20.

45. VESTEX (1999).

46. Jennifer Paredes, "Industria de Maquila y Vestuario," *Siglo Ventiuno*, July 26, 1999: 54.

47. The phase-out of the Multi-Fiber Agreement (MFA) in December 31, 2004 is expected to further undermine the country's (and region's) *maquila* industry. For more on this critical issue, see Sweatshop Watch, *Free Trade's Looming Threat to the World's Garment Workers* (Working Paper). October 30, 2003. This document can be accessed at the following Web site: http://www.sweatshopwatch.org/ global/SWtradepaper.

48. Petersen (1992), 139.
49. Interview with Teresa Casertano, FITTIV Representative. Guatemala City, Guatemala. January 18, 1997.
50. Interview with Teresa Casertano (1997).
51. Cerigua, *Maquilas in Guatemala: Ladder To Development or Overexploitation?* (Guatemala City: Cerigua, 1994).
52. AVANCSO (1994); Cerigua (1994).
53. Interview with Guatemalan *maquila* worker, Guatemala City, Guatemala. January 30, 1997.
54. Interview with Rosalinda Galacia López, INEXPORT Union Member, Guatemala City, Guatemala, January 30, 1997.
55. Interview with Flor de María Salguero, Mujeres en Solidaridad, Guatemala City, Guatemala, January 30, 1997.
56. The information included in this paragraph comes from a variety of sources—the Guatemalan *Codigo de Trabajo* (see especially Article 51), internal documents and memos from UNSITRAGUA (on file with the author), and interviews with Julio Coj, UNSITRAGUA Secretary of International Relations, (July 27, 1999), Rigoberto Dueñas, CGTG Assistant General-Secretary (August 9, 1999), Juan Francisco Alfaro, CUSG General-Secretary (August 10, 1999). Two-thirds of the twenty *maquila* unions established in the 1980s and 1990s were affiliated with UNSITRAGUA. See AVANCSO (1994), chapter seven, for more on labor conflicts and unions within specific factories. There is no single source, yet, that comprehensively examines the history of resistance and unionization in the Guatemalan *maquiladora* industry.
57. This draft was initially written before workers at the two Guatemala-based, Korean-owned Choi and Shin factories organized themselves into a union in 2001 and negotiated a contract on July 9, 2003. This is the only collective bargaining agreement in the country's *maquila* industry. For more on the Choi and Shin campaign, see http:// www.usleap.org.
58. These two factories merged into one plant in January 1997. *Maquila* unions are, incidentally, usually named after the factory they are located in. Because PVH's two factories were initially known as *Camosa* I and II, the union was called the Camosa Workers' Union (STECAMOSA). Since the names "Camosa" and "Camisas Modernas" were used so interchangeably, the union was also called (and legally registered as) the Camisas Modernas Workers' Union. For clarity's sake, STECAMOSA refers to the Camosa/Camisas Modernas (PVH) Workers' Union.
59. Interview with Teresa Casertano (1997).
60. Interview with STECAMOSA Union Member, Guatemala City, Guatemala, July 28, 1999.
61. Interview with STECAMOSA Union Member, Guatemala City, Guatemala, July 28, 1999.
62. Wendy Bounds, "Critics Confront a CEO Dedicated to Human Rights," *Wall Street Journal,* February 24, 1997: B1.
63. The phrase, "crown jewels" of the Guatemalan *maquiladora* industry, comes from Petersen (1992), 108–109.
64. For more on these events, see Rebecca Johns, "International Solidarity: Space and Class in the U.S. Labor Movement," (Ph.D. Dissertation, Rutgers University, 1994), 169–76; Petersen (1992), 111.
65. Petersen (1992), 111.
66. Interviews with Julio Coj (UNSITRAGUA) and Juan Francisco Alfaro (CUSG). Dates mentioned above.
67. Petersen (1992), 111.
68. Moberg (1998), 40–42.
69. See Human Rights Watch, *Corporations and Human Rights: Freedom of Association in a Maquila in Guatemala* (New York: Human Rights Watch, 1997), 15.
70. Petersen (1992), 112.
71. Petersen (1992), 112. Rodríguez lost part of one ear. PVH officials were not involved in the shooting. Human Rights Watch (1997: 15) states U.S. Embassy and Guatemalan police reports concluded the incident was not politically motivated. It was, apparently, the result of "casual violence." Rodríguez and some her co-workers claimed, nevertheless, that the shooting was designed to intimidate workers and weaken the union (Petersen 1992: 112).
72. *Report on Guatemala,* "Phillips Van-Heusen Campaign," Spring 1992, 13(1): 13.
73. Moberg (1998), 41.

74. Interview with Byron Padilla, STECAMOSA Secretary of Organization, Guatemala City, Guatemala, August 4, 1999.
75. The other organizations that signed this petition were—the International Union of Electrical Workers (IUE), the United Food and Commercial Workers (UFCW), the North American Regional Office of the International Union of Food Workers (IUF), the United Electrical Workers (UE), the National Council of Churches Human Rights Office, and the Washington Office on Latin America (WOLA). The AFL-CIO later filed its own separate petition in the case.
76. Over the next three months (October-December 1992) three more *maquila* unions obtained legal recognition because of GSP pressure. See Stephen Coats, "Trade Pressure Brings Gains in Worker Rights," *Report on Guatemala*, Winter 1993, 14(4): 12–13. For more on how GSP pressure was used during this phase of the PVH campaign, see Stephen Coats, "Free Trade and Labor Cooperation Across Borders: Recent U.S./Guatemalan Experiences," *Latin American Labor News* Issue 8 (1993): 10–11.
77. Interview with STECAMOSA Union Members. Guatemala City, Guatemala. August 5, 1999. I should mention here that CUSG General-Secretary Juan Francisco Alfaro denied these claims.
78. Petersen (1992: 112) notes that the union, based on documents submitted with the Guatemalan Labor Ministry, reportedly had 150 members in September 1991. Given the rough estimate that the two factories employed, at that time, between 700–800 workers, this means that about 15–20 percent of them were union members. As the campaign progressed that number declined significantly as a result of the company's anti-union activities.
79. Interview with Teresa Casertano (1997).
80. Interview with Teresa Casertano. Guatemala City, Guatemala, September 25, 1996.
81. Interview with Teresa Casertano (1996).
82. Interview with Teresa Casertano (1996).
83. Phone Interview with Jeff Hermanson. UNITE Director of Organizing, August 15, 1997.
84. Phone Interview with Jeff Hermanson (1997).
85. Interview with Teresa Casertano (1997) and STECAMOSA Union Members, July 28, 1999. See also U.S./GLEP, "PVH Union Launches Blitz," (October, Update #17): 1–2.
86. Human Rights Watch (1997), 23.
87. Interview with STECAMOSA Union Members. July 28, 1999.
88. See Human Rights Watch (1997), 25–27 and 37–55 for more specific details concerning discriminatory actions taken against STECAMOSA members.
89. The union's 1995 membership list actually stated that the union had 131 members, while the general assembly meeting minutes claimed that it had 135. This latter number was correct. The union had 135 members, at the *start* of the meeting. The union officially welcomed its new members, however, after the meeting began, stating that it *now* had 177 members. Unfortunately, this information was left out of the meeting's original minutes that were submitted to the Labor Ministry. For more on this incident, see Human Rights Watch (1997), 24–28.
90. This was a very difficult decision for the union and it undoubtedly played into the company's hands. Human Rights Watch investigators stated that the union had legitimate concerns for not including the membership list, but also said that this was a "strategic error." See Human Rights Watch (1997), 28.
91. Human Rights Watch (HRW) (1997), 28–29. An official within the Labor Ministry's office reiterated this claim, stating, "The union [STECAMOSA] simply did not follow the legal procedures. There's nothing we can do." Interview with Zoila González, 2nd Deputy Minister of Labor, Guatemala City, Guatemala, February 5, 1997.
92. HRW (1997), 30–35.
93. HRW (1997), 8–9.
94. Petersen (1992), chapter two.
95. Interview with John Cushing, U.S. Embassy Labor Attaché, Guatemala City, Guatemala, January 29, 1997.
96. See U.S./GLEP, "PVH Agrees to Negotiate!" (April 1997, Update #18): 1–2, for more information on these U.S.-based actions.
97. Phone Interview with David Parker, Economist, U.S. Department of Labor, April 2, 1997.
98. Moberg (1998), 45.

99. Moberg (1998), 45.
100. HRW (1997), 27. HRW investigators actually discovered that STECAMOSA could have claimed that it had 189 members, rather than 177.
101. See U.S./GLEP, "USTR Ends Trade Probation on Guatemala," (July 1997, Update #19), 1–2.
102. Interview with Byron Padilla, August 4, 1999.
103. Interview with STECAMOSA Union Member. July 28, 1999.
104. See U.S./GLEP, "PVH Contract Signed in Guatemala!" (October 1997, Update #20), 1–2, for more information concerning these points.
105. Interview with Byron Padilla, July 28, 1999.
106. This quote appears in U.S./GLEP (October 1997, #20).
107. See chapters one and six for a more thorough analysis and critique of Keck and Sikkink's (1998) model.
108. Keck and Sikkink (1998), 23–24.
109. Interview with Bruce Fieldman, FITTIV Representative, San Pedro Sula, Honduras, September 1999.
110. Letter from Allen Sirkin to author, December 22, 1998.
111. See U.S./GLEP, People of Faith Network, USAS, "Phillips Van-Heusen: An Industry 'Leader' Unveiled: An Investigative Report into the Closing of a Model Maquiladora Factory in Guatemala," January 15, 1999.
112. Interview with Byron Padilla, August 4, 1999.
113. U.S./GLEP Press Release, December 18, 1998.
114. Campaign for Labor Rights Update, "PVH Union Lives," January 9, 1999.
115. Campaign for Labor Rights, "PVH Union Lives."
116. Some of these actions took place before Christmas in December 1998, while others occurred during the first few months of 1999.
117. This information comes from the USAS list-serve.
118. U.S./LEAP Press Release, June 15, 1999.
119. See U.S./LEAP, "PVH Union Ends Vigil; Re-Opening Hope Remains," (August, Issues 1 & 2): 1–2
120. Campaign for Labor Rights, "Guatemalan Union Leader's Family Receives Death Threats While She Visits New York to Protest PVH Practices," June 21, 1999.
121. Interview with STECAMOSA Union Members, July 28, 1999.
122. Interview with STECAMOSA Union Members, July 28, 1999.
123. Interview with STECAMOSA Union Members, July 28, 1999.
124. Interview with STECAMOSA Union Members, August 6, 1999.
125. COVERCO stands for the Guatemalan Commission for the Monitoring of Codes of Conduct. It is currently monitoring several Liz Claiborne and Gap factories in Guatemala.
126. Interview with Juan Francisco Alfaro, August 10, 1999.
127. Interview with Byron Padilla, July 28, 1999.
128. See footnote 57 for more on the recent successful unionization and contract ratification at the two Choi and Shin factories in Guatemala.

Chapter 3

1. Mark Anner, *Maquilas and Independent Monitoring in El Salvador* (San Salvador: Independent Monitoring Group of El Salvador [GMIES], 1998), 15.
2. Author interview with unidentified *maquila* worker, outside the San Marcos Free Trade Zone, San Salvador, El Salvador, August 28, 1999.
3. Even though SETMI was ousted from the factory, it continued holding meetings, organizing protests, and working with non-governmental organizations (NGOs) from El Salvador and the United States.
4. Author interview with Pedro Mancíllas, Corporate Director, Mandarin International. San Salvador, El Salvador, September 10, 1999.
5. Author interview with SETMI's Secretary of Organization, San Salvador, El Salvador, August 28, 1999.
6. For an overview of the "early" history of the Salvadoran labor movement as well as the PCS, see Thomas Anderson, *Matanza: El Salvador's Communist Revolt of 1932* (Lincoln: University of Nebraska Press, 1971); William Bollinger, "El Salvador," in Michael Greenfield and Sheldon Maram (eds.), *Latin American Labor Organizations* (Westport, CT: Greenfield

Press, 1987); Roque Dalton, *Miguel Mármol* (Willimantic, CT: Curbstone Press, 1987); Equipo Maíz. *Historia de El Salvador* (San Salvador: Equipo Maíz, 1998); Rafael Menjívar, *Formación y Lucha Proletariado Industrial Salvadoreño* (San Salvador: UCA Editores, 1979).

7. The president, Arturo Araujo, often described as a "liberal reformer," arrested key labor and communist party activists in 1931, including PCS leader Farabundo Martí. These activities helped spark massive protests against the Araujo administration. Martínez overthrew Araujo in December 1931. The popular insurrection occurred several weeks later. For more on these events see Anderson (1971); Dalton (1987); Tommie Sue Montgomery, *Revolution in El Salvador: From Civil Strife to Civil Peace* (2nd ed.) (Boulder, CO: Westview Press, 1995).

8. See Anderson (1971) for the definitive account of the *matanza*. Farabundo Martí was one of many people executed during the uprising. Miguel Mármol, a shoemaker and key PCS activist, survived the attack. See Dalton (1987) for his *testimonio* and description of the *matanza*. The 1932 massacre left a permanent mark on the labor movement as well as the entire society.

9. Although the PCS was banned under the Martínez dictatorship, activists regrouped clandestinely and organized the National Union of Workers (*Unión Nacional de Trabajadores—* UNT) in the early 1940s. The UNT and the General Association of Salvadoran University Students (AGEUS) held major protests and a general strike against Martínez in April-May 1944, leading to his eventual resignation. Several years later, a new labor federation, the Salvadoran Trade Union Reorganizing Committee (*Comité de Reorganización Obrero Sindical Salvadoreño—*CROSS) was established. A military junta legally recognized the CROSS, but it later was banned in the early 1950s. See Bollinger (1987) for more on these organizations.

10. Some of these federations included the leftist General Confederation of Salvadoran Workers (*Confederación General de Trabajadores Salvadoreños—*CGTS) and the conservative, Inter-American Regional Organization of Workers (ORIT)-supported General Confederation of Unions (*Confederación General de Sindicatos—*CGS). The military crushed the CGTS and consolidated its power through electoral fraud in the early 1960s. CGTS activists later formed the Unitary Trade Union Federation of El Salvador (*Federación Unitaria Sindical de El Salvador—*FUSS), which worked closed with the militant Acero textile workers union and helped organize, along with the CGS rather surprisingly, a general strike in 1967. See Bollinger (1987) for details on these organizations and events. For more on ORIT and later the American Institute for Free Labor Development's (AIFLD) activities in El Salvador in the late 1950s and early 1960s, see Serafino Romualdi, *Presidents and Peons: Recollections of Labor Ambassador in Latin America* (New York: Funk and Wagnalls, 1967).

11. See Montgomery (1995) for more on the 1972 election and its aftermath.

12. For more information on these organizations and the period that preceded the emergence of El Salvador's civil war in the 1980s, see James Dunkerley, *The Long War: Dictatorship and Revolution in El Salvador* (London: Junction Books, 1982); James Dunkerley, *Power in the Isthmus: A Political History of Modern Central America* (London: Verso, 1988); Montgomery (1995); Marío Lungo Uclés, *El Salvador in the Eighties: Counterinsurgency and Revolution* (Philadelphia: Temple University Press, 1996).

13. Montgomery (1995); Uclés (1996).

14. Author interview with Roger Guitiérrez, FEASIES General-Secretary, San Salvador, El Salvador, August 25, 1999. See also Montgomery (1995).

15. Bollinger (1987), 357–59.

16. For more on this wave of violence, along with the relationship between the Salvadoran military, death squads, and the United States, see Michael McClintock, *The American Connection: State Terror and Popular Resistance in El Salvador* (London: Zed Books, 1985).

17. Robert S. Leiken, "The Salvadoran Left," in Marvin E. Gettleman, Patrick Lacefield, Louis Menashe, and David Mermelstein (eds.), *El Salvador: Central America and the Cold War* (New York: Grove Press, 1986), 187–99.

18. See Dunkerley (1982); Leiken (1986); Montgomery (1995) for more on these events.

19. This new umbrella organization was called the Revolutionary Coordination of the Masses (*Coorinadora Revolucionaria de Masas—*CRM).

20. Leiken (1986), 191.
21. For more on the life of Romero, see James Brockman, *Romero: A Life* (Maryknoll, NY: Orbis Books, 1989); María López Vigil, *Oscar Romero: Memories in Mosaic* (Washington, DC: Ecumenical Program on Central America and the Caribbean [EPICA], 2000); Oscar Romero, *Voice of the Voiceless: Four Pastoral Letters and Other Statements* (Maryknoll, NY: Orbis Books, 1985).
22. See Americas Watch (1991); Montgomery (1995); Truth Commission of El Salvador (1993).
23. Bollinger (1987), 319. Interview with Roger Guitiérrez (1999). Progressive and radical labor activists continued organizing on a clandestine basis between 1980–1983. In 1983, they established the Unitary Trade Union and Guild Movement of El Salvador (*Movimiento Unitario Sindicalista y Gremial de El Salvador*—MUSYGES). After several of its leaders were assassinated, MUSYGES was disbanded. Conflicts within the FSR also led to its demise. Some its activists later helped create the Workers Solidarity Coordinating Committee (*Coorinadora de Solidaridad de los Trabajadores*—CST) in 1985. The CST was one the key groups behind the formation of the UNTS in 1986. See Bollinger (1987) for more details surrounding these events.
24. Bollinger (1987), 338–41, 374.
25. Ibid., 340.
26. Ibid., 340–42.
27. For a devastating critique of AIFLD's activities during this period, see Robert Armstrong, Henry Frundt, Hobart Spalding, and Sean Sweeney, *Working Against Us: AIFLD and the International Policy of the AFL-CIO* (New York: North American Congress on Latin America, 1987); Tom Barry and Deborah Preusch, *AIFLD in Latin America: Agents as Organizers* (Albuquerque: Resource Center, 1990); Bollinger (1987); Beth Sims, *Workers of the World Undermined* (Boston: South End Press, 1992). Some labor union officials from AIFLD-backed federations, incidentally, criticized the AFL-CIO's heavy-handed role during the 1980s. Nevertheless, they wistfully noted that "those were the days" when they received substantial funding (Interview with CTD Representatives. San Salvador, El Salvador. September 6, 1999).
28. Barry and Preusch (1990), 36. Bollinger (1987), 363–64.
29. Barry and Preusch, 37.
30. Ibid.
31. Ibid., 37–38; Bollinger (1987), 347–48, 363.
32. Not all UPD affiliates left the UNTS. For more on the reasons why the CTS and UPD joined UNOC, see Barry and Preusch (1990), 37; Bollinger (1987), 364, 374. See also Rubén Zamora, "The Popular Movement," in Anjali Sundaram and George Gelber (eds.), *A Decade of War: El Salvador Confronts the Future* (New York: Monthly Review Press, 1991), 189.
33. Montgomery (1995), 216, 242.
34. For more on the assassination of the Jesuits and their two assistants, see Salvador Caranza (ed.), *Martires de la UCA: 16 de Noviembre de 1989* (San Salvador: UCA Editores, 1990); Teresa Whitfield. *Paying the Price: Ignacio Ellacuría and the Murdered Jesuits of El Salvador* (Philadelphia: Temple University Press, 1994). See also John Hasset and Hugh Lacey, *Toward a Society That Serves its People: The Intellectual Contributions of El Salvador's Murdered Priests* (Washington, DC: Georgetown University Press, 1991) for a concise overview of the Jesuits' work, which challenged the ruling political and economic elite in El Salvador.
35. Montgomery (1995), chapter 7.
36. Mark Anner, "Hacia la sindicalización de los sindicatos?" *ECA (Estudios Centroamericanos)*, July-August 1996: 599–615. I should mention here that Anner was a key player in the Gap campaign. He worked for several years with the Human Rights Project of the International Union of Food Workers (IUF) and later served as the coordinator of the Independent Monitoring Group of El Salvador. Anner is currently pursuing his doctorate in political science at Cornell University.
37. Author interview with Roger Guitiérrez (1999). Anner (1996), 608 claims that FENASTRAS lost 80 percent of its members after it left the UNTS.
38. Almost every single labor union official or activist that I interviewed in August–September 1999 described FENASTRAS in this manner.

39. A fairly recent report, *Situación de las Organizaciones Sindicales en El Salvador* (San Salvador: CENTRA, 1999), indicates that FESTES had 1,100 members, while FEASIES had 589 in 1996. FUSS, another left-wing labor federation, had 2000 members. See Anner (1996), 603 for a graphic description of the decline of leftist labor unions and federations.

40. Nonetheless, FEASIES and FESTES have worked, over the last several years with Danish labor unions to develop a *maquila* organizing model. At this time it is too soon to tell whether or not this collaboration will be successful. It is interesting to note, that these federations, which briefly joined forces with the American Center for International Labor Solidarity in 1997, are currently not working with U.S. unions, but they are collaborating with the NLC (Interview with Sergio Muñoz, NLC Representative, San Salvador, El Salvador, August 30, 1999).

41. Anner (1996: 607) claims that these organizations were created as part of a "counter-insurgency based model of unionism" that was designed by AIFLD to create a "popular" base of support for the ruling Christian Democratic Party in the 1980s. This strategy flopped, however, because many AIFLD-backed affiliates grew weary of its divisive tactics and joined the UNTS. After the war, the remaining unions within UNOC left it and became independent or joined conservative, pro-government labor federations.

42. Anner (1996), 602. Interview with CTD Representatives, September 6, 1999. I should mention here that the CTD, like the AFL-CIO, is affiliated with the International Confederation of Free Trade Unions (ICFTU) and its regional arm, Inter-American Regional Organization of Workers (ORIT).

43. Anner (1996), 611.

44. Author interview with STIASSYC General-Secretary Juan Hernández, San Salvador, El Salvador, September 9, 1999. In 1996, FUGTS had more than 45,000 members (CENTRA, 1999: 21).

45. Anner (1998), 601; Procuraduría para la defensa de los Derechos Humanos (PDDH). *Los Derechos Humanos y la Maquila en El Salvador* (San Salvador: PDDH, 1998).

46. Anner (1998), 19.

47. Menjívar (1979), 149–50.

48. Montgomery (1995).

49. Anner (1998), 15.

50. For more on the development and differences between free trade zones and *recintos fiscales* (or fiscal "precincts"), see Carolina Quinteros, Gilberto García, Roberto Góchez, and Norma Molina, *Dinámica de la Actividad Maquiladora y Derechos Laborales en El Salvador* (San Salvador: CENTRA/ACILS, 1998), 18–20.

51. For more on the GSP and CBI, see Edna Bonacich and David Waller, "Mapping a Global Industry: Apparel Production in the Pacific Rim Triangle," in *Global Production: The Apparel Industry in the Pacific Rim* (Philadelphia: Temple University Press, 1994). Edna Bonacich, Lucie Cheng, Norma Chinchilla, Nora Hamilton, and Paul Ong (eds.), 21–41. The internationally recognized worker rights standards are the right of association, the right to organize and collectively bargain, the prohibition of forced labor, a minimum age for the employment of children, and "acceptable minimum conditions" for wages, work hours, and occupational health and safety standards. Nations that receive GSP and CBI benefits must protect these standards. If they do not, then they may be placed "under review" until they "take steps" to do so. For more on this latter process, see Peter Dorman, "Worker Rights and U.S. Trade Policy: An Evaluation of Worker Rights Conditionality Under the Generalized System of Preferences," (Washington, DC: Department of Labor, 1989); Mike Witt, "The Real Trade Wars: Solidarity and Worker Rights," *Labor Research Review* 8(1): 93–98.

52. Melissa Connor, Tara Gruzen, Larry Sacks, Jude Sunderland, and Darcy Tromanhauser, *The Case for Corporate Responsibility: Paying a Living Wage to Maquila Workers in El Salvador* (Study Conducted for the National Labor Committee) (New York: Columbia University, May 14, 1999), 5.

53. Anner (1998), 17.

54. Connor et al. (1999), 5.

55. Connor et al. (1999), 6.

56. Quinteros et al. (1998), 21, 26.

57. Ibid., 20–22.

58. See Rolando Arévalo and Joaquín Arriola, "El Caso de El Salvador," in *La Situación Sociolaboral en las Zonas Francas de Centroamérica y República Dominicana* (Geneva: International Labor Organization, 1996).

59. Connor et al. (1999), iv.

60. Quinteros et al. (1998), 34–35.

61. See the National Labor Committee (NLC), *Fired for Crying to the Gringos: The Women in El Salvador Who Sew Liz Claiborne Garments Speak Out for Justice* (New York: NLC, 1999).

62. PDDH (1998).

63. Quinteros et al. (1998), 41–42. This study cogently points out that this percentage may be too low because sexual harassment is an extremely delicate issue that many women fear speaking about in an open and candid manner.

64. U.S. State Department, *El Salvador Country Report on Human Rights Practices for 1998* (Released by the Bureau of Democracy, Human Rights, and Labor. February 26, 1999).

65. Anner (1998), 19.

66. See Quinteros et al. (1998), 52–58 for a complete listing of various *maquila* organizing campaign drives between the 1970s and late 1990s. The two active unions are SETMI and the *Sindicato de Empresa Maquisal*. The former union is currently affiliated with the CTS, while the latter has ties with the CNTS. FEASIES's industrial textile workers' union, the *Sindicato de Trabajadores de la Industria Textile*—STIT) has one active *secciónal* (at a factory named INSINCA), but many of its members have been fired and it is currently very weak (Interview with Daniel García, STIT Director of Organizing, San Salvador, El Salvador, August 25, 1999). Since this draft was initially written, another union, at a Taiwanese-owned *maquila* named Tainan, was established in 2000–2001. This organization, affiliated with STIT, surpassed the 50% level and requested contract negotiations with the company. Tainan responded with firings and factory closure in April 2002. Ironically, one of the factory's main buyers, the Gap, put pressure on Tainan to reopen it under new ownership, which agreed to rehire all the fired workers and negotiate a contract with the union. The new company, named Just Garments, was slated to open mid-2003, but various issues have delayed the process. This entire campaign involved Tainan's workers and NGOs from the United States, El Salvador, and Taiwan. For future updates and more information on this case, see www.usleap.org and Human Rights Watch, *Deliberate Indifference: El Salvador's Failure to Protect Workers' Rights* (New York: Human Rights Watch, 2003). The latter source is essential for understanding the legal obstacles that impede Salvadoran workers, regardless of industry, from organizing.

67. Author interview with Sergio Muñoz (1999). See also Anner (1998); Arévalo and Arriola (1996).

68. Author interview with Otilio Candido. CTS Director of Organizing, San Salvador, El Salvador, September 7, 1999; Gilberto García, CENTRA Director, San Salvador, El Salvador, August 24, 1999; Roger Guitiérrez (1999).

69. See Julia Evelína Martínez and Carolina Quinteros, *Situación de las Mujeres en las Organizaciónes Laborales Salvadoreñas* (Fundación Paz y Solidaridad, CENTRA, y Cooperación Española, Proyecto Escuela Formación Sindical en Centroamérica II Fase, 1997). Marlene López, an attorney with the Mélida Anaya Montes Women's Movement (Interview, San Salvador, El Salvador, August 20, 1999) also discussed how the "double-shift" affected women *maquila* workers, and the prospects for unionization.

70. Anner (1998), 19–20.

71. This information comes from the flyers and informational leaflets distributed by Global Exchange (GX), a San Francisco-based labor and human rights organization. For additional information on GX and the Gap, see (www.globalexchange.org).

72. Information regarding the wages and working conditions inside Mandarin comes from the following sources: Interviews with SETMI leaders and members, San Salvador, El Salvador, August 28, 1999. Jill Esbenshade, "The Gap Campaign: Enforcing Labor Standards Across Borders," *Labor Center Reporter* (Fall 1996): 4–7; Jon Pattee, "Gapatistas Win a Victory," *Labor Research Review* (Summer 1996: 77–85).

73. Author interview with Juan Hernández (1999).

74. Author interview with Gilberto García (1999).

75. See Article 271, *Código de Trabajo* (Salvadoran Labor Code, 1999). The Salvadoran Labor Ministry is responsible for determining whether or not this level has been reached based on the union's records.
76. Author interview with Juan Hernández (1999).
77. Author interview with Otilio Candido (1999).
78. I tried several times to interview Juan José Hueso for this study. Unfortunately, he was unavailable for comment. The information, therefore, regarding this phase of the campaign comes from interviews with Otilio Candido and Juan Hernández.
79. Many Salvadoran-based labor activists mentioned these activities. Representatives from U.S.-based labor and solidarity organizations made similar statements. I asked Juan José Hueso's wife about these allegations and she denied them. Despite her comments, it is clear that FENASTRAS has signed favorable agreements with *maquila* owners to block organizing campaigns and to obtain financial gain. This is a tragic development for those activists and organizations that supported the radical labor federation before and during the civil war, but officials within the *maquiladora* industry are pleased with its transformation. Indeed, Mandarin's Pedro Mancíllas said FENASTRAS is the kind of union that "we can work with."
80. Author interview with Otilio Candido (1999).
81. Author interview with Otilio Candido (1999).
82. See *Código de Trabajo* (Salvadoran Labor Code), Articles 213, 214, 219.
83. Author interview with Otilio Candido (1999).
84. See Quinteros et al. (1998), 52–58 for more details on these unions. This overview does not stipulate whether or not these organizations obtained legal recognition.
85. Author interview with CTS General-Secretary, Felix Blanco, San Salvador, El Salvador, August 23, 1999.
86. The Salvadoran Labor Code (Article 204) clearly states workers have the right to organize. These firings contradicted that statute, making them "illegal."
87. Author interviews with SETMI leaders and members (1999). See also Marisol Ruiz and Gilberto García, *Condiciones Laborales de Mujeres y Menores en Las Plantas de la Maquila Coreana y Taiwanesa en El Salvador* (San Salvador: CENTRA, 1996). The Salvadoran Labor Code (Article 537) states that workers should not be fired for going on strike. Mandarin's actions were, therefore, once again "illegal" based on this provision.
88. Anner (1998), 21. Interview with Otilio Candido (1999).
89. Author interview with Otilio Candido (1999).
90. Ruiz and García (1996), 36–40.
91. SETMI made this demand even though it did not represent more than 50 percent of all workers inside the factory at this time. It claimed, nevertheless, that it would have reached that level if the company had not fired its members and intimidated virtually the entire labor force. The union hoped that these considerations would be taken into account, paving the way for contract negotiations. Interview with Otilio Candido (1999).
92. Author interviews with SETMI leaders and members (1999).
93. Author interviews with SETMI leaders and members (1999). See also Ruiz and García (1996). I should mention that ATEMISA remained active inside the factory (until 2000 when it disappeared) after SETMI was basically ousted.
94. Anner (1998), 22.
95. Anner (1998), 22; Pattee (1996), 81.
96. The trip was paid for by the NLC and UNITE. Claudia Molina worked for a Honduran-based Maquila named Orion that produced clothes for Gitano, a label sold in Wal-Mart stores. For more details on the speaking tour, see Brooks (2002); Esbenshade (1996); Pattee (1996).
97. Pattee (1996).
98. For more on these activities, see *Working Together: Labor Report on the Americas*, Issues 13–16, 18 (July 1995–June 1996).
99. *Working Together*. "Minnesota GAP Effort Focuses on Students," (January–February 1996), 2. *Zoned for Slavery* can be directly obtained from the NLC (www.nlcnet.org).
100. Larry Weiss, "Maquila Workers' Tour, California Sweatshop Case, Put Heat on Retailers," *Working Together* (September-October 1995), 1–2. See also Pattee (1996), 82.
101. Pattee (1996), 81.

102. Anner (1998), Appendix 1, The Human Rights Project of the International Union of Food Workers and the International Labor Organization also signed this letter.
103. Ibid., 23.
104. Ibid., Appendix 2.
105. Ibid., 23.
106. Ibid., Appendix 3.
107. Pattee (1996), 83.
108. Larry Weiss, "Gap Agreement Proceeds Along Torturous Path," *Working Together* (May–June 1996), 4–5.
109. Anner (1998), Appendix 4.
110. The NLC later dropped out of the IMWG (Anner, 1998, 27).
111. Anner (1998), Appendix 6.
112. Author interview with Norma Molina, GMIES Representative, San Salvador, El Salvador, August 24, 1999.
113. Anner (1998), Appendix 7.
114. Anner (1998), Appendix 8.
115. Universidad de El Salvador (Facultad de Ciencias Economicas), "El Grado Mejoramiento de las Condiciones Laborales de las Trabajadoras(es) de la Maquila Mandarin Internacional de la Zona Franca de San Marcos a Partir del Funcionamiento del Grupo Monitoreo Indpendiente" (Vitelio Henriques Mejia, Project Director; San Salvador, June 11, 1999) .
116. This is one of Charles Kernaghan's favorite phrases.
117. Naomi Klein, *No Logo: Taking on the Brand Bullies* (New York: Picador, 2000).
118. Klein (2000), 345.
119. Author interview with Mandarin workers outside the San Marcos Free Trade Zone. San Salvador, El Salvador. September 2, 1999.
120. Author interview Mandarin workers (1999).
121. Open discussion of these issues is extremely difficult. The representatives from the NLC, ACILS, and other labor and solidarity organizations that I spoke with specifically asked that their names not be used for this study. Most of these conversations involved sensitive material and so the presentation here is rather broad and general, but I think it captures the essence of what was said during these interviews.
122. See the previous footnote. Again, all respondents requested anonymity.
123. Daniel Cantor and Juliet Schor, *Tunnel Vision: Labor, the World Economy, and Central America* (Boston: South End Press, 1987); Hobart Spalding, "The Two Latin American Foreign Policies of the U.S. Labor Movement: The AFL-CIO Versus the Rank-and-File," *Science and Society* (Winter 1992–1993): 421–39.
124. Anonymous conversations with NLC representatives. After FENASTRAS underwent its ideological transformation in the early 1990s, the NLC stopped working with it.
125. Anonymous conversations with ACILS representatives.
126. Keck and Sikkink (1998), 206–09.
127. What occurs next is unclear. Mandarin moved and became Charter in 2000. SETMI subsequently changed its name to STECHAR. Esbershade (2004: 244) reports that STECHAR membership is growing and that ATEMISA has "disappeared."

Chapter 4

1. This phrase comes from the title of James Scott's book, *Weapons of the Weak: Everyday Forms of Peasant Resistance* (New Haven: Yale University Press, 1985). Scott claims that oppressed groups do not typically manifest overt signs of resistance, but they often do so covertly through conversation, jokes, songs, and other cultural practices. He calls these everyday acts of resistance "infrapolitics" because they are largely invisible—they occur "below the surface." Robin D. G. Kelley suggests that these "tactical choices born of a prudent awareness of the balance of power" (this quote comes from James Scott, *Domination and the Art of Resistance: Hidden Transcripts* [New Haven: Yale University Press, 1990], 183) have a "cumulative effect on power relations." Kelley's book, *Race Rebels: Culture, Poiltics, and the Black Working Class* (Free Press: New York, 1994) explores "race rebels" (particularly African-American men) that wore zoot suits, created hip-hop culture and "gangsta rap," joined the Communist Party in the 1920s and the Abraham Lincoln Brigades during the Spanish Civil War, and tested the limits of "Jim Crow" legislation in the U.S.

South. Américo Paredes (*With a Pistol in His Hand*. Austin: University of Texas, 1958) and José E. Limón's (*Dancing with the Devil*. Madison: University of Wisconsin, 1994) work shows how working-class Chicanos resisted racial oppression (although these practices reinscribed sexism) through *corridos*, jokes, polka dances, and other cultural traditions, while Vicki Ruiz's *From Out of the Shadows* (New York: Oxford, 1998) illustrates how twentieth century working-class Mexicanas challenged racism and sexism with "pickets, baskets, and ballots." Devon Peña *(Terror of the Machine*. Austin: Center for Mexican-American Studies, 1997) discovered that Mexican *maquiladora* workers often worked slowly (a process called *tortuguismo*, or working at the pace of turtles), resisting ever-faster production schedules (the "speed-up"). These examples indicate that the "weak" (or the "wretched of the earth" as Franz Fanon called them) have many "weapons." In this union "office" in Honduras, their "arsenal" included tangible items (tape, pens, maps, etc.) for a much larger battle against Kimi and other *maquila* factories, but they also told jokes and exchanged gossip during this all-important strategy session. I witnessed many examples of this type of "infrapolitics," but did not examine them fully. Future studies will hopefully capture these rich histories (or "hidden transcripts" as Scott calls them) of resistance.

2. I mention this point because most Honduran *maquila* workers are women, although men make up 15–20 percent of the industry's labor force. Most *maquila* labor activists are women—SITRAKIMIH's entire executive committee, for instance, included women.

3. Kimi de Honduras is Korean-owned. It is spelled with capital or lowercase letters. I prefer the latter and use that spelling throughout this chapter.

4. Yoo Yang is a Korean-owned maquila that produces clothing for Phillips Van-Heusen and Kohl's, among other companies. On August 16, 1999, just two days before the strike at Kimi began, the union filed papers asking for legal recognition as an industrial union (that latter union is known as the Union of Maquila Workers and Similar Industries of Honduras—SITRAIMASH). The Yoo Yang and Kimi workers both felt that organizing along industrial lines, which could potentially include all the *maquila* workers in Continental Park, made more sense than organizing factory-by-factory. The Honduran Labor Code stipulates that industrial unions must include at least two local-level unions. In this situation, the two local unions were from Kimi and Yoo Yang. Understanding just how potent this new union could be, the Honduran Labor Ministry delayed acting on its application for legal recognition for several months. On March 10, 2000, Yoo Yang, however, agreed to tacitly recognize the union and pledged to begin contract negotiations once the Labor Ministry formally granted SITRAIMASH legal recognition. Unfortunately, the Ministry rejected the petition, saying that the Kimi workers could not have two unions—SITRAKIMIH and SITRAIMASH—representing them at the same time. Union leaders claimed that this decision was based on a misinterpretation of the labor code. The ruling gave Yoo Yang the opening that it was looking for, however, and it refused to begin contract negotiations with the union since it was not legally recognized. Yoo Yang has also threatened to close down the factory and move to another location. After nine long months of foot-dragging and near-total intransigence, the Yoo Yang Workers Union (*Sindicato de Trabajadores de Empresa Yoo Yang*—STEYY) obtained legal recognition in December 2000. One year later, on December 10, 2001, the union signed a collective bargaining agreement after receiving assistance from U.S./LEAP and the International Textile, Garment, and Leather Workers Federation (ITGLWF), STITCH, and the AFL-CIO. Coming on the heels of the Kimi and PVH defeats, the Yoo Yang victory is crucial for the broader anti-sweatshop movement. For more details on the Yoo Yang campaign, see the U.S./LEAP April 2002 newsletter as well as the organization's Web site, (www.usleap.org).

5. Interviews with Kimi and Yoo Yang workers, La Lima, Honduras, September 23, 1999.

6. For more on these strikes as well as the early history of the Honduran labor movement, see Victor Meza, *Historia del Movimiento Obrero Hondureño* (Tegucigalpa: Centro de Documentación de Honduras, 1997); Mario Posas, *Luchas del Movimiento Obrero Hondureño* (San Jose, Costa Rica: Editorial Universitaria Centroaméricana, 1981). Both texts are essential for understanding the dynamics and trajectory of the Honduran labor movement, but they do not discuss events from the 1980s and 1990s.

7. I am not suggesting that Honduras was actually a "banana republic." The country had "limited autonomy" in the early twentieth century. Local capitalists and labor unions in the Northern Coast influenced policy-making. Nevertheless, U.S. banana companies had

tremendous power and influence during this time period. For a fresh and provocative analysis of these issues, see Darío Euraque, *Reinterpreting the Banana Republic: Region and State in Honduras, 1870–1972* (Chapel Hill: University of North Carolina Press, 1996).

8. The FSH maintained ties with the Honduras Communist Party and the Soviet Union-supported Latin American Union Confederation (CSLA). For more on the FSH, see Meza (1997), 18–20, 31–39 and Posas (1981), 87–89. Also see the *testimonio* of FSH activist and feminist Graciela García in Rina Villars, *Porque Quiero Seguir Viviendo . . . Habla Con Graciela García* (Tegucigalpa: Editorial Guyamuras, 1991), especially 70–166.

9. For an analysis of the labor movement under Carías' rule, see Meza (1997), 49–66.

10. For more on these events, see Euraque (1996), 68–70; Donald E. Schulz and Deborah Sundloff Schulz, *The United States, Honduras, and the Crisis in Central America* (Boulder, CO: Westview Press, 1994), 18. Schulz and Schulz (1994: 18) note that even the U.S. State Department distanced itself from Carías after the massacre took place.

11. Schulz and Schulz (1994: 18) make this claim, while Euraque (1996: 170) points out that there is disagreement over this issue. Whatever Gálvez's role may have been, the San Pedro Sula massacre deeply affected Honduran politics for many years. See Euraque (1996: 68–70) for more on these consequences.

12. For more on Gálvez's policies toward the labor movement and banana worker organizing campaigns and strikes, see Mario Argueta, *La Gran Huelga Bananera: 69 Días que Conmovieron a Honduras* (Tegucigalpa: Editorial Universitaria, 1995), 23–54; Meza (1997), 67–85.

13. For more on the "great banana strike," see Argueta (1995), 55–255; Meza (1997), 86–98; Posas (1981), 95–186.

14. See Cullather (1999) for more on the CIA-backed coup.

15. Kinzer and Schlesinger (1982).

16. This is a fairly controversial issue. After Carías banned the Honduras Communist Party (PCH) in 1933, some members remained, but it fell apart. Meza (1997: 65–66) contends that the "new" PCH was formed in 1948. Some party members undoubtedly played a role within the Central Strike Committee (CCH), but they did not "control" it. Argueta (1995: 145-175) suggests that CCH members had closer ties with the reform-oriented Honduran Revolutionary Democratic Party (PDRH) than the PCH.

17. For more on ORIT's involvement in the 1954 strike, see Argueta (1995), 65–108; Euraque (1996), 96; Posas (1981), 158–62. For more on ORIT's activities in Latin America, see Buhle (1999); Herod (2001); Kofas (1992); Radosh (1969); Romualdi (1967); Scott (1978); Spalding (1977).

18. Schulz and Schulz (1994), 21.

19. For more on ORIT and the AFL-CIO's involvement with these unions, see Euraque (1996), 99–100; Meza (1997), 99–117.

20. For more on the ties between the CTH and AIFLD, see Argueta (1995), 250–51; Meza (1997), 128–30. *Centrales* are broad-based organizations. They often include labor, *campesino,* indigenous, and women's groups. The CTH, for instance, initially encompassed two labor federations (FESITRANH and FECESITLIH), and a campesino organization (the National Association of Honduran Peasants [ANACH]). For more on CTH's origins, see Neale J. Pearson, "Honduras," in *Latin American Labor Organizations* (Westport, CT: Greenfield Press, 1987). Michael Greenfield and Sheldon Maram (eds.), 477–78.

21. Euraque (1996), 97.

22. Meza (1997), 161–67; Pearson (1987), 475–76, 491–93.

23. Pearson (1987), 482–83. The CGT actually emerged from an earlier organization called the Authentic Syndical Federation of Honduras (*Federación Auténtica Sindical de Honduras*—FASH). FASH was established in 1963 and had ties with the Confederation of Latin American Workers (CLAT). The CGT was formed in 1970, but did not receive legal recognition until 1984. The CGT also has links with CLAT. The CGT was initially fairly progressive. Thus, in the late 1970s and early 1980s, the trade union ideological spectrum was as follows: FUTH (left), CGT (centrist), and CTH (conservative). Honduran labor activists like CUTH Secretary of Organization Efraín Aguilar contend that the CGT and CTH switched positions in the mid-1980s.

24. In October 1978, Honduran Communist Party activists and various leftists created the Committee of Syndical Unity (CUS). Three years later, the CUS, the Independent Syndical

Front (FSI), and the Inter-Syndical Committee of Labor Unity (CUL) established the FUTH. See Pearson (1987), 494 for a more elaborate analysis of these events. CUTH Secretary of Organization Efraín Aguilar (San Pedro Sula, Honduras. September 14, 1999) largely "confirmed" this organizational chronology.

25. Schulz and Schulz (1994), 69–72, 122–33.
26. Ibid., 64–69 for more on the early ties between the United States, Honduras, and the Contras.
27. See Americas Watch, *Honduras: Central America's Sideshow* (New York: Americas Watch, 1987); Schulz and Schulz (1994), 64–69.
28. Interview with CUTH Secretary of Organization, Efraín Aguilar, San Pedro Sula, Honduras, September 14, 1999. Tom Barry and Kent Norsworthy's, *Honduras: A Country Guide* (Albuquerque: Resource Center, 1990) suggests that the CGT became more conservative after the government granted it legal recognition in 1984.
29. Author interview with Efraín Aguilar (1999).
30. Ibid.
31. Schulz and Schulz (1994), 275–76.
32. Ibid., 190–201, 273–76.
33. Mario Posas, *Diagnostico del Movimiento Sindical Hondureño: Situación Actual y Perspectivas* (Tegucigalpa: Friedrich Ebert Foundation, 2000), 8.
34. The following classification system reflects how these labor confederations view the broader political economy. Ever since the mid-1980s, Honduras has embraced free market-oriented, neoliberal policies that favor domestic and foreign investors. The CGT has strongly supported these policies. This explains its "conservative" designation. The CGT has also worked with *maquila* owners to limit dissent within the industry. The CTH has called for more state regulation of the economy and been marginally involved in organizing *maquila* workers. These two positions illustrate the confederation's "moderate" orientation. The CUTH has openly challenged the neoliberal model, holding strikes and demonstrations, advocating progressive socioeconomic reforms, and organizing *maquila* workers. These views explain its "leftist" description. Bluntly speaking, the CGT backs neoliberal global capitalism, the CTH favors smoothing out its rough edges, and CUTH supports substantially transforming it. These categories are based on information obtained from interviews with Honduran labor activists.
35. The following analysis (185–209) appeared in Armbruster-Sandoval (2003). The author thanks *Social Science History* for granting permission to reprint pages 90–106.
36. For more on the development of the Honduran *maquila* industry and the export-led development model, see Efraín Moncada Valladares, *Las Dos Caras de La Maquila en Honduras* (Documentos de Trabajo, No. 10, July 1995. Universidad Nacional Autónoma de Honduras); Barry and Norsworthy (1990), 47–60.
37. Valladares (1995), 18–22.
38. Barry and Norsworthy (1990), 49–50.
39. Schulz and Schulz (1994), 273–76.
40. Honduran Apparel Manufacturers Association (HAMA), *Apparel Industry in Honduras* (San Pedro Sula: Honduras, 1999).
41. These statistics can be found in *Apparel Industry in Honduras* (1999).
42. Nelly del Cid, Carla Castro, and Yadira Rodriguez, "Trabajadoras de Maquila: Nuevo Perfil de Mujer?" *Envío*, September 1999: 35–41.
43. See *Apparel Industry in Honduras* (1999).
44. del Cid et al. (1999), 35.
45. See Friedrich Ebert Stiftung, *Las Maquilas en Honduras y el Monitoreo Independiente en Central America* (Tegucigalpa: Friedrich Ebert Foundation, 1998).
46. del Cid et al. (1999), 38.
47. Author interview with Efraín Aguilar (1999).
48. Information on wages comes from *Las Dos Caras* (1995) and *Las Maquilas en Honduras y el Monitoreo Independiente* (1998) and interviews with *maquila* workers and union officials.
49. See *Las Maquilas en Honduras y el Monitoreo Independiente*, 11–12 and Valladares (1995), 28.
50. See EMI, "Ponencia Sobre Experiencias y Reflexiones del Equipo de Monitoreo Independiente (EMI) en La Empresa KIMI de Honduras," Paper Delivered at Taller Sobre Monitoreo Independiente, San Salvador, El Salvador. January 12–15, 1998.

51. Código de Trabajo, Articulo 475.

52. See *Las Maquilas en Honduras y el Monitoreo Independiente* (1998), 11–12.

53. U.S. State Department, *1999 Country Reports on Human Rights Practices: Honduras*. Released by the Bureau of Democracy, Human Rights, and Labor. February 25, 2000, 18.

54. See International Labor Organization, *Que Ha Pasado Con La Maquila? Actualización del Estudio sobre la Situación en las Empresas Maquiladoras del Istmo Centroamericano y Republica Dominicana* (Geneva: ILO, 1999), 14 and U.S. State Department (2000), 18.

55. Author unterviews with Efraín Aguilar, Israel Salinas, and Nelly del Cid (the latter was conducted in El Progreso, Honduras. September 21, 1999).

56. Author interview with Efraín Aguilar (1999). I was not able to determine, with any degree of certainty, just how many FITH-affiliated *maquila* unions had collective bargaining agreements.

57. Author interview with CTH-FESITRANH Assistant General Secretary David Cisneros. San Pedro Sula, Honduras. September 23, 1999, and Israel Salinas (CUTH) (1999).

58. Author interviews with Hugo Maldonado, CODEH Director, San Pedro Sula, Honduras. September 16, 1999; and Maritza Paredes, CODEMUH Director, San Pedro Sula, Honduras, September 28, 1999.

59. Author interview with Maritza Paredes (1999).

60. Author interview with SITRAKIMI General-Secretary Sara Aguillón, La Lima, Honduras, September 25, 1999.

61. Author interview with Sara Aguillón (1999).

62. STITCH and the Maquila Solidarity Network (MSN), *Women Behind the Labels: Worker Testimonies from Central America* (STITCH and MSN, 2000), 21.

63. Author interview with FITTIV Representative Bruce Fieldman, San Pedro Sula, Honduras, September 24, 1999. The Honduran Labor Code states that employers must negotiate with legally recognized unions, no matter how members they might have.

64. The previous footnote explains the thinking behind this position.

65. Author interview with Sara Aguillón (1999).

66. Ibid.

67. See Larry Weiss, "Sweatshop Task Force Report Fuels Controversy," *Working Together Newsletter*, May–June 1997. 1.

68. Benjamin (1999); Howard (1999).

69. Author interview with Bruce Fieldman (1999).

70. *Código de Trabajo*, Article 54.

71. EMI, "Ponencia Sobre Experiencias," 3.

72. Author interview with NLC Executive Director, Charles Kernaghan. San Salvador, El Salvador. August 22, 1999.

73. See *Firma De Convenio: Acuerdo Para El Monitoreo Independiente en la Empresa KIMI de Honduras* (the text of this accord can be found in EMI's "Ponencia Sobre Experiencias").

74. Phone Interview with anonymous sources from J.C. Penney, September 12, 2000.

75. Phone Interview with anonymous sources from J.C. Penney, September 12, 2000.

76. Phone Interview with Stephen Coats, U.S./LEAP Executive Director, September 12, 2000. I should point out here that U.S./GLEP changed its name to the United States/Labor in the Americas Project (U.S./LEAP) in 1999.

77. Because of the sensitive nature of this conflict, I cannot attribute the statements in this paragraph to specific individuals, only to organizations. For a fuller explanation of this issue, see the following note.

78. This is a very complicated and controversial story. I have merely sketched out the broad contours of this debate. Each side of this conflict spoke harshly about the other. Virtually everyone involved told me that they preferred that their names and comments not be used. Others said that I could mention their remarks, but not use their names. I believe that I have honored these requests and I hope that all sides involved this conflict will come together and unite—for the good of all parties.

79. For more on Hurricane Mitch, see Jeff Boyer and Aaron Pell, "Mitch in Honduras: A Disaster Waiting to Happen," *NACLA: Report on the Americas* (September–October, 1999): 36–41.

80. This quote comes from Jon Bilbao's unpublished paper (dated November 29, 1999), "La Fabrica Kimi and El Sindicato SITRAKIMIH." This document is on file with the author. Bilbao works with ERIC in El Progreso.

81. Dorman (1989).
82. Author interview with Alan Howard (2000).
83. Ibid.
84. Author interview with Stephen Coats (2000).
85. See *Working Together*, "Workers Win Contract at Honduran Maquila, But Union's Victory Under Threat," (May–June 1999): 3.
86. *Working Together*, "Workers Win Contract. . . .", 3.
87. Author interview with Maritza Paredes (1999).
88. Author interview with Sara Aguillón (1999).
89. See the following articles for more on the three-day strike: Jackie Cole, "Policía Desaloja a Pacificamente a Huelguistas de Maquiladora," *La Tribuna* (August 31, 1999): 138; Herbert Rivera, "Por Toma de Zona Industrial No Laboran 6 Mil Obreros," *La Prensa* (August 28, 1999): 7A; Herbert Rivera, "Chocan Huelguistas y Policía en toma Parque Industrial," *La Prensa* (August 31, 1999): 1A.
90. Campaign for Labor Rights Action Alert, "Honduras: Kimi Victory (for now)," September 4, 1999.
91. Campaign for Labor Rights Action Alert, "Honduras: Kimi Cuts and Runs," May 25, 2000.
92. CLR Action Alert, "Honduras: Kimi Cuts and Runs."
93. Author interview with J.C. Penney anonymous sources, September 12, 2000.
94. This information on Modas Cielo and J.C. Penney comes from author interview with US/LEAP staffer Joan Axthelm, July 20, 2000.
95. For a summary of these activities, see U.S./Labor in the Americas Project, "Kimi Closes, Runs to Guatemala; Yoo Yang Union Remains Strong," August 2000: 1–2. This article also points out that the American Friends Service Committee, Bangor (Maine) Clean Clothes Campaign, Campaign For Labor Rights, Global Exchange, International Labor Rights Fund, Maquila Solidarity Network (Canada), Resource Center of the Americas, Support Team for International Textileras (STITCH), Sweatshop Watch, UNITE, and the United Students Against Sweatshops (USAS) took out a paid ad in Honduran newspapers promising to "follow Kimi to Guatemala" and to "work vigorously to persuade Kimi to re-open its unionized factory in Honduras."
96. In the U.S./LEAP August 2000 newsletter, the organization states that one of Kimi's main customers, Bodek and Rhodes, supplies clothing to the Collegiate Licensing Company (CLC), which distributes the clothing to major colleges like Duke University and Indiana University. These schools have codes of conduct stipulating that the right to organize a union must be upheld in factories where they buy their clothing from. Kimi's decision to shut down its unionized factory violated this provision. Campus anti-sweatshop activists initially thought that this opening might provide them with leverage, but nothing materialized. The factory remains closed.
97. Kathryn Sikkink and Margaret Keck, *Activists Beyond Borders: Advocacy Networks in International Politics* (Ithaca, NY: Cornell University Press, 1998), 12–13.

Chapter 5

1. Witness For Peace (WFP) Group Delegation Interview with Gladys Mananzares, CST Chentex Workers' Union, General-Secretary, Managua, Nicaragua, August 1, 2000.
2. Miriam Ching Yoon Louie, *Sweatshop Warriors: Immigrant Women Workers Take on the Global Factory* (Boston: South End Press, 2001), 3–4.
3. Author interview with Gladys Manzanares, Managua, Nicaragua, August 1, 2000.
4. This free trade zone was actually constructed in the late 1970s under the Somoza dictatorship. The Sandinistas converted it into a center for nationally-based production, along with a penitentiary, in the 1980s, but when they were voted out of power, the new government turned it into a corporate-oriented "free trade zone." For more details on this process, see Witness for Peace, *Behind the Seams: Maquilas and Development in Nicaragua* (Washington, DC: Witness for Peace, 2001), 8–9.
5. Author interview with Gladys Manzanares (2000).
6. *Hard Copy: Maquila in Nicaragua.* November 11–13, 1997. For a copy of this video, contact the National Labor Committee (www.nlcnet.org).
7. This union was the one at Fortex International, a Taiwanese-owned *maquila*. It was affiliated with the Sandinista-linked (CST) Textile Workers Union and received legal recogni-

tion in 1997. Shortly after the CST Chentex Workers Union obtained legal recognition, a CST union was recognized at a U.S.-owned plant named JEM III. Thus, by early 1998, three CST unions were officially functioning within Las Mercedes. See *Behind the Seams* (18–19) for more details on these unions.

8. "Company unions" are typically called "white unions" or *sindicatos blancos* in Latin America because they exist on paper only. Workers are often unaware that they are "members" of these organizations. They never see their representatives and have limited knowledge about the union's activities. Company unions usually sign "protection contracts" with employers that safeguard their interests. The legal and organizational process for replacing a company union is arduous. Indeed, company union officials typically appear when labor strife emerges. Their primary function is to limit the establishment of a truly independent union that will work legitimately on behalf of its members' best interests. *Behind the Seams* (23) suggests that Nicaraguan *maquila* owners have used company unions as a co-optive strategy for sparking divisions amongst workers and creating the impression that they are "pro-labor."

9. The four unions (all affiliated with the CST) were at the following factories: JEM III, Chih Hsing, Mil Colores, and Chentex.

10. For more on the historical development of the Nicaraguan labor movement, see Armando Amador, *Un Siglo de Lucha de los Trabajadores de Nicaragua, 1880-1979* (Managua: Universidad Centroamericana, 1992); Carlos Pérez Bermúdez and Onofre Guevara López, *ElMovimiento Obrero en Nicaragua* (Parts I and II). (Managua: Editorial El Amanecer, 1985); Richard Stahler-Sholk, "Nicaragua," in *Latin American Labor Organizations* (Westport, CT: Greenwood Press, 1987), 549–75.

11. For a good historical overview of U.S.-Nicaraguan relations during this time period, see Karl Bermann, *Under the Big Stick: Nicaragua and the United States since 1848* (Boston: South End Press, 1986).

12. In September 1925, soldiers and military officials, for example, killed Cuyamel Fruit Company workers after they petitioned the company for better wages and working conditions. See Amador (1992), 60–61; Stahler-Sholk (1987), 550.

13. For more on Sandino and the Sandinista uprising, see Gregorio Selser, *Sandino: General of the Free* (New York: Monthly Review Press, 1981). Sandino favored "nationalist-internationalism" over "proletarian internationalism" (the Third International's strategy [1928–1935] of a world-wide revolution led exclusively by the working class). This position sometimes placed him at odds with some radicals and communists like Julio Antonio Mella (Cuba) and Farabundo Martí (El Salvador). For more on these ideological debates, see Rodolfo Cerdas-Cruz, *The Communist International in Central America, 1920-1935* (London: Macmillan, 1993).

14. Selser (1981), 174–79. Selser suggests that the U.S. may have been involved in Sandino's assassination.

15. For an excellent overview of this period, see Knut Walker, *The Regime of Anastasio Somoza, 1936-1956* (Chapel Hill: University of North Carolina Press, 1993). I should note that although Somoza repressed virtually all left-leaning unions during his rule, some continued organizing even after they were driven underground. For more on the labor movement during Somoza's reign, see Amador (1992), 101–50.

16. The CGT, like most labor organizations during the Somoza regime, was divided into different factions. Some supported, while others (mostly tied with unions affiliated with the Nicaraguan Socialist Party [PSN]) opposed, Somoza. Despite these internal differences, the CGT, for the most part, strongly backed the dictator. See Walker (1993), 134–44 for a fuller discussion of Somoza's relationship toward labor.

17. Stahler-Sholk (1987), 551–52.

18. Ibid., 552.

19. For more on the relationship between CUS and AIFLD, see Tom Barry and Deb Preusch, *AIFLD in Central America: Agents As Organizers* (Albuquerque: Resource Center, 1990), 25–30; Stahler-Sholk (1987), 552.

20. The FSLN, of course, like the labor movement, was not without its divisions. For an overview of the FSLN and the different positions within it, see George Black, *Triumph of the People: The Sandinista Revolution in Nicaragua* (London: Zed Press, 1981); James Dunkerley, *Power in the Isthmus* (London: Verso, 1988); Sergio Ramírez, *Adiós Muchachos:*

Una Memoria de la Revolución Sandinista (México, D.F.: Aguilar, 1999); Matilde Zimmerman, *Carlos Fonseca and the Nicaraguan Revolution* (Durham, NC: Duke University Press, 2000).

21. Stahler-Sholk (1987), 553.
22. Dunkerley (1988), 247–60; Ramírez (1999), 163–223.
23. These categories are taken from Stahler-Sholk (1987).
24. The FO, a small Maoist-oriented splinter group kicked out of the FSLN in the early 1970s, used violence after Somoza fell. The FO declined sharply after the FSLN took over its arms supplies in 1980. For its part, there is no evidence that CAUS used violence after the Sandinistas took power. The federation did, however, continue holding strikes against the FSLN's wishes in the early 1980s. The FO and CAUS both took part in the armed insurrection against Somoza. See Stahler-Sholk (1987), 572–75 for more details on these two federations.
25. The CTN and CUS claimed that the FSLN harassed and repressed their members. Two AIFLD reports in the mid-1980s documented these activities. In response, the National Lawyers Guild dispatched a delegation of U.S. labor lawyers to Nicaragua. They found, "virtually every claim of trade union repression made in the AIFLD report is disputed by representatives of CUS and CTN, by respected human rights groups, or by credible evidence provided by the Nicaraguan government." Barry and Preusch (1990: 28–29) state that these two federations were harassed and that all labor organizations, including the Sandinista-linked CST, opposed the FSLN ban on the strikes, but allegations of repression against CTN and CUS activists were unfounded.
26. Stahler-Sholk (1987), 555.
27. Ibid., 555.
28. Trish O' Kane, "New Autonomy, New Struggle: Labor Unions in Nicaragua," in *The New Politics of Survival: Grassroots Movements in Central America* (New York: Monthly Review Press, 1995), 182–207.
29. From the outset, the CTN had ties with the anti-communist Social Christian Party (PSC). The CTN has links regionally with the Latin American Confederation of Workers (CLAT) and internationally with the World Confederation of Labor (WCL). In 1982, a split occurred within the CTN. One group stayed with the CTN and PSC, while the other formed the CTN-A, which became associated with the "centrist" Popular Social Christian Party (PPSC). For more on these two organizations, see Stahler-Sholk (1987), 569–70.
30. See William I. Robinson, *A Faustian Bargain: U.S. Intervention in the Nicaraguan Elections and American Foreign Policy in the Post-Cold War World.* (Boulder, CO: Westview, 1992) for a discussion of the CPT and FNT. See also "El Frente Nacional de los Trabajadores (FNT): Origen, Concepción, y Estrategia de Municipalizacion." No Date. Unpublished Paper. On file with author.
31. For a discussion of these events, see O'Kane (1995), 189–90.
32. For an excellent analysis of Nicaragua's shift towards neoliberalism, see William I. Robinson, *Promoting Polyarchy: Globalization, US Intervention, and Hegemony* (Cambridge: Cambridge University Press, 1996). See also these three Witness For Peace reports: *Bitter Medicine: Structural Adjustment in Nicaragua* (Washington, DC: Witness For Peace, 1994); *A High Price to Pay: Structural Adjustment and Women in Nicaragua* (Washington, DC: Witness For Peace, 1995); *A Bankrupt Future: The Human Cost of Nicaragua's Debt* (Washington, DC: Witness for Peace, 2000).
33. See O'Kane (1995), 196–198 for more details on the politics surrounding these strikes. As her analysis makes clear, FNT and CTN leaders came around very slowly.
34. The Alemán administration has been involved in a number of embarrassing scandals over the past four years. For a detailed analysis, see "A Society Scandalized," *Envío*, June 2000: 3–11. The law finally caught up with Alemán in December 2003 when a judge sentenced him to a twenty-year term and a $17 million fine. He is serving his time under house arrest and is believed to still be influencing political events, although he is barred from doing so. The former president reportedly took more than $100 million in public funds during his time in office. For more on these events, see Nicaragua Network's Web site (www.nicanet. org/hotline).

35. For a comprehensive overview of Nicaragua's debt crisis, see *A Bankrupt Future: The Human Cost of Nicaragua's Debt* (Washington, DC: Witness For Peace, 2000).
36. These statistics come from a September 1999 study by the Institute For Nicaraguan Studies, cited in *A Bankrupt Future* (2000), 2.
37. "Poverty in Cold Numbers," *Envío*, June 2000: 12.
38. "El Frente Nacional de los Trabajadores (FNT)," No Date.
39. *Bitter Medicine* (1994); *A High Price to Pay* (1995).
40. See Leia Raphaelidis, "Sewing Discontent in Nicaragua: The Harsh Reality of Asian Garment Factories in Nicaragua," *Multinational Monitor*, September 1997: 24–26, for a discussion of free trade zone incentives and subsidies.
41. See *Country Commercial Guide For Nicaragua* (July 2000). Economic/Commercial Section, U.S. Embassy, Managua, Nicaragua, for information on the inflation and export figures. It should be noted that most of the statistics in this guide are taken from Nicaraguan government and bank reports. Also, in October–November 1998, Hurricane Mitch hit Nicaragua, killing thousands of people and creating tremendous economic damage, particularly in the export sector.
42. See *Bitter Medicine* (1994); *A High Price to Pay* (1995); and *A Bankrupt Future* (2000) for a fuller discussion of these issues and statistics.
43. Reliable information on the value of apparel exports and the overall number of *maquila* workers is hard to come by. The *County Commercial Guide For Nicaragua* July 2000 report claims that Nicaragua shipped $198 million of apparel exports into the United States in 1999, while a National Labor Committee Many 31, 2000 Press Release, "Serious and Systematic Worker Rights Violations at Chentex Garment Factory," cites a figure of $277.4 million. On a Witness For Peace Delegation (2000), the figure, $203 million, was also mentioned. Given all these different numbers, it is safe to say the overall number of Nicaraguan apparel exports to the U.S. in 1999 topped $200 million. Apparel exports are expected to top $300 million in 2000.
44. Most of the thirty factories are Asian-owned—with Taiwanese and Korean investors leading the way. Discussion with Witness For Peace Nicaragua Long-Team Members. Managua, Nicaragua. July–August 2000.
45. The names of these four free trade zones are: Index, Saratoga, Siglo XXI, and Unisebaco.
46. Alys Willman, "Bearing a Double Burden—Women and Work in Nicaragua," *Horizons* (March/April 1999): 20–23.
47. Jeff Shriver, "Human Slavery in Nicaragua's 'Free Zones,'" *Nicaragua Developments* (Spring 1997): 2–3.
48. Willman (1999).
49. The information contained within this paragraph comes from the following sources: Raphaelidis (1997); Shriver (1997); Willman (1999). See also Movimiento de Mujeres Trabajadores y Desempleadas "María Elena Cuadra." *Diagnóstico Sobre Las Condiciones Sociolaborales de las Empresas de las Zonas Francas* (Managua: María Elena Cuadra, 1999).
50. The CST Textile Workers Union saw its membership fall from 10,000 in 1989 to just 1,500 in 1996. The union is affiliated with the International Textile, Garment, and Leather Workers Federation (ITGLWF), the international trade secretariat for almost all garment worker unions around the world.
51. Tom Ricker and Dale Wimberley, "Global Networking in the 21st Century: Labor Rights Movements and Nicaragua's Maquilas, 2000-2001," in *Emerging Issues in the 21st Century World-System* (New York: Praeger, 2003). Wilma Dunaway (ed.), 3.
52. *Behind the Seams* (2001), 19; Ricker and Wimberley (2003), 3.
53. *Behind the Seams* (2001), 19; Ricker and Wimberley (2003), 3.
54. Ricker and Wimberley (2003), 5–8.
55. Ricker and Wimberley (2003), 8, 10. It is not clear why the CST Mil Colores union stopped operating inside the factory nor what the terms of the contract are between the CTN-A affiliated union and Mil Colores.
56. The María Elena Cuadra Women's Movement is a community-based organization that focuses on educating and training women workers. It also facilitates leadership development and publishes reports for workers as well as the general public.
57. These figures are drawn from the National Labor Committee (NLC), "Urgent Action Alert." November 25, 1997, 25.

58. NLC "Urgent Action Alert," 13.
59. See NLC "Urgent Action Alert," and *Hard Copy: Maquila in Nicaragua* (November 11–13, 1997) for an in-depth discussion of these findings.
60. NLC "Urgent Action Alert," 16–17.
61. Author Interview with Gladys Manzanares (2000).
62. NLC "Urgent Action Alert," 11.
63. This paragraph is drawn from the Campaign For Labor Rights, "Nicaragua Sweatshop Action Alert," December 3, 1997.
64. NLC "Urgent Action Alert," 17.
65. Ibid.
66. Author interview with Gladys Manzanares (2000).
67. Ibid.
68. Ibid.
69. The Chentex workers, in collaboration with the CST Textile Workers Federation, FITTIV, and the ACILS, led the organizing drive. Gladys Manzanares and her fellow *compañeras/os* did much of the actual organizing inside and outside the factory.
70. Nicaraguan Labor Code, Article 206.
71. *Working Together*, "Nicaragua Maquila Workers Win Union," March–April 1998: 1–2.
72. Author interview with Gladys Manzanares (2000). Also see *Working Together*, "Nicaragua Maquila Workers."
73. *Working Together*, "Nicaragua Maquila Workers."
74. Ibid.
75. Ibid.
76. *Behind the Seams* (2001), 16.
77. *Working Together*, "Nicaragua Maquila Workers."
78. Author interview with Gladys Manzanares (2000).
79. Ricker and Wimberley (2003, 2–3) note that in 1996, U.S.-based organizations contacted CST Textile Workers Federation General Secretary Pedro Ortega about the possibility of establishing a *maquila* workers rights project. These talks sparked the creation of the initial transnational advocacy network, which included four organizations: Witness for Peace, Nicaragua Network, the United States/Guatemala Labor Education Project (U.S./GLEP), and the Campaign for Labor Rights. The National Labor Committee joined the network shortly before the *Hard Copy* series was aired. In January 1998, the Quixote Center/Quest for Peace, TecNica, and the Upper Westside/Tipitapa Sister City Project joined the network. These eight organizations provided funding for a *maquila* organizing program led by the CST Textile Workers Union. The ACILS funded this program between May 1998 and July 1999.
80. *Working Together*, "Contract Victory at Nicaraguan Maquila," September–October 1998: 5.
81. National Labor Committee (NLC) Press Statement, "Serious and Systematic Worker Rights Violations at Chentex Garment Factory," May 31, 2000, 5.
82. Ibid.
83. Author interview with fired Chentex worker, Managua, Nicaragua, August 1, 2000.
84. Witness For Peace Group Delegation Discussion with Alys Willman, Managua, Nicaragua, July 30, 2000.
85. NLC Urgent Action Alert, "Union Movement Under Attack: Chentex Union, Textile Workers Federation, and Center for Human Rights (CENDIH) in Nicaragua Appeal for International Campaign," June 6, 2000, 2.
86. Rodney Ortiz, "A Union Struggles in Nicaragua's Free Trade Zone," *Solidaridad: News and Analysis From Central America and Mexico*, June 1, 2000.
87. *Nicaragua Network*, "Labor Crisis in the Free Trade Zone Continues," August 2000.
88. The Nicaraguan Labor Code stipulates that workers may strike after they have shown that they have "just cause" to do so and have exhausted all other mechanisms for resolving the dispute. In this instance the Chentex workers had used every available legal remedy, but the company and Labor Ministry consistently rebuffed them. The workers then held the one-hour strike, which the Ministry claimed was "illegal." Under this ruling, Chentex was "legally" entitled to fire the union leaders. This whole affair illustrates how the Nicaraguan government and foreign investors, with apparent backing from the U.S. and Taiwanese

governments, have collaborated to undermine and crush unions in the *maquila* sector. It would seem, broadly speaking, that the powerful have appropriated the legal system as an "instrument" to use as a blunt force against the powerless. If all strikes are, by definition, "illegal" then the right to strike does not really exist. Without one of their most potent weapons, the right to strike, garment workers face an uphill battle to bring about social and economic justice in the *maquiladora* industry.

89. The U.S. State Department 1999 Human Rights Report on Nicaragua states that only two strikes have been declared "legal" since the 1970s. One other strike, within the free trade zone, at JEM III, was remarkably declared legal in December 1999.

90. Witness For Peace Group Delegation Interview with U.S. Embassy Labor Attaché Marío Fermández, Managua, Nicaragua, August 2, 2000.

91. Author interview with Gladys Manzanares (2000).

92. Quote from Ricker and Wimberley (2003), 4.

93. This is not hyperbole. The Chentex campaign had far-ranging implications for garment workers all over the world. A defeat here would mean achieving better wages and working conditions would be much more difficult. The never-ending "race to the bottom" with corporations pitting workers all over the world would continue if this campaign failed.

94. Aryneil Pantoja. "United States Unionists Threaten Commercial Boycott of Nicaragua." *La Prensa*. June 1, 2000, 5A.

95. The Caribbean Basin Trade Partnership Act extends North American Free Trade Agreement (NAFTA)-style benefits to countries that receive assistance under the Caribbean Basin Initiative (CBI). These countries had complained that NAFTA would lead garment factories to move to Mexico. Hence, they lobbied for Caribbean Basin Trade Partnership Act, also called CBI Parity.

96. NLC Press Statement, "Serious and Systematic Worker Rights Violations," 1–2.

97. The term "political opportunity structure" comes from Doug McAdam's classic work, *The Political Process and the Development of Black Insurgency* (Chicago: University of Chicago Press, 1982).

98. Aryneil Pantoja's June 1, 2000 (Page 5A) piece in *La Prensa*, for instance, carried this headline, "United States Unionists Threaten Commercial *Boycott* of Nicaragua." As evidence, Pantoja cited Kernaghan as saying the NLC will launch an "international campaign to win the closure of the company" if Chentex does not rehire the nine fired union leaders. In the same article, Kernaghan was later quoted, "we are going to launch an international campaign in support of the Chentex workers." These two statements are contradictory—on the one hand Kernaghan looks like he was backing a boycott, while on the other, he was supporting more vigorous international solidarity activities. Kernaghan consistently denied during the campaign that the NLC favored a boycott, making his latter statement appear more accurate. *La Prensa* often mistakenly and purposively claimed that Kernaghan and ITGLWF General-Secretary Neil Kearney favored a "boycott" to generate nationalist sentiment. These articles were designed to blame the NLC and other solidarity groups for creating more unemployment within Nicaragua. For two clear examples of *La Prensa's* ideological slant, see "A Quiénes Defienden?" *La Prensa*, June 6, 2000, 10A; Gabriella Roa Romero. "Amenzan a Textileras con Boicot," *La Prensa*, August 3, 2000, 2A. In all fairness to *La Prensa*, *El Nuevo Diario* also suggested many times that the NLC and ITGLWF supported a "boycott" of Nicaraguan garment exports through the CBI Parity process and international solidarity activities.

99. Pedro Ortega later changed his position towards supporting using the worker rights language in the CBI Parity as a mechanism for obtaining leverage in the Chentex campaign. E-Mail correspondence with Witness for Peace Long-Term Members. Managua, Nicaragua. August 2000.

100. This is a very sensitive issue. I prefer to not use the names of people that disagreed with the NLC, but I will say that this dispute ran very deep. Some groups, on the one hand, praised Charles Kernaghan for his brilliant media attacks, but, on the other hand, they complained he was too authoritarian and did not work well with other groups. The chapters on El Salvador and Honduras highlighted these issues and conflicts as well.

101. Campaign For Labor Rights, "Nicaragua; The Struggle Intensifies," September 9, 2000, 5. This is an excellent overview of the campaign since May 2000.

102. During the July 21-August 3, 2000 Witness For Peace Nicaragua Delegation, U.S. Embassy Labor Attaché Marío Fernández reiterated the claim that Ortega was a "terrorist" and a "bad guy." He stated that the Embassy had "proof" that Ortega had "incited violence" during a militant protest at Mil Colores in January 2000. Fernández also expressed concern that so many solidarity groups in the United States rallied behind Ortega and the CST. Ortega, incidentally, has denied all criminal charges and accusations of terrorism that have been leveled against him. I believe that entire campaign against Pedro Ortega, which involves anachronistic Cold War rhetoric, is basically a ploy to discredit the union and the broader anti-sweatshop movement. Indeed, during our delegation, I felt that the Embassy completely downplayed limitations on the right to organize, alleging that unemployment, rather than repression, was the cause of low rates of unionization within the *maquilas*. I agree—unemployment is an issue, but to deny the fact that workers are being fired and unions are being crushed is absurd.

103. Douglas Grow, "Presented with Unfair Labor Issues, Target Turns Away," *Minneapolis Star-Tribune*, June 21, 2000. Georgia Pabst, "Nicaraguan Union Leader Seeks Support for Garment Workers," *Milwaukee Journal Sentinel*, June 20, 2000.

104. For a vivid account of the delegation's findings, see Robert Ross and Charles Kernaghan, "Countdown in Managua," *The Nation* (September 4/11, 2000): 25–27. See also Congressional Letter Signed by 64 Congressional Representatives to President Clinton. July 21, 2000.

105. Under Nicaraguan labor law, workers are entitled to severance pay. The amount is tied to their length of service. For instance, for every year worked, employers must pay workers one month of severance pay. In the case of many Chentex workers, they had worked within the factory for one or two years. Faced with the prospect of being laid off (fired) with no pay, or quitting with severance pay, many chose the latter in order to support their families. For more information on these firings, see Moises Castillo Zeas, "700 Corridos en La Chentex." *El Nuevo Diario*, September 5, 2000.

106. Personal communication with delegation members. The chant, "*ni un paso atrás* (not one step back)" emerged in 1990 as a result of President Violeta Chamorro's call for austerity measures and structural adjustment programs.

107. Congressional Letter Signed by sixty-four Congressional Representatives to U.S. President Bill Clinton, July 21, 2000.

108. This was a very close call. The NLC was apparently asked to leave the coalition (and did for several days), but the Chentex workers and the CST, who had great respect for the organization, worked hard to keep it together and the rift was healed. Witness for Peace (WFP) pulled out of the coalition because it feared that given the NLC's negative reputation within the Nicaraguan press and among *maquila* owners that its role as "informal mediator" might be jeopardized. In the "heat of the moment," the transnational coalition, which included the NLC and WFP, was working on the Chentex and Mil Colores campaigns. In mid-August 2000, WFP quietly brought Mil Colores owner Craig Miller and Pedro Ortega to the negotiating table. WFP worried that the organization might not be able to set up future meetings with Miller and other *maquila* industry and free trade zone officials if it was seen as too closely associated with the NLC. Thus, on August 14, 2000, when separate NLC and WFP delegations arrived at Las Mercedes, the WFP group stayed outside the free trade zone gates, while the NLC mission passed through. For more on these issues, see Ricker and Wimberley (2003), 7–8. WFP later "rejoined" the transnational coalition.

109. Campaign For Labor Rights, "Strategy Shift Proposed for Nicaragua Campaign," August 2, 2000.

110. UNITE, the Steelworkers, and USAS joined the transnational coalition in July 2000. The NLC, FITTIV, ITGLWF, ACILS, Nicaragua Network, U.S./LEAP, Campaign for Labor Rights, WFP, Quest for Peace, TecNica, and the Upper Westside/Tipitapa Sister City project were also members at that time.

111. WFP Group Delegation Interview with Pedro Ortega. Managua, Nicaragua. August 1, 2000.

112. For Kearney's comments, see Moises Castillo Zeas, "Puede Haber Boicot en EU a la Maquila Nica," *El Nuevo Diario*, August 3, 2000: 8, and Gabriela Roa Romero, "Amenzan a Textileras Con Boicot," *La Prensa Grafica*, August 3, 2000: 2A.

113. WFP Group Delegation Interview with Marío Fernández. August 2, 2000.

114. Nicaragua Network Hotline, "Religious Leaders 'Asked to Leave' After Protesting Sweatshops," August 21, 2000.

115. For more on these events see Nicaragua Network Hotline, August 21 and 28, 2000. I should mention here that on the very same day that the religious delegation was "expelled," they were scheduled to leave on a morning flight to New York City with Gladys Manzanares and Rosa Esterlina Ocampo.

116. The NPR piece ran on August 18, 2000 and the Pacifica one on August 21, 2000.

117. Campaign For Labor Rights, "Nicaragua: The Struggle Intensifies," 4.

118. Campaign For Labor Rights, "Nicaragua: The Struggle Intensifies," 3.

119. Ricker and Wimberley (2003), 8.

120. Ibid., 9.

121. Campaign for Labor Rights, "Update from Nicaragua," October 27, 2000. Nicaraguan Foreign Minister Francisco Aguirre Sacasa traveled to Washington D.C. and met with Barshefsky shortly after receiving her letter.

122. Ricker and Wimberley (2003), 9.

123. Ibid.

124. Ibid.

125. In November 2000, a new labor rights organization called Taiwan-Nicaragua Solidarity emerged. This group coordinated the protests inside and outside Nien Hsing's Taipei-based headquarters. For more on these actions, see the National Labor Committee, "Nica Alert: An Inside Look at Nien Hsing." November 20, 2000.

126. Because Taiwan and the United States do not have diplomatic relations, Taiwan has no ambassador here. Chen is the highest-ranking Taiwanese official in the country.

127. Ricker and Wimberley (2003), 9–10.

128. National Labor Committee, "Nien Hsing Now Challenging the U.S. Embassy/Lucas Huang Attempts Once Again to Sabotage the Agreement/Nien Hsing Increasingly Isolated," January 12, 2001; Nicaragua Network, "Hopes May Be Dashed in Chentex Struggle," January 2001. Hernández's role represented a major shift from his earlier statements and actions in the campaign. It should be recalled that he claimed several months before (in August 2000) that the April 27, 2000 strike was "illegal" and that even though the unions at Mil Colores, Chih Hsing, and JEM III were crushed, maquila workers could still organize freely. See footnote 102 for more on Hernández's involvement in the campaign.

129. National Labor Committee, "Nien Hsing Now Challenging the U.S. Embassy."

130. Nien Hsing also produces in Lesotho. In mid-September 2000, Macafea Billy, General-Secretary of the Lesotho Clothing and Allied Workers Union, visited Nicaragua and signed an agreement with the CST Textile Workers Federation, pledging its support (See Moises Castillo Zeas, "Gringos Intervienen en Zona Franca," La Prensa, September 15, 2000). It is not known how involved he and other Lesotho garment workers were in the broader Chentex campaign.

131. Ricker and Wimberley (2003), 10.

132. Steve Greenhouse, "Critics Calling U.S. Supplier a 'Sweatshop.'" New York Times, December 3, 2000. Section 1, 9.

133. Campaign for Labor Rights, "Victory for Chentex Workers!" April 6, 2001.

134. Ibid.

135. Ibid.

136. Campaign for Labor Rights, "Chentex Accord Signed—An Update on This Unprecedented Victory," May 11, 2001.

137. Parsons' testimony can be found on the Nicaragua Network and U.S./LEAP websites. Witness for Peace Long-Term Member, Melinda St. Louis interviewed her on July 5, 2001. For more on her remarks, see "Testimony on the Busting of Union at Chentex," U.S./LEAP Web site (www.usleap.org/maquilas/nica/parsontestimony).

138. Maura Parsons, "Testimony on the Busting of the Union at Chentex."

Chapter 6

1. Harvey (1982); (2000).

2. Francis Fukuyama and Margaret Thatcher are responsible for coining these statements. They both focus on the notion that after the Cold War ended and the Soviet Union collapsed, "history ended." The forty-five year (1945–1990) Cold War "proved" that capitalism

supposedly defeated socialism. Thatcher believed that these events illustrated that "there was no alternative;" capitalism was *the* superior political and economic system. This viewpoint became increasingly popular in the 1990s (see Thomas Frank, *One Market Under God* [New York: Doubleday, 2000]). Frank contends that during the nineties virtually no one questioned the sanctity of the free-market—politicians, business leaders, and government officials all made far-reaching claims about its prowess—it provided jobs and consumer goods, broke down the barriers of race, class, and gender, conquered communism, fostered democracy, and brought about liberty and freedom for all. There was seemingly nothing that it could not do. The "left" often tacitly embraced these views, fostering a sense of defeatism or fatalism. In the middle and late 1990s, the "fair trade," anti-sweatshop, and global justice movements emerged, however, challenging those views and sparking some oppositional (counter-hegemonic) activity. Social justice activists "made history" on November 30, 1999, shutting down the World Trade Organization (WTO) in Seattle, Washington. The "Battle in Seattle" reframed the debate around the "benefits" of the free-market and globalization and showed that alternatives *do* exist. These events indicate that Fukuyama and Thatcher's views are experiencing a "hegemonic crisis," although they remain fairly potent.

3. The phrase, "people before profit," is one of the leading chants of the global justice movement. It is also the recent title of Charles Derber's book *People Before Profit: The New Globalization in the Age of Terror, Big Money, and Economic Crisis* (New York: St. Martin's Press, 2002).

4. For more on the World Social Forum, see William F. Fisher and Thomas Ponniah (eds.), *Another World Is Possible: Popular Alternatives to Globalization at the World Social Forum* (London: Zed Press, 2003).

5. Robin Cohen. *Contested Domains: Debates in International Labor Studies* (London: Zed Press, 1991).

6. For more on this debate, see Liza Featherstone, "Response to Isaac," *Dissent* (Fall 2001): 109–111; Jeffrey Isaac, "Thinking About the Anti-Sweatshop Movement: A Proposal for Modesty," *Dissent* (Fall 2001): 100–8; Rachel Neumann (ed.), *Anti-Capitalism: A Field Guide to the Global Justice Movement* (New York: The New Press, 2004); Amory Starr, *Naming the Enemy: Anti-Corporate Movements Confront Globalization* (London: Zed Press, 2000).

7. See, for instance, Marco Giugni, "Was It Worth the Effort? The Outcomes and Consequences of Social Movements," *Annual Review of Sociology* (1998): 371–93; Doug McAdam, John D. McCarthy, and Mayer N. Zald, "Social Movements," in *Handbook of Sociology*, Neil Smelser (ed.). Beverly Hills: Sage, 1988), 695–737.

8. Marco Giugni, "How Social Movements Matter: Past Research, Present Problems, and Future Developments," in *How Social Movements Matter* (Minneapolis: University of Minnesota Press, 1999). Marco Giugni, Doug McAdam, Charles Tilly (eds.). xv.

9. William Gamson, *The Strategy of Social Protest* (Homewood, IL: Dorsey Press, 1975), 28.

10. Paul Almeida and Linda Brewster Stearns. "Political Opportunities and Local Grassroots Environmental Movements: The Case of Minamata." *Social Problems* (February 1998): 37–60.

11. Almeida and Stearns (1998), 43–44.

12. Sidney Tarrow, *Power in Movement: Social Movements and Contentious Politics* (Cambridge: Cambridge University Press, 1998).

13. Frances Fox Piven and Richard Cloward, *Poor People's Movements: Why They Succeed, How They Fail* (New York: Vintage, 1979).

14. Almeida and Stearns (1998), 43.

15. Ibid., 44–48.

16. Ibid., 48–51.

17. Ibid., 51–53.

18. Ibid., 53.

19. Margaret Keck and Kathryn Sikkink, *Activists Beyond Borders: Advocacy Networks in International Politics* (Ithaca, NY: Cornell University Press, 1998), 12–13.

20. Sanjeev Khagram, James V. Riker, and Kathryn Sikkink, "From Santiago to Seattle: Transnational Advocacy Groups Restructuring World Politics," in *Restructuring World Politics: Transnational Social Movements, Networks, and Norms* (Minneapolis: Univer-

sity of Minnesota Press, 2002). Khagram, Riker, and Sikkink (eds.), 3-23.

21. William Gamson and David Meyer, "Framing Political Opportunity," in *Comparative Perspectives on Social Movements* (Cambridge: Cambridge University Press, 1996). McAdam, McCarthy, and Zald (eds.), 275–90. For a devastating critique of the political opportunity or political process model, see Jeff Goodwin and James Jasper, "Caught in a Winding, Snarling Vine: The Structural Bias of Political Process Theory," *Sociological Forum* (June 1999): 27–54.

22. Doug McAdam, "Conceptual Origins, Current Problems, Future Directions," in *Comparative Perspectives on Social Movements* (Cambridge: Cambridge University Press, 1996). McAdam, McCarthy, and Zald (eds.), 23–40.

23. For more on Central America's "transition towards democracy," see Jorge Dominguez and Marc Lindenberg (eds.), *Democratic Transitions in Central America* (Gainesville, FL: University Press of Florida, 1997); James Dunkerley, *The Pacification of Central America: Political Change in the Isthmus, 1987–1993* (London: Verso, 1994); Rachel Sieder (ed.), *Central America: Fragile Transition* (New York: St. Martin's Press, 1996); Thomas Walker and Ariel Armony (eds.), *Repression, Resistance, and Democratic Transition in Central America* (Wilmington, DE: Scholarly Resources, 1999).

24. Noam Chomsky, *Turning the Tide: U.S. Intervention in Central America and the Struggle for Peace* (Boston: South End Press, 1986). James Dunkerley, *Power in the Isthmus: A Political History of Modern Central America* (London: Verso, 1988); Walter LaFeber, *Inevitable Revolutions: The United States and Central America* (2nd ed.) (New York: W.W. Norton, 1993); Lars Schoultz, *Human Rights and U.S. Policy Towards Latin America* (Princeton, NJ: Princeton University Press, 1987).

25. Bill Robinson, *Promoting Polyarchy: Globalization, U.S. Intervention, and Hegemony* (Cambridge: Cambridge University Press, 1996).

26. Ibid., 67.

27. Ibid., 48–72.

28. Ibid., 49.

29. Robinson's argument particularly challenges the work of Guillermo O' Donnell, *Modernization and Bureaucratic Authoritarianism: Studies in South American Politics* (Berkeley: University of California Press, 1973); Guillermo O' Donnell, Philippe Schmitter, and Laurence Whitehead, *Transitions from Authoritarian Rule* (Baltimore, MD: Johns Hopkins University Press, 1986).

30. For more on the relationship between export-led development policies, the United States, the IMF, the World Bank, and labor repression in these four countries, see chapters 2–5 this volume. Also see Dunkerley (1994); Robinson (1996); Walker and Armony (1999) for more on how neoliberal restructuring has affected social movement mobilization and union organizing.

31. Henry Frundt, "Central American Unions in the Era of Globalization," *Latin American Research Review* (2002): 7–54

32. Paul Drake, *Labor Movements and Dictatorships: The Southern Cone in Comparative Perspective* (Baltimore, MD: Johns Hopkins University Press, 1996).

33. Ibid., 12–24.

34. Ibid., 29–56.

35. Ibid., 181–93.

36. Witness for Peace, *In Our Name? The Cycles of Economic and Military Violence in Latin America* (Washington, DC: Witness for Peace, 2002); Witness for Peace, *A Bankrupt Future: The Human Cost of Nicaragua's Debt* (Washington, DC: WFP, 2001).

37. See Mark Anner, "Hacia la Sindicalización de los Sindicatos?" *ECA (Estudios Centroaméricanos)* (July–August 1996): 599–615; Frundt (2002); and chapters 2–5 of this volume for more a deeper analysis of these weaknesses.

38. Susanne Jonas, *Of Centaurs and Doves: Guatemala's Peace Process* (Boulder, CO: Westview, 2000); Tommie Sue Montgomery, *Revolution in El Salvador: From Civil Strife to Civil Peace* (2nd ed.) (Boulder, CO: Westview, 1995).

39. Keck and Sikkink (1998), 18–25.

40. Tarrrow (1998), 30–32; Charles Tilly. *From Mobilization To Revolution* (Reading, MA: Addison-Wesley, 1978), 151.

41. McAdam, McCarthy, and Zald (1996), 1–22.

42. McAdam, McCarthy, and Zald (1996), 3.
43. David A. Snow, E. Burke Rochford Jr., Steven K. Worden, and Robert D. Benford, "Frame Alignment Processes, Micro-mobilization, and Movement Participation," *American Sociological Review* (August 1986): 464–81.
44. McAdam, McCarthy, and Zald (1996), 6.
45. For more on the concept of "transnational moral entrepreneurs," see Nathan Edelman, "Global Prohibition Regimes: The Evolution of Norms in International Society," *International Organization* (Fall 1990): 479–526. "Transnational moral entrepreneurs" are social movement activists or organizations that make "normative demands," like a "living wage" for all *maquila* workers.
46. See Keck and Sikkink (1998), 13. See chapter one (20–26) for a fuller discussion about this issue.
47. Naomi Klein, *No Logo: Taking on the Brand Bullies* (New York: Picador, 2000), 345–64. Klein also notes that brand-based politics have certain limitations, see 421–38.
48. The phrase "naming the enemies" comes from Amory Starr's book *Naming the Enemy*. She notes that while academic discourse considers this terminology passé, global justice activists openly pepper their speech with catchwords like "the enemy" and "the system." Radical academics and activists that used these terms before World War II usually identified capitalism as the "enemy." Post-structuralist and post-modern scholars in the post-war period showed that social inequality involved more than just class; race, gender, and sexuality were also key sites of struggle and oppression. This literature thus demonstrated that there were many enemies, not just one. I prefer the phrase "naming the enemies" (plural) rather than "naming the enemy" (singular) for this reason. I should also note that labor organizers often talk colloquially about "the enemy" or "the target" when discussing campaign strategies and tactics.
49. Featherstone and USAS (2002).
50. For more on SNCC, see Clayborne Carson. *In Struggle* (Cambridge: Cambridge University Press, 1981).
51. See Featherstone and USAS (2002) for more on these conferences.
52. I should explain this point. Most USAS conferences do not include NGOs like the Campaign for Labor Rights, Witness for Peace, UNITE, U.S./LEAP, Global Exchange, and so on. These are USAS-specific events. A broad-based conference, involving all these organizations, is from my perspective, sorely needed.
53. For clarification purposes, *maquila* workers have been involved in these conversations within Central America. The Central American Women Maquiladora Workers Network has been especially active in this area. See Bickham Mendez (2002).
54. Ethel Brooks, "The Ideal Sweatshop? Gender and Transnational Protest," *International Labor and Working-Class History* (Spring 2002): 91–111; Featherstone and USAS (2002); Kitty Krupat, "Rethinking the Sweatshop: A Conversation About USAS with Charles Eaton, Marion Traub-Werner, and Evelyn Zepada," *International Labor and Working-Class History* (Spring 2002): 112–27.
55. See Marion Traub-Werner's comments on this issue, Krupat (2002), 121.
56. See Evelyn Zepada's comments on this issue, Krupat (2002), 120.
57. Brooks (2002), 106.
58. Ibid., 102–04.
59. Ibid., 103.
60. Ibid., 95.
61. Ibid., 95.
62. Nelson Lichtenstein, "A Race Between Cynicism and Hope: Labor and Academia," *New Labor Forum* (Spring–Summer 2002): 71–80.
63. For more on these recent victories and the movement's current activities, access the following organization's websites—U.S./LEAP, United Students Against Sweatshops, Maquila Solidarity Network, Sweatshop Watch, UNITE, and the National Labor Committee. Also see, Eileen Boris, "Consumers of the World Unite, Campaigns Against Sweating, Past and Present," in *Sweatshop USA: The American Sweatshop in Historical and Global Perspective* (New York: Routledge, 2003). Daniel E. Bender and Richard A. Greenwald (eds.), 203–24.

64. This is not to say that this case has not generated any media coverage. Indeed, the NLC's website claims that this story sparked over five hundred news stories. Despite this fact, Combs' clothing line, called Sean John, has not elicited a national and global uproar like the Kathie Lee case did. On a tangible level, working conditions have improved in one of the Honduran-based factories that produces the Sean John line. For more on this campaign, see www.nlcnet.org/campaigns/setisa.

65. bell hooks, *Feminist Theory: From Margins to Center* (Boston: South End, 1984).

66. Frundt (2002), 18.

67. Ralph Armbruster, "Globalization and Cross-Border Labor Organizing in the Automobile and Garment Industries." (PhD Dissertation, Univesity of California Riverside, 1998), 177–210.

68. Leigh Strope, "Union Membership Falls to Lowest Level in Two Decades," *Associated Press* (February 25, 2003).

69. For more on the MFA phase-out, see Richard Appelbaum, "Assessing The Impact of the Phasing Out of the Agreement on Textiles and Clothing on Apparel Exports on the Least Developed and Developing Countries." Working Paper (November 2003) (www.sweatshop watch.org/global/appelbaum). See also Sweatshop Watch, "Globalization and Free Trade's Looming Threat to the World's Garment Workers." Working Paper (October 2003) (www.sweatshopwatch.org/global/analysis).

70. For more on "world company councils," see Burton Bendiner, *International Labour Affairs* (Oxford: Claredon Press, 1987); Charles Levinson. *International Trade Unionism* (London: George Allen and Unwin, 1972).

71. For more on "popular democracy" and re-shaping neoliberal capitalism, see Robinson (1996), 380–85.

72. David Cole, *Enemy Aliens: Double Standards and Constitutional Freedoms in the War on Terrorism* (New York: New Press, 2003).

73. See the following reports for more these issues, Center on Budget and Policy Priorities, "Poverty Increases and Median Income Declines for 2nd Consecutive Year," September 29, 2003 (www.cbpp.org/9-26-03/pov.htm); Center for Budget and Policy Priorities, "Number of Americans Without Insurance Rose in 2002," October 8, 2003 (www.cbpp.org/9-30-03/health.htm).

74. Center on Budget and Policy Priorities, "Deficit Picture Grimmer Than New CBO Projections Suggest," February 1, 2004 (www.cbpp.org/1-28-04/bud.htm).

75. Witness for Peace (2002).

76. Hello NYC, *2/15: The Day the World Said No To War.* (San Francisco: AK Press, 2003).

77. Rank-and-file workers and union activists from all across the United States established "US Labor Against the War" in January 2003. This group actively opposed the war before AFL-CIO President John Sweeney went on record adopting a similar position in February 2003. This latter decision was surprising when one considers Sweeney had supported the "war on terrorism" after September 11 and given the fact that no AFL-CIO president had ever opposed a U.S. president's decision to go to war.

Bibliography

Books and Reports

Albizures, Miguel Angel. *Tiempo de Sudor y Lucha*. Mexico City: Talleres de Praxis., 1987.

Amador, Armando. *Un Siglo de Lucha de los Trabajadores de Nicaragua (1880–1979)*. Managua: Universidad Centroaméricana. 1992.

Americas Watch. *El Salvador's Decade of Terror: Human Rights Since the Assassination of Archbishop Romero*. New Haven, CT: Yale University Press, 1991.

———. *Honduras: Central America's Sideshow*. New York: Americas Watch, 1987.

Amin, Samir. *Capitalism in the Age of Globalization*. London: Zed Books, 1997.

Anderson, Sarah and John Cavanagh (with Thea Lee). *Field Guide to the Global Economy*. New York: New Press, 2000.

Anderson, Thomas. *Matanza: El Salvador's Communist Revolt of 1932*. Lincoln: University of Nebraska, 1971.

Andrews, Gregg. *Shoulder To Shoulder: The American Federation of Labor, the United States, and Mexico*. Berkeley: University of California Press, 1992.

Anner, Mark. *Maquilas and Independent Monitoring in El Salvador*. San Salvador: Independent Monitoring Group of El Salvador (GMIES), 1998.

Arévalo, Rolando and Joaquín Arriola. *Situación Sociolaboral en las Zonas Francas y Maquiladoras en Centroamérica y Republicana Dominicana*. Geneva: International Labor Organization, 1996.

Argueta, Mario. *La Gran Huelga Bananera: 69 Días que Conmoverion a Honduras*. Tegucigalpa: Editorial Universitaria, 1995.

Armstrong, Robert, Henry Frundt, Hobart Spalding, and Sean Sweeney. *Working Against Us: AIFLD and the International Policy of the AFL-CIO*. New York: North American Congress on Latin America (NACLA), 1987.

Arriola, Joaquín and José Victor Aguilar. *Globalización de la Economía*. San Salvador: Equipo Maíz, 1999.

Asociación Para el Avance de las Ciencias Sociales en Guatemala (AVANCSO). *El Significado de la Maquila en Guatemala*. Guatemala City: AVANCSO, 1994.

Bao, Xiolan. *Holding Up Half the Sky: Chinese Women Garment Workers in New York City, 1948–1992*. Urbana: University of Illinois Press, 2001.

Barnet, Richard and John Cavanagh. *Global Dreams: Imperial Corporations and the New World Order*. New York: Touchstone, 1994.

Barnet, Richard and Ronald E. Müller. *Global Reach: The Power of Multinational Corporations*. New York: Simon and Schuster, 1994.

Barry, Tom and Deb Preusch. *AIFLD in Latin America: Agents as Organizers* (2nd Edition). Albuquerque: Resource Center, 1990.

Barry, Tom and Kent Norsworthy. *Honduras: A Country Guide*. Albuquerque: Resource Center, 1990.

Bello, Walden. *Dark Victory: The United States and Global Poverty* (2nd ed.). San Francisco: Food First Books, 1999.

Bender, Daniel. *Seated Work, Weak Bodies: Anti-Sweatshop Campaigns and Languages of Labor.* New Brunswick, NJ: Rutgers University PRess, 2004.

———— and Richard A. Greenwald. *Sweatshop USA: The American Sweatshop in Historical and Global Perspective.* New York: Routledge, 2003.

Bendiner, Burton. *International Labour Affairs.* Oxford: Claredon Press, 1987.

Bermann, Karl. *Under the Big Stick: Nicaragua and the United States Since 1848.* Boston: South End Press, 1986.

Bermúdez, Carlos Pérez and Onofre Guevara López. *El Movimiento Obrero en Nicaragua* (Parts I and II). Managua: El Amanecer, 1985.

Black, George. *Triumph of the People: The Sandinsta Revolution in Nicaragua.* London: Zed Press, 1981.

Blake, William. *Milton.* Boulder, CO: Shambhala Publications, 1978.

Bonacich, Edna and Richard Appelbaum. *Behind the Label: Inequality in the Los Angeles Apparel Industry.* Berkeley: University of California Press, 2000.

Bonacich, Edna, Lucie Cheng, Norma Chinchilla, Nora Hamilton, and Paul Ong (eds.). *Global Production: The Apparel Industry in the Pacific Rim.* Philadelphia: Temple University Press, 1994.

Boris, Eileen. *Home To Work: Motherhood and the Politics of Industrial Homework in the United States.* Cambridge: Cambridge University Press, 1994.

Brecher, Jeremy and Tim Costello. *Global Village or Global Pillage* (2nd ed.). Boston: South End Press, 1998.

Brecher, Jeremy, Tim Costello, and Brendan Smith. *Globalization From Below: The Power of Solidarity.* Boston: South End Press, 2000.

Brockman, James. *Romero: A Life.* Maryknoll, NY: Orbis Books, 1989.

Buhle, Paul. *Taking Care of Business: Samuel Gompers, George Meany, Lane Kirkland, and the Tragedy of American Labor.* New York: Monthly Review Press, 1999.

Cantor, Daniel and Juliet Schor. *Tunnel Vision: Labor, the World Economy, and Central America.* Boston: South End Press, 1987.

Caranza, Salvador (ed.). *Martires de la UCA: 16 de Noviembre de 1989.* San Salvador: UCA Editores, 1990.

Carmack, Robert (ed.). *Harvest of Violence: The Maya Indians and the Guatemalan Crisis.* Norman: University of Oklahoma Press, 1988.

Carson, Clayborne. *In Struggle.* Cambridge: Cambridge University Press, 1981.

Centra de Estudios del Trabajo (CENTRA). *Situación de las Organizaciones Sindicales en El Salvador.* San Salvador: CENTRA, 1999.

Cerdas-Cruz, Rodolfo. *The Communist International in Central America, 1920–1936.* Oxford: Macmillan, 1993.

Cerigua. *Maquilas in Guatemala: Ladder to Development or Over-Exploitation?* Guatemala City: Cerigua, 1994.

Chomsky, Noam. *Turning the Tide: U.S. Intervention in Central America and the Struggle for Peace.* Boston: South End Press, 1986.

Cockburn, Alexander, Jeffrey St. Clair, and Allan Sekula. *5 Days That Shook the World: Seattle and Beyond.* London: Verso, 2000.

Cohen, Robin. *Contested Domains: Debates in International Labour Studies.* London: Zed Press, 1991.

Cole, David. *Enemy Aliens: Double Standards and Constitutional Freedoms in the War on Terrorism.* New York: New Press, 2003.

Collins, Chuck and Felice Yeskel. *Economic Apartheid in the United States: A Primer on Economic Inequality and Insecurity.* New York: New Press, 2000.

Collins, Henry and Chimen Abramsky. *Karl Marx and the British Working Class Movement: Years of the First International.* New York: Macmillan, 1965.

Collins, Jane L. *Threads: Gender, Labor, and Power in the Global Apparel Industry.* Chicago: University of Chicago Press, 2003.

Comisíon Para Esclarecimiento Histórico (CEH). *Guatemala: Memoria del Silencio.* Guatemala City: CEH, 1999.

Compa, Lance and Stephen Diamond (eds.). *Human Rights, Labor Standards, and International Trade: Law and Policy.* Philadelphia: University of Pennsylvania, 1996.

Connor, Melissa, Tara Gruzen, Larry Sacks, Jude Sutherland, and Darcy Tromanhauser. *The Case for Corporate Responsibility: Paying a Living Wage to Maquila Workers in El Salvador* (Study for the National Labor Committee). New York: NLC, 1999.

Connor, Tim. *Still Waiting for Nike to do it.* San Francisco: Global Exchange, 2001.

Cowie, Jefferson. *Capital Moves: RCA's Seventy-Year Quest for Cheap Labor.* New York: New Press, 2000.

Cullather, Nick. *Secret History: The CIA's Classified Account of Its Operations in Guatemala, 1952–1954.* Stanford: Stanford University Press, 1999.

Dalton, Roque. *Miguel Mármol.* Wilmantic, CT: Curbstone Press. 1987.

Danaher, Kevin (ed.). *Democratizing the Global Economy: The Battle Against the IMF and World Bank.* Monroe, ME: Common Courage Press, 2000.

————. *Corporations Are Gonna Get Your Mama.* Monroe, ME: Common Courage Press, 1996.

————. *Fifty Years is Enough: The Case Against the World Bank and the International Monetary Fund.* Boston: South End Press, 1994.

Derber, Charles. *People Before Profit: The New Globalization in An Age of Terror, Big Money, and Economic Crisis.* New York: St. Martin's Press, 2002.

Dominguez, Jorge and Marc Lindenberg (eds). *Democratic Transitions in Central America.* Gainesville: University of Florida Press, 1997.

Dossal, Paul. *Doing Business With Dictators: A Political History of United Fruit, 1899–1914.* Wilmington, DE: Scholarly Books, 1993.

Drake, Paul. *Labor Movements and Dictatorships: The Southern Cone in Comparative Perspective.* Baltimore: Johns Hopkins University Press, 1996.

Dubb, Steve. *Logics of Resistance: Globalization and Telephone Unionism in Mexico and British Columbia.* New York: Garland, 1999.

Dubofsky, Melvyn. *We Shall Be All.* New York: Quadrangle, 1969.

Dunkerely, James. *The Pacification of Central America: Political Change in the Isthmus, 1987–1993.* London: Verso, 1994.

————. *Power in the Isthmus.* London: Verso, 1988.

————. *The Long War: Dictatorship and Revolution in El Salvador.* London: Junction Books, 1982.

Dye, Nancy. *As Equals and As Sisters: Feminism, the Labor Movement, and the Women's Trade Union League of New York.* Columbia: University of Missouri Press, 1980.

Engels, Fredrich. *The Condition of the Working Class in England.* Stanford: Stanford University Press, 1958.

Esbenshade, Jill. *Monitoring Sweatshops: Women, Consumers, and the Global Apparel Industry.* Philadelphia: Temple University Press, 2004.

Equipo Maíz. *Historia de El Salvador.* San Salvador: Equipo Maíz, 1998.

Euraque, Darío. *Reinterpreting the Banana Republic: Region and State in Honduras, 1870-1972.* Chapel Hill: University of North Carolina Press, 1996.

Falla, Ricardo. *Massacres in the Jungle, 1975-1982.* Boulder, CO: Westview Press, 1994.

Featherstone, Liza and United Students Against Sweatshops (USAS). *Students Against Sweatshops.* London: Verso, 2002.

Fernbach, David. *Karl Marx: The First International and After.* New York: Penguin, 1992.

Fisher, William and Thomas Ponniah (eds). *Another World Is Possible: Popular Alternatives to Globalization at the World Social Forum.* London: Zed Books, 2003.

Flores, Marco Antonio. *Fortuny: Un Comunista Guatemalteco.* Guatemala City: Editorial Oscar de León Palacios, 1994.

Foner, Phillip. *U.S. Labor and Latin America: A History of Workers' Responses to Intervention: Volume I, 1848–1919.* South Hadley, MA: Bergin and Garvey, 1988.

Frank, Dana. *Buy American: The Untold Story of Economic Nationalism.* Boston: Beacon Press, 1999.

Frank, Thomas. *One Market Under God: Extreme Capitalism, Market Populism, and the End of Economic Democracy.* New York: Doubleday, 2000.

French, John, Jefferson Cowie, and Scott Littlehale. *Labor and NAFTA: A Briefing Book.* Report Prepared for National Trade Union Responses in a Transnational World Conference. Duke University, 1996.

Friedrich Ebert Stiftung Foundation. *Las Maquilas en Honduras y Monitoreo Independiente en Central América*. Tegucigalpa, Honduras: Friedrich Ebert Foundation, 1998.

Frundt, Henry. *Trade Conditions and Rights: U.S. Initiatives and Dominican and Central American Responses*. Gainesville: University of Florida Press, 1999.

———. *Refreshing Pauses: Coca-Cola and Human Rights*. New York: Praeger, 1987.

Fukuyama, Francis. *The End of History and the Last Man*. New York: Free Press, 1992.

Fung, Archon, Dara O'Rourke, and Charles Sabel. *Can We Put an End to Sweatshops?* Boston: Beacon Press, 2001.

Gamson, William. *The Strategy of Social Protest*. Homewood, IL: Dorsey Press, 1975.

Gatehouse, Mike and Miguel Angel Reyes. *Soft Drink, Hard Labour: Guatemala Workers Take on Coca-Cola*. London: Latin American Bureau, 1987.

Gibson-Graham, J. K. *The End of Capitalism (As We Knew It): A Feminist Critique of Political Economy*. Cambridge: Blackwell, 1996.

Gleijeses, Piero. *Shattered Hope: The Guatemalan Revolution and the United States*. Princeton: Princeton University Press, 1991.

Goldston, James. *Shattered Hope: Guatemalan Workers and the Promise of Democracy*. Boulder, CO: Westview Press, 1989.

Gordon, Michael E. and Lowell Turner (eds.). *Transnational Cooperation Among Unions*. Ithaca, NY: ILR Press, 2000.

Guidry, John, Michael Kennedy, and Mayer Zald (eds.). *Globalizations and Social Movements: Culture, Power, and the Transnational Sphere*. Ann Arbor: University of Michigan Press, 2000.

Handy, Jim. *Gift of the Devil*. Boston: South End Press, 1984.

Hart, John. *Anarchism and the Mexican Working Class, 1860–1931*. Austin: University of Texas Press, 1978.

Harvey, David. *Spaces of Hope*. Berkeley: University of California Press, 2000.

———. *Limits To Capital*. London: Verso, 1982.

Hasset, John and Hugh Lacy. *Towards A Society That Serves Its People: The Intellectual Contributions of El Salvador's Murdered Jesuits*. Washington, DC: Georgetown University Press, 1991.

Hathaway, Dale. *Allies Across the Border: Mexico's Authentic Worker Front and Global Solidarity*. Boston: South End Press, 2001.

Heintz, James, Nancy Folbre, and the Center for Popular Economics. *The Ultimate Field Guide to the U.S. Economy*. New York: New Press, 2000.

Hello NYC. *2/15: The Day the World Said No to War*. San Francisco: AK Press, 2003.

Herod, Andrew. *Labor Geographies: Workers and the Landscape of Capitalism*. New York: Guilford Press, 2001.

Hirst, Paul and Grahame Thompson. *Globalization in Question*. Cambridge: Polity Press, 1996.

Holthoon, Frits and Marcel Van der Linden (eds.). *Internationalism in the Labor Movement, 1830–1940*. London: E.J. Brill, 1988.

Honduran Apparel Manufacturers Association. *Apparel Industry in Honduras*. San Pedro Sula, Honduras: Honduran Apparel Manufacturers Association, 1999.

———. *Code of Conduct of the Honduran Apparel Manufacturers Association*. San Pedro Sula, Honduras: Honduran Apparel Manufacturers Association, 1999.

Hoogvelt, Ankie. *Globalization and the Postcolonial World: The New Political Economy of Development*. Baltimore: Johns Hopkins University Press, 1997.

hooks, bell. *Feminist Theory: From Margin to Center*. Boston: South End Press, 1984.

Human Rights Watch. *Deliberate Indifference: El Salvador's Failure to Protect Workers' Rights*. New York: Human Rights Watch, 2003.

———. *From the Household to the Factory: Sex Discrimination in the Guatemala Labor Force*. New York: Human Rights Watch, 2002.

———. *Corporations and Human Rights: Freedom of Association in a Maquila in Guatemala*. New York: Human Rights Watch, 1997.

Immerman, Richard. *The CIA in Guatemala*. Austin: University of Texas, 1982.

International Confederation of Free Trade Unions (ICFTU). *Behind the Wire: Anti-Union Repression in Export Processing Zones*. Brussels: ICFTU, 1996.

International Labor Organization (ILO). *Labor Practices in the Footwear, Leather, Textile, and Clothing Industries*. Geneva: ILO, 2000.

———. *Que Ha Pasado Con la Maquila? Actualización del Estudio Sobre la Situación en las Empresas Maquiladoras del Istmo Centroaméricano y República Domicana.* Geneva: ILO, 1999.

———. *The Globalization of the Footwear, Textiles, and Clothing Industries.* Geneva: ILO, 1996.

Jensen, Joan and Sue Davison (eds.). *A Needle, A Bobbin, and A Strike: Women Needleworkers in America.* Philadelphia: Temple University Press, 1984.

Joll, James. *The Second International, 1889–1914.* New York: Praeger, 1956.

Jonas, Susanne. *Of Centaurs and Doves: Guatemala's Peace Process.* Boulder, CO: Westview Press, 2000.

———. *The Battle for Guatemala: Rebels, Death Squads, and U.S. Power.* Boulder, CO: Westview Press, 1991.

Juravich, Tom and Kate Bronfenbrenner. *Ravenswood: The Steelworkers Victory and the Revival of American Labor.* Ithaca, NY: ILR Press, 1999.

Keck, Margaret and Kathryn Sikkink. *Activists Beyond Borders: Advocacy Networks in International Politics.* Ithaca: Cornell University Press, 1998.

Kelley, Robin D. G. *Race Rebels: Culture, Politics, and the Black Working Class.* New York: Free Press, 1994.

Khagram, Sajeev, James V. Riker, and Kathryn Sikkink. *Restructuring World Politics: Transnational Social Movements, Networks, and Norms.* Minneapolis: University of Minnesota Press, 2002.

Kinzer, Stephen and Stephen Schlesinger. *Bitter Fruit: The Untold Story of the American Coup in Guatemala.* New York: Doubleday, 1982.

Klein, Naomi. *No Logo: Taking on the Brand Bullies.* New York: Picador, 2000.

Kofas, Jon. *The Struggle for Legitimacy: Latin American Labor and the United States, 1930–1960.* Center for Latin American Studies, Arizona State University: Tempe, 1992.

Kornbluh, Joyce (ed.). *Rebel Voices: An IWW Anthology.* Chicago: Charles Kerr, 1988.

Korten, David. *When Corporations Rule the World.* West Hartford, CT: Kumarian Press, 1995.

La Botz, Dan. *Made in Indonesia: Indonesian Workers Since Suharto.* Boston: South End Press, 2001.

———. *Mask of Democracy: Labor Suppression in Mexico Today.* Boston: South End Press, 1992.

LaFeber, Walter. *Inevitable Revolutions.* New York: Norton, 1993.

Larrave, Marío López. *Breve Historia del Movimiento Sindical Guatemalteco.* Guatemala City: Editorial Universitaria, Colección Popular, 1979.

Leung, Trini Wing-yue. *Smashing the Iron Rice Pot: Workers and Unions in China's Market Socialism.* Hong Kong: Asia Resource Monitor Center, 1988.

Levenson-Estrada, Deborah. *Trade Unionists Against Terror, 1954–1985.* Chapel Hill: University of North Carolina Press, 1994.

Levinson, Charles. *International Trade Unionism.* London: George Allen and Unwin, 1972.

Lichtenstein, Nelson. *Walter Reuther: The Most Dangerous Man in Detroit.* Urbana: University of Illinois, 1995.

Liebhold, Peter and Harry R. Rubenstein. *Between a Rock and a Hard Place: A History of American Sweatshops, 1820–Present.* Los Angeles: UCLA Asian American Studies Center and Simon Wiesenthal Museum of Tolerance, 1999.

Límon, José E. *Dancing with the Devil.* Madison: University of Wisconsin Press, 1994.

Logue, John. *Toward a Theory of Trade Union Internationalism.* University of Gothenburg, Sweden: Research Section on Post-War History, 1980.

Louie, Miriam Ching Yoon. *Sweatshop Warriors: Immigrant Women Workers Take on the Global Factory.* Boston: South End Press, 2001.

MacShane, Denis. *International Labor and the Origins of the Cold War.* Oxford: Claredon Press, 1992.

Manz, Beatriz. *Refugees of a Hidden War: The Aftermath of the Counterinsurgency in Guatemala.* Albany: SUNY Press, 1988.

Martínez, Julia Evelína and Carolina Quinteros. *Situación de las Mujeres en las Organizaciones Laborales Salvadoreñas.* Fundación Paz y Solidaridad, Centra, y Cooperación Española, Proyecto Escuela Formación Sindical en Centroamérica Fase II, 1997.

Marx, Karl. *The Eighteenth Brumaire of Louis Bonaparte.* New York: International Publishers, 1984.

———. *Capital.* New York: Vintage, 1977.

McAdam, Doug, John D. McCarthy, and Mayer N. Zald. *Comparative Perspectives on Social Movements: Political Opportunities, Mobilizing Structures, and Framing Processes*. Cambridge: Cambridge University Press, 1996.

McAdam, Doug. *Freedom Summer*. New York: Oxford University Press, 1988.

———. *The Political Process Model and the Development of Black Insurgency, 1930–1979*. Chicago: University of Chicago Press, 1982.

McClintock, Michael. *The American Connection, Volume I: State Terror and Popular Resistance in El Salvador*. London: Zed Press, 1985b.

———. *The American Connection, Volume II: State Terror and Popular Resistance in Guatemala*. London: Zed Press, 1985a.

Menchú, Rigoberta. *I, Rigoberta Menchú*. London: Verso, 1984.

Menjívar, Rafael. *Formación y Lucha Proletariado Industrial Salvadoreño*. San Salvador: UCA Editores., 1979.

Messer-Kruse, Timothy. *The Yankee International, 1848–1872: Marxism and the American Reform Tradition*. Chapel Hill: University of North Carolina, 1998.

Meza, Victor. *Historia del Movimiento Obrero Hondureño*. Tegucigalpa: Centro de Documentación de Honduras, 1997.

Midwest Center for Labor Research. *No More Business as Usual: Taking a Comprehensive Approach*. Chicago: Salsdeo Press, 1993.

Montejo, Victor. *Voices from Exile: Violence and Survival in Modern Maya History*. Norman: University of Oklahoma Press, 1999.

Montgomery, Tommie Sue. *Revolution in El Salvador: From Civil Strife to Civil Peace* (2nd Edition). Boulder, CO: Westview Press, 1994.

Moody, Kim. *Workers in a Lean World*. London: Verso, 1997.

Morgan, Ted. *Jay Lovestone: Communist, Anti-Communist, and Spymaster*. New York: Random House, 1999.

Morris, George. *CIA and American Labor: The Subversion of the AFL-CIO's Foreign Policy*. New York: International Publishers, 1967.

Movimiento de Mujeres Trabajadores y Desempleadas (María Elena Cuadra). *Diagnóstico Sobre las Condiciones Sociolaborales de las Empresas de las Zonas Francas*. Managua: María Elena Cuadra, 1999.

National Labor Committee. *Fired For Crying To The Gringos: The Women in El Salvador Who Sew Liz Claiborne Garments Speak Out For Justice*. New York: NLC, 1999.

———. *Help End The Race To The Bottom*. New York: NLC, 1999.

———. *The Search for Peace in Central America*. New York: NLC, 1985.

Neumann, Rachel, Emma Bircham, Andrew Hsiao, and John Charlton (eds.). *Anti-Capitalism: A Field Guide to the Global Justice Movement*. New York: New Press, 2004.

O'Brien, Robert, Anne Marie Goetz, Jan Aard Scholte, and Marc Williams. *Contesting Global Governance: Multilateral Economic Institutions and Global Social Movements*. New York: Cambridge University Press, 2000.

O'Donnell, Guillermo. *Modernization and Bureaucratic Authoritarianism: Studies in Latin American Politics*. Berkeley: University of California Press, 1973.

O' Donnell, Guillermo, Philippe Schmitter, and Laurence Whitehead. *Transitions from Authoritarian Rule*. Baltimore: Johns Hopkins University Press, 1986.

Paredes, Américo. *With a Pistol in His Hands*. Austin: University of Texas Press, 1958.

Peña, Devon. *The Terror of the Machine: Technology, Work, Gender, and Ecology on the U.S. Border*. Center for Mexican-American Studies (CMAS) Books: University of Texas Press, 1997.

Perera, Victor. *Unfinished Conquest: The Guatemalan Tragedy*. Berkeley: University of California Press, 1993.

Petersen, Kurt. *The Maquiladora Revolution in Guatemala*. New Haven, CT: Schell Center for Human Rights, Yale University Law School, 1992.

Piven, Frances Fox and Richard A. Cloward. *Poor People's Movements: Why They Succeed and How They Fail*. New York: Vintage, 1979.

Porta, Donatella della, Hanspeter Kriesi, and Dieter Rucht. *Social Movements in a Globalizing World*. London: Macmillan, 1999.

Posas, Marío. *Diagnostico del Movimiento Sindical Hondureño: Situación Actual y Perspectivas*. Tegucigalpa, Honduras: Friedrich Ebert Stiftung, 2000.

————. *Luchas del Movimiento Obrero Hondureño.* San Jose, Costa Rica: Editorial Universitaria Centroaméricana, 1981.

Procuraduría Para la Defensa de los Derechos Humanos (PDDH). *Los Derechos Humanos y la Maquila en El Salvador.* San Salvador: PDDH, 1998.

Prokosch, Mike and Laura Raymond (United for a Fair Economy) (eds.). *The Global Activists Manual: Local Ways to Change the World.* New York: Thunder Mouth/Nation Books, 2002.

Quinteros, Carolina, Gilberto García, Roberto Góchez, and Norma Molina. *Dinamica de la Actividad Maquiladora y Derechos Laborales en El Salvador.* San Salvador: CENTRA/ACILS, 1998.

Raat, Dirk. *Revoltosos: Mexican's Rebels in the United States, 1903–1923.* College Station: Texas A & M University Press, 1981.

Radosh, Ronald. *American Labor and U.S. Foreign Policy.* New York: Random House, 1969.

Ramírez, Sergio. *Adiós Muchachos: Una Memoria de la Revolución Sandinista.* México, D.F.: Aguilar, 1999.

Recovery of Historical Memory Project (REMHI). *Guatemala: Never Again!* Maryknoll, NY: Orbis Books, 1999.

Reed, Thomas and Karen Brandow. *The Sky Never Changes: Testimonies From the Guatemalan Labor Movement.* Cornell: ILR Press, 1996.

Renshaw, Patrick. *The Wobblies: The Story of the IWW and Syndicalism in the United States.* Chicago: Ivan R. Dee, 1967.

Robinson, William. *Promoting Polyarchy: Globalization, U.S. Intervention, and Hegemony.* Cambridge: Cambridge University Press, 1996.

————. *A Faustian Bargain: U.S. Intervention in the Nicaraugan Elections.* Boulder, CO: Westview Press, 1992.

Romero, Oscar. *Voice of the Voiceless: Four Pastoral Letters and Other Statements.* Maryknoll, NY: Orbis Books, 1985.

Romualdi, Serafino. *Presidents and Peons.* New York: Funk and Wagnalls, 1967.

Rosen, Ellen. *Making Sweatshops: Globalization of the U.S. Apparel Industry.* Berkeley: University of California Press, 2002.

Ross, Andrew. *Low Pay, High Profile: The Global Push for Fair Labor,* New York: Free Press, 2004.

———— (ed.). *No Sweat: Fashion, Free Trade, and the Rights of Garment Workers.* London: Verso, 1997.

Rosswurm, Steve (ed.). *The CIO's Left-Led Unions.* New Brunswick, NJ: Rutgers University Press, 1992.

Ruiz, Marisol and Gilberto García. *Condiciones Laborales de Mujeres y Menores en las Plantas de la Maquila Coreana y Taiwanesa en El Salvador.* San Salvador: CENTRA, 1996.

Ruiz, Vicki. *From out of the Shadows.* New York: Oxford, 1998.

Sánchez, Antonio Obando. *Memorias: La Historia del Movimiento Obrero.* Guatemala City: Editorial Universitaria, 1978.

Schirmer, Jennifer. *The Guatemala Military Project.* Cambridge: Cambridge University Press, 1999.

Scott, Jack. *Yankee Unions Go Home: How the AFL Helped the U.S. Build an Empire in Latin America.* Vancouver: New Star, 1978.

Scott, James. *Domination and the Art of Resistance: Hidden Transcripts.* New Haven: Yale University Press, 1990.

————. *Weapons of the Weak: Everyday Forms of Peasant Resistance.* New Haven: Yale University Press, 1985.

Schoenberger, Karl. *Levi's Children: Coming to Terms with Human Rights in the Global Marketplace.* New York: Atlantic Monthly, 2000.

Schoultz, Lars. *Human Rights and U.S. Policy Towards Central America.* Princeton: Princeton University Press, 1987.

Schulz, Donald and Deborah Sundolff Schulz. *The United States, Honduras, and the Crisis in Central America.* Boulder, CO: Westview Press, 1994.

Selser, Gregorio. *Sandino: The General of the Free.* New York: Monthly Review Press, 1981.

Shaw, Randy. *Reclaiming America: Nike, Clean Air, and the New National Activism.* Berkeley: University of California Press, 1999.

Sieder, Rachel (ed). *Central America: Fragile Transition.* New York: St. Martin's Press, 1996.

Silverman, Victor. *Imaging Internationalism in American and British Labor, 1939–1949.* Urbana: University of Illinois Press, 2000.

Sims, Beth. *Workers of the World Undermined*. Boston: South End, 1992.

Smith, Jackie, Charles Chatfield, and Ron Pagnucco (eds.). *Transnational Social Movements and Global Politics: Solidarity Beyond the State*. Syracuse: Syracuse University Press, 1997.

Sobrino, Jon. *Archbishop Romero: Memories and Reflections*. Maryknoll, NY: Orbis Books, 1990.

Spalding, Hobart. *Organized Labor in Latin America*. New York: NYU Press, 1977.

Starr, Amory. *Naming the Enemy: Anti-Corporate Movements Confront Globalization*. London: Zed Books, 2000.

Stein, Leon (ed.). *Out of the Sweatshop: The Struggle for Industrial Democracy*. New York: Quadrangle, 1977.

———. *The Triangle Fire*. New York: Carroll and Graf, 1962.

Storrs, Landon R. Y. *Civilizing Capitalism: The National Consumers League, Women's Activism, and Labor Standards in the New Deal Era*. Chapel Hill: University of North Carolina Press, 2000.

STITCH (Support Team for Textileras) and Maquila Solidarity Network (MSN). *Women Behind the Labels: Worker Testimonies from Central America*. STITCH and MSN: Chicago and Toronto, 2000.

Tabb, William. *The Amoral Elephant: Globalization and the Struggle for Social Justice*. New York: Monthly Review Press, 2001.

Tarrow, Sidney. *Power in Movement* (2nd ed.). Cambridge: Cambridge University Press, 1998.

Thomas, Janet. *The Battle in Seattle: The Story Behind and Beyond the WTO Demonstrations*. Golden, CO: Fulcrum, 2000.

Tilly, Charles. *From Mobilization to Revolution*. Reading, MA: Addison-Wesley, 1978.

Truth Commission of El Salvador. 1993. *De la Locura a la Esperanza*. New York: United Nations.

Tyler, Gus. *Look for the Union Label: A History of the International Ladies Garment Workers Union*. Armonk, NY: M.E. Sharpe, 1995.

Uclés, Mario Lungo. *El Salvador in the Eighties: Counterinsurgency and Revolution*. Philadelphia: Temple University Press, 1996.

Universidad de El Salvador (Facultad de Ciencias Economicas). *El Grado de Mejoramiento de las Condiciones Laborales de las Trabajadoras(es) de la Maquila Mandarín International de las Zona Franca de San Marcos a Partir del Funcionamiento del Grupo Monitoreo Independiente* (Vitelio Henriques Mejia, Director). San Salvador. June, 1999.

Vallardes, Efraín Moncada. *Las Dos Caras de la Maquila en Honduras* (Documentos de Trabajo, #10). Universidad Nacional Autónoma de Honduras, 1995.

Varley, Pamela (ed.). *The Sweatshop Quandary: Corporate Responsibility on the Global Frontier*. Washington, DC: Investor Responsibility Research Center, 1998.

Verité. *Comprehensive Factory Evaluation Report on Kukdong International Mexico*. Verité, 2001.

VESTEX (Non-Traditional Products Exporters Association). *Apparel and Textile Industry*. Guatemala City: VESTEX, 1999.

Vigil, María López. *Oscar Romero: Memories in Mosaic*. Washington, DC: EPICA, 2000.

Villars, Rina. *Porque Quiero Seguir Viviendo....Habla Con Graciela García*. Tegucigalpa: Editorial Guaymuras, 1991.

Von Drehle, David. *Triangle: The Fire That Changed America*. New York: Atlantic Monthly Press, 2003.

Walker, Knut. *The Regime of Anastasio Somoza, 1936–1956*. Chapel Hill: University of North Carolina Press, 1993.

Walker, Thomas and Ariel Armony (eds). *Repression, Resistance, and Democratic Transition in Central America*. Wilmington, DE: Scholarly Resources, 1999.

Wallach, Lori and Michelle Sforza. *Whose Trade Organization? Corporate Globalization and the Erosion of Democracy*. Washington, DC: Public Citizen, 1999.

Waterman, Peter. *Globalization, Social Movements, and the New Internationalisms*. London: Continuum, 2001.

Welton, Neva and Linda Wolf (eds.). *Global Uprising: Confronting the Tyrannies of the 21st Century*. Gabriola Island, British Columbia: New Society, 2001.

Whitfield, Teresa. *Paying the Price: Ignacio Ellacuría and the Murdered Jesuits of El Salvador*. Philadelphia: Temple University Press, 1994.

Windmuller, John. *American Labor and the International Labor Movement, 1940 To 1953*. Ithaca: Cornell University Press, 1954.

Witness For Peace (WFP). *In Our Name? The Cycles of Economic and Military Violence in Latin America*. Washington, DC: WFP, 2002.

———. *Behind the Seams: Maquilas and Development in Nicaragua*. Washington, DC: WFP, 2001.

———. *A Bankrupt Future: The Human Cost of Nicaragua's Debt*. Washington, DC: WFP, 2000.

———. *From the Maquila To the Mall*. Washington, DC: WFP, 1996.

———. *A High Price To Pay: Structural Adjustment and Women in Nicaragua*. Washington, DC: WFP, 1995.

———. *Bitter Medicine: Structural Adjustment in Nicaragua*. Washington, DC: WFP, 1994.

Witzel de Cuidad, Renate. *Más de 100 Años del Movimiento Obrero Urbano en Guatemala (Tomo IV: Recomposición y Busqueda de Unidad del Movimiento Sindical, 1982–1990)*. Guatemala City: Asociación de Investigación y Estudios Sociales (ASIES), 1996.

———. *Mas de 100 Años del Movimiento Obrero Urbano en Guatemala (Tomo III: Reorganizacíon, Auge, y Desarticulacíon del Movimiento Sindical, 1954–1982)*. Guatemala City: ASIES, 1994.

———. *Mas de 100 Años del Movimiento Obrero Urbano en Guatemala (Tomo II: El Protagonismo Sindical en la Construccíon de la Democracia, 1944–1954)*. Guatemala City: ASIES, 1992.

———. *Mas de 100 Años del Movimiento Obrero Urbano en Guatemala (Tomo I: Arteasnos y Obreros en el Periodo Liberal, 1877–1944)*. Guatemala City: ASIES, 1991.

Wolensky, Kenneth C., Nicole H. Wolensky, and Robert P. Wolensky. *Fighting for the Union Label: The Women's Garment Industry and the ILGWU*. University Park: Pennsylvania State University Press, 2002.

Worker Rights Consortium (WRC). *WRC Investigation: Complaint Against Kukdong (Mexico)*. Washington, DC: WRC. (June 20), 2001.

———. *Report by the WRC on the Kukdong Investigation*. Washington, DC: WRC. (January 24), 2001.

Yuen, Eddie, George Katsiaficas, and Daniel Burton Rose (eds.). *The Battle of Seattle: The New Challenge to Capitalist Globalization*. New York: Soft Skull Press, 2001.

Zieger, Robert. *The CIO, 1935–1955*. Chapel Hill: University of North Carolina, 1995.

Zimmerman, Matilde. *Carlos Fonseca and the Nicaraguan Revolution*. Durham: Duke University Press, 2000.

Articles and Book Chapters

Alexander, Robin and Peter Gilmore. "The Emergence of Cross-Border Labor Solidarity," *NACLA: Report on the Americas* 28(1): 42–48, 1994.

Almeida, Paul and Linda Brewster Stearns. "Political Opportunities and Local Grassroots Environmental Movements," *Social Problems* (February): 37–60, 1998.

Anner, Mark. "Defending Labor Rights Across Borders: Central American Export Processing Plants," in *Struggles for Social Rights in Latin America*, Susan Eva Eckstein and Timothy Wickham-Crowley (eds.), 147–166. New York: Routledge, 2003.

———. "Transnational Campaigns to Defend Labor Rights in Export Processing Zones in El Salvador, Guatemala, Honduras, and Haiti," Paper Presented at Latin American Studies 21st International Congress, 1998.

———. "Hacia la sindicalización de los sindicatos?" *ECA (Estudios Centroaméricanos)* (July-August 1996): 599–615.

Arévalo, Rolando and Joaquín Arriola. "El Caso de El Salvador." In *La Situación Sociolaboral en las Zonas Francas de Centroamérica y República Domincana*, Arévalo and Arriola (eds.). Geneva: ILO, 1996.

Armbruster, Ralph. "Cross-National Organizing Strategies," *Critical Sociology* 21(2) (1995): 75–89.

Armbruster-Sandoval, Ralph. "The Honduran Maquiladora Industry and the Kimi Campaign," *Social Science History* 27(4) (2003): 551–76.

———. "Globalization and Cross-Border Labor Organizing: The Guatemala Maquiladora Industry and the Phillips Van Heusen Workers' Movement," *Latin American Perspectives* 26(2) (1999): 108–28.

Bandy, Joe and Jennifer Bickham Mendez. "A Place of Their Own? Women Organizers in the Maquilas of Nicaragua and Mexico." *Mobilization* 8(2) (2003): 173–88.

Benjamin, Medea. "What's Fair About the Fair Labor Association? Putting the Fox in Charge," *Against the Current* (March-April) (1999): 8–9.

Bickhham Mendez, Jennifer. "Creating Alternatives From a Gender Perspective: Central American Women's Transnational Organizing for Maquila Workers Rights." In *Women's Activism and Globalization: Linking Local Struggles and Transnational Politics*, Nancy Naples and Manisha Desai (eds.), 121–41. New York: Routledge, 2002.

Bollinger, William. "El Salvador." In *Latin American Labor Organizations*, Michael Greenfield and Sheldon Maram (eds.). Westport, CT: Greenwood Press, 507–88, 1987.

Bonacich, Edna. "The Past, Present, and Future of Split-Labor Market Theory," *Research in Race and Ethnic Relations* (Volume I): 17–64, 1979.

———. "Advanced Capitalism and Black/White Relations in the United States," *American Sociological Review* (February) (1976): 34–51.

———. "A Theory of Ethnic Antagonism: The Split Labor Market," *American Sociological Review* (October) (1979): 547–59.

Bonacich, Edna and David Waller. "Mapping A Global Industry: Apparel Production in the Pacific Rim Triangle." In *Global Production*, Bonacich et al. pgs. 21–41, 1994.

Boris, Eileen. "Consumers of the World Unite: Campaigns Against Sweating, Past and Present," in *Sweatshop USA*, Bender and Greenwald (eds.), 203–24, 2003.

Bounds, Wendy. "Critics Confront a CEO Dedicated To Human Rights," *Wall Street Journal* (February 24) (1997): B1.

Bowden, Charles. "Keeper of the Fire," *Mother Jones* (July/August) (2003): 68–73.

Boyer, Jeff and Aaron Pell. "Mitch in Honduras: A Disaster Waiting To Happen," *NACLA: Report on the Americas* (September-October) (1999): 36–41.

Bronfenbrenner, Kate and Tom Juravich. "Evolution of Strategic and Coordinated Bargaining Campaigns in the 1990s: The Steelworkers' Experience" In *Rebuilding the Movement: Labor's Quest for Relevance in the 21ˢᵗ Century*, Lowell Turner, Harry Katz, and Richard Hurd (eds.), 211–37, 2001.

Brooks, Ethel. "The Ideal Sweatshop? Gender and Transnational Protest," *International Labor and Working-Class History* (Spring) (2002): 91–111.

Campaign for Labor Rights (CLR) Action Alert. 2001. "Chentex Accord Signed—An Update on the This Unprecedented Victory," May 11.

———. "Victory for Chentex Workers!" April 6, 2001.

———. "Update From Nicaragua," October 27, 2000.

———. "New Leaflets! 76 Actions in 69 Cities!" October 2, 2000.

———. "Honduras: Kimi Cuts and Runs," May 25, 2000.

———. "Honduras: Kimi Victory (for now)," September 4, 1999.

———. "New Honduran Union Victory in Jeopardy," June 21 1999.

———. "Nicaragua Sweatshop Action Alert," December 3, 1997.

CLR Update. "Nicaragua: The Struggle Intensifies," September 9, 2000.

———. "Strategy Shift Proposed for Nicaragua Campaign," August 2, 2000.

———. "Guatemalan Union Leader's Family Receives Death Threats While She Visits New York To Protest PVH Practices," June 21, 1999.

———. "PVH Union Lives," January 9, 1999.

Center for Budget and Policy Priorities. "Deficit Picture Grimmer Than New CBO Projections Suggest," February 1. www.cbpp.org/1-28-04/bud.htm (2004).

———. "Number of Americans Without Health Insurance Rose in 2002," October 8. www.cbpp.org/9-30-03/health.htm (2003a).

———. "Poverty Increases and Median Income Declines for 2nd Consecutive Year," September 29. www.cbpp.org/9-26-03/pov.htm (2003b).

Cid, Nelly del, Carla Castro, and Yadira Rodriquez. "Trabajadoras de la Maquila: Neuvo Perfil de Mujer?" *Envío* (September, 1999): 35–41.

Cleeland, Nancy and Evelyn Iritani, and Tyler Marshall. "Scouring the Globe To Give Shoppers $8.63 Polo Shirt," *Los Angeles Times*, November 24, 2003: A1.

Coats, Stephen. "Central American Labor Solidarity: Lessons for Activists?" In *The Global Activists Manual*, Mike Prokosch and Laura Raymond (eds.), 199–208, 2002.

———. "Trade Pressure Brings Gains in Workers' Rights," *Report on Guatemala* 14(4) (1993): 12–13.

———. "Free Trade and Labor Cooperation Across Borders: Recent U.S./Guatemalan Experiences," *Latin American Labor News* (#8) (1993): 10–11.

Coen, Rachel. "Whitewash in Washington: Media Provide Cover as Police Militarize D.C.," *Extra!* (July/August) (2000): 9–12.

Cole, Jackie. "Policia Desaloja Pacificamente a Huelguistas de Maquiladora," *La Tribuna* (August 30) (1999): 138.

Corea, Martha Danelia. "In Chentex and Mi Colores, North American Delegation Verifies Mistreatment," *La Prensa* (July 16) (2000).

Davis, Terry. 1995. "Cross-Border Labor Organizing Comes Home," *Labor Research Review* (#23) (1995): 23–29.

Edelman, Nathan. "Global Prohibition Regimes: The Evolution of Norms in International Society," *International Organization* (Autumn) (1990): 479–526.

Emmanuel, Arrighi. "The Delusions of Internationalism," *Monthly Review* (June) (1970): 13–18.

Envío. "A Society Scandalized," (June) (2000): 3–11.

———. "Poverty in Cold Numbers," (June) (2000): 12.

Epstein, Barbara. "Anarchism and Anti-Globalization," *Monthly Review* (September) (2001): 1–14.

Esbenshade, Jill. "The Gap Campaign: Enforcing Labor Standards Across Borders," *Labor Center Reporter* (Fall) (1996): 4–7.

Esbenshade, Jill and Edna Bonacich. "Can Codes of Conduct and Monitoring Combat America's Sweatshops?" *Working USA* (May-June) (1999): 21–33.

Featherstone, Liza. "Response To Isaac," *Dissent* (Fall) (2001): 109–11.

Frundt, Henry. "Four Models of Cross-Border Maquila Organizing." In *Unions in a Globalized Environment*, Bruce Nissen (ed.), Armonk, NY: M.E, Sharpe, 45–75, 2002a.

———. "Central American Unions in the Era of Globalization," *Latin American Research Review* (2002b): 7–54.

———. "Cross-Border Organizing in Apparel: Lessons from the Caribbean and Central America." *Labor Studies Journal* 24(1) (1999): 89–106.

———. "Trade and Cross-Border Labor Organizing Strategies in the Americas," *Economic and Industrial Democracy* (Issue 21) (1996): 387–417.

———. "AIFLD in Guatemala: End or Beginning of a New Regional Strategy?" *Interamerican Studies and World Affairs* 32(3) (1995): 287–317.

Goldman, Abigail and Nancy Cleeland. "An Empire Built on Bargains Remakes the Working World," *Los Angeles Times*, November 23, 2003: A1.

Goodwin, Jeff and James Jasper. "Caught in a Winding, Snarling Vine: The Structural Bias of Political Process Theory," *Sociological Forum* (June) (1999): 27–54.

Graeber, David, "For a New Anarchism," *New Left Review* (January-February, 2002): 61–73.

Grafico (Guatemala). "Maquila: Fabrica de Empleo o Atropellos?" (June 18) (1996): 15.

Greenhouse, Steve. "Critics Calling U.S. Supplier a 'Sweatshop,'" *New York Times* (December 3) (2000): Section 1, Page 9.

Grow, Douglas. "Presented with Unfair Labor Practices, Target Turns Away," *Minneapolis Star-Tribune* (June 21) (2000).

Guigni, Marco. "How Social Movements Matter: Past Research, Present Problems, Future Developments." In *How Social Movements Matter*, Marco Guigni, Doug McAdam, and Charles Tilly (eds.), xii–xxxii. Minneapolis: University of Minnesota Press, 1999.

———. "Was It Worth The Effort? The Outcomes and Consequences of Social Movements," *Annual Review of Sociology* (1998): 371–94.

Haworth, Nigel and Harvey Ramsay. "Workers of the World Undermined: International Capital and Some Dilemmas in Industrial Democracy" In *Trade Unions and the New Industrialization of the Third World*, Roger Southall (ed.), 306–31. London: Zed, 1987.

———. "Grasping the Nettle: Problems in the Theory of International Labor Solidarity." In *For a New Labour Internationalism*, Peter Waterman (ed.), pgs. 60–85. The Hague: International Labor Education Research and Information Foundation, 1984.

Herman, Edward. "Globalization in Question?" *Z Magazine* (April) (1997): 8–11.

Herod, Andrew. "Labor As An Agent of Globalization and As A Global Agent" In *Spaces of Globalization: Reasserting the Power of the Local*, Kevin Cox (ed.), 167–200. New York: Guilford Press, 1997.

Hogness, Peter. "One More Hole in the Wall: The Lunafil Strikers in Guatemala," *Labor Research Review* 13 (1989): 1–13.

Howard, Alan. "Why Unions Can't Support the Apparel Industry Sweatshop Code," *Working USA* (May-June) (1999): 34–50.

———. "Labor, History, and Sweatshops in the New Global Economy," In *No Sweat*, Ross (ed.), 151–72, 1997.

Ibarra, Elosia. "Wong: Hay Que Mejorar Condiciones," *El Nuevo Diario* (September 5).

———. "Violencia Institutucionalizada Contra la Mujer en las Zonas Francas," *El Nuevo Diario* (September 5, 2000).

Isaac, Jeffrey C. "Thinking About the Anti-Sweatshop Movement: A Proposal for Modesty," *Dissent* (Fall 2001): 100–9.

Jeffcoat, Bob and Lynda Yanz. "Voluntary Codes of Conduct: Do They Strengthen or Undermine Government Regulations and Worker Organizing?" *Maquila Solidarity Network* (October 1999).

Johns, Rebecca. "Bridging the Gap Between Class and Space: U.S. Worker Solidarity with Guatemala," *Economic Geography* 74(3) (1998): 252–71.

Khagram, Sanjeev, James V. Riker, and Kathryn Sikkink. "From Santiago to Seattle: Transnational Advocacy Groups Restructuring World Politics." In *Restructuring World Politics: Transnational Social Movements, Networks, and Norms.* Khagram, Riker, and Sikkink (eds.), 3–23, 2002.

Khor, Martin. "The World Trade Organization, Labor Standards, and Trade Protectionism," *Third World Resurgence* (May 1994) 30–34.

Klein, Naomi. "Reclaiming the Commons," *New Left Review* (May-June) (2001) 81–89.

Kristoff, Nicholas and Sheryl WuDunn. "Two Cheers for Sweatshops," *New York Times Magazine* (September 24, 2000).

Krupat, Kitty. "Rethinking the Sweatshop: A Conversation About USAS with Charles Eaton, Marion Traub-Werner, and Evelyn Zepada," *International Labor and Working-Class History* (Spring 2002): 112–27.

———. "From War Zone To Free Trade Zone: A History of the National Labor Committee" In *No Sweat*, Andrew Ross (ed.), 51–78, 1997.

La Prensa (Honduras). "Por Diez Delitos: Procesan a Dirigentes Sindicales de Maquiladora," (August 21, 1999): 30A.

La Prensa (Nicaragua). "A Quiénes Defienden?" (June 6, 2000): 10A.

La Tribuna. "Se Enfrenten Policías y Trabajadores de Maquila," (August 31, 1999): 118.

Leiken, Robert S. "The Salvadoran Left." In *El Salvador: Central America and the Cold* War, Marvin E. Gettleman, Patrick Lacefield, Louis Menashe, and David Mermelstein (eds.), pgs. 187–199. New York: Grove Press, 1986.

Levenson-Estrada, Deborah and Henry Frundt. "Toward A New Inter-Nationalism," *NACLA: Report on the Americas* 28(5) (1995): 16–21.

Lichtenstein, Nelson. "A Race Between Cynicism and Hope: Labor and Academia," *New Labor Forum* (Spring/Summer) (2002): 71–80.

Linden, Marcel Van der. "The Rise and Fall of the First International: An Interpretation." In *Internationalism in the Labor Movement, 1830–1940*, Holthoon and Van der Linden (eds.) 323–336, 1988.

Maney, Gregory. "Transnational Structures and Protest: Linking Theories and Assessing Evidence," *Mobilization* (Spring 2001): 83–100.

Maquila Solidarity Network. "The Labour Behind the Label: How Are Our Clothes Made?" Spring (2000).

Martínez, Elizabeth. "Where Was the Color in Seattle." In *Globalize This! The Battle Against the WTO and Corporate Rule*, Kevin Danaher and Roger Burbach (eds.), 74–81. Monroe, ME: Common Courage Press, 2000.

McAdam, Doug, John D. McCarthy, and Mayer N. Zald. "Introduction: Opportunities, Mobilizing Structures, and Framing Processes—Toward a Synthetic Perspective on Social Movements" In *Comparative Perspectives on Social Movements*, McAdam, McCarthy, and Zald (eds.), 1–22, 1996.

———. "Social Movements." In *Handbook of Sociology*, Neil Smelser (ed.), 695–737. Beverley Hills: Sage, 1988.

McAdam, Doug. "Conceptual Origins, Current Problems, Future Directions." In *Comparative Perspectives on Social Movements*, McAdam, McCarthy, and Zald, 23–40, 1996.

McAdam, Doug. "The Biographical Consequences of Activism," *American Sociological Review* (October 1989): 744–60.

McLeod, Marc Christian. "Maintaining Unity: Railway Workers and the Guatemalan Revolution." In *Workers Control in Latin America, 1930–1979*. Jonathan Brown (ed.). Chapel Hill: University of North Carolina Press, 1997.

Moberg, David. "Lessons From the Victory at Phillips Van-Heusen," *Working USA* (May-June 1998): 39–50.

Monthly Review. "After Seattle: A New Internationalism?" (July–August 2000): Entire Issue.

Narin, Allen. "Behind the Death Squads," *The Progressive* (May 1984): 20–29.

National Labor Committee (NLC). "Nica Alert: An Inside Look at Nien Hsing," November 20, 2000.

NLC. "Serious and Systematic Worker Rights Violations at Chentex Garment Factory," May 31 (2000) (Press Release).

NLC Action Alert.. "Union Movement Under Attack: Chentex Union, Textile Workers Federation, and Center for Human Rights (CENDIH) in Nicaragua Appeal for an International Campaign," (June 6, 2000) (Press Release).

NLC. "Urgent Action Alert," (November 25 , 1997).

Nevarez, Roberto Collardo. "Democratic Congressman Horrified by Abuses in Free Trade Zone: Gross Exploitation," *El Nuevo Diario* (July 16, 2000).

New Labor Forum. "Let There Be One, Two, Many Seattles: Observations and Reflections," (Spring/Summer 2000): 4–40.

Nicaragua Network. "Labor Crisis in the Free Trade Zone Continues." August (2000).

Nicaragua Network (Hotline). "Glimmers of Light or Smoke and Mirrors in Free Trade Zones?" (August 28, 2000).

———. "Religious Leaders 'Asked To Leave' After Protesting Sweatshops," (August 21, 2000).

Olle, Werner and Wolfgang Scholler. "World Market Competition and Restrictions Upon International Trade Union Policies," *Capital and Class* (#2) (1977): 56–75.

O'Kane, Trish. "New Autonomy, New Struggle: Labor Unions in Nicaragua." In *The New Politics of Survival: Grassroots Movements in Central America*. Minor Sinclair (ed.). New York: Monthly Review Press, 1995.

Ortiz, Rodney. "A Union Struggles in Nicaragua's Free Trade Zone," *Solidaridad: News and Analysis from Central America and Mexico* (June 2000).

Pabst, Georgia. "Nicaraguan Union Leader Seeks Support for Garment Workers," *Milwaukee Journal Sentinel* (June 20, 2000).

Pantoja, Aryneil. "United States Unionists Threaten Commercial Boycott of Nicaragua," *La Prensa* (June 1, 2000): 5A.

Paredes, Jennifer. "Industria de Maquila y Vestuario," *Siglo Veintiuno*, July 26,1999: 54.

Pattee, Jon. "'Gapatistas' Win A Victory," *Labor Research Review* (Summer): 77–85.

———. "Sprint and the Shutdown of La Conexión Familiar," *Labor Research Review* 23 (1995): 13–21.

Pearson, Neale J. "Honduras." In *Latin American Labor Organizations*, Michael Greenfield and Sheldon Maram (eds.), 463–94, 1987.

Pooley, Eric. "The IMF: Dr. Death? A Case Study of How the Global Banker's Shock Therapy Helps Economies But Hammers the Poor," *Time* (April 24,2000): 47.

Raphaelidis, Leia. "Sewing Discontent in Nicaragua: The Harsh Reality of Asian Garment Factories in Nicaragua," *Multinational Monitor* (September 1997)): 24–27.

Ramsay, Harvie. "Know Thine Enemy: Understanding Multinational Corporations as a Requirement for Strategic International Laborism" In *Transnational Cooperation Among Labor Unions*, Michael E. Gordon and Lowell Turner (eds.), 26–43, 2000.

Reflection, Research, and Communication Team of the Jesuits of Honduras (ERIC). "Maquila: The Swallow That Lays the Golden Eggs." *Envío* (September 1997): 4–9.

Report on Guatemala.. "Phillips Van-Heusen Campaign," 13(1) (1992): 13.

Ricker, Tom and Dale Wimberley. "Global Networking in the 21st Century: Labor Rights Movements and Nicaragua's Maquilas." In *Emerging Issues in the 21st Century World-System*, Wilma Dunaway (ed.). New York: Praeger, 2003.

Rivera, Herbert. "Chocan Huelguistas y Policía en Toma Parque Industrial," *La Prensa* (August 31, 1999).

————. "Contigente Policial Desaloja a Huelguistas de Parque Industrial," *La Prensa* (August 30, 1999).

————. "Por Toma de Zona Industrial No Laboran 6 Mil Obreros," *La Prensa* (August 28, 1999): 7A.

Romero, Gabriela Roa. "Amenzan a Textileras Con Boicot," *La Prensa* (August 3, 2000): 2A.

Ross, Robert and Charles Kernaghan. "Countdown in Nicaragua," *The Nation* (September 4–11, 2000): 25–27.

Shriver, Jeff. "Human Slavery in Nicaragua's 'Free Zones,'" *Nicaragua Developments* (Spring) (1997): 2–3.

Slaughter, Jane. "Which Side Are They On? The AFL-CIO Tames Guatemala's Unions," *The Progressive* 52 (1987): 32–36.

Smith, Jackie. "Globalizing Resistance: The Battle of Seattle and the Future of Social Movements," *Mobilization* (Spring 2001): 1–20.

Snow, David A., E. Burke Rochford Jr., Steven K. Worden, and Robert D. Benford. "Frame Alignment Processes, Micro-mobilization, and Movement Participation," *American Sociological Review* (August 1986): 464–81.

Spalding, Hobart. "The Two Latin American Foreign Policies of the U.S. Labor Movement: The AFL-CIO Versus the Rank-and-File," *Science and Society* (Winter 1992–93): 421–39.

Stahler-Sholk, Richard. "Nicaragua." In *Latin American Labor Organizations*, Michael Greenfield and Sheldon Maram (eds.), 549–75, 1987.

Stiglitz, Joseph. "What I Learned at the World Economic Crisis: An Insider's Perspective," *New Republic* (April 17, 2000): 56–61.

Su, Julie. "El Monte Thai Garment Workers: Slave Sweatshops." In *No Sweat*, Andrew Ross (ed.), 143–49, 1997.

Sweatshop Watch. "Frequently Asked Questions," (http://www.sweatshopwatch.org/swatch/questions.html), 2002.

Sweatshop Watch. "Mexican Workers Win Unprecedented Victory," December: 2–3, 2001.

Traub-Werner, Marion and Altha Cravey. "Spatiality, Sweatshops, and Solidarity in Guatamala." *Social and Cultural Geography* 3(4) (2002): 383–400.

U.S./LEAP. "Victory at Yoo Yang!" (April, Issue #1) (2002): 6.

————. "Nike Workers Win Increase," (April, Issue #1) (2002): 8.

————. "Independent Union Wins at Nike Supplier!" (December, Issue #3) (2001): 1, 4.

————. "Testimony on the Busting of the Union at Chentex: An Interview with Maura Parsons," (July 5) (2001): 1–4.

————. "Yoo Yang Wins Recognition," (December, Issue #3) (2000): 1–2.

————. "Kimi Still Closed in Honduras," (December, Issue #3) (2000): 7.

————. "Kimi Closes, Runs To Guatemala; Yoo Yang Maquila Union Remains Strong," (August, Issue #2) (2000): 1–2.

————. "PVH Struggle Ends in Guatemala, But New Campaign Begins in Honduras," (December, Issues 3 & 4) (1999): 5–6.

————. "Honduran Maquila Workers Tear-Gassed!" (December, Issues # 3 & 4) (1999): 1, 6–7.

————. "PVH Union Ends Vigil; Re-Opening Hope Remains," (August, Issues 1 & 2) (1999): 1–2.

————. "Honduran Maquila Victory at Risk!" (August, Issues 1 & 2) (1999): 1–5.

U.S./LEAP, People of Faith Network, USAS. "Phillips Van-Heusen: An Industry "Leader" Unveiled: An Investigation into the Closing of a Model Maquiladora Factory in Guatemala," June 15 (1999).

U.S./LEAP. Press Release. June 15 (1999).

U.S. GLEP. Press Release. December 18 (199.)

————. "Fighting for Worker Justice in the Global Economy: 10 Years of Leadership by the United States/Guatemala Labor Education Project," December (1997).

————. "PVH Contract Signed in Guatemala!" (October, Issue #3) (1997): 1–2.

————. "USTR Ends Trade Probation on Guatemala," (July, Issue #2) (1997): 1–2.

————. "PVH Agrees To Negotiate," (April) (1997): 1–2.

————. "PVH Union Launches Blitz," (October) (1996): 1–2.

Weiss, Larry. "Sweatshop Task Force Fuels Controversy," *Working Together* (May-June) (1997): 1.

————. "Maquila Workers' Tour, California Sweatshop Case, Put Heat on Retailers," *Working Together* (September-October) (1996): 1–2.

————. "Gap Agreement Proceeds Along Torturous Path," *Working Together* (May-June) (1996): 4-5.

Williams, Matthew. "Towards More Democracy or More Bureaucracy: Civil Society, NGOs, and the Global Justice Movement," *Social Anarchism* (#30) (2001): 5–26.

Wilman, Alys. "Bearing A Double Burden: Women and Work in Nicaragua," *Horizons* (March/April) (1999): 20–23.

Wood, Ellen Meiksins. "Globalization and Epochal Shifts: An Exchange," *Monthly Review* (February) (1997): 21–32.

———. "Modernity, Postmodernity, or Captialism?" *Monthly Review* (July-August) (1996): 21–39.

Working Together. "Workers Win Contract at Honduran Maquila, But Union's Victory Under Threat," (May-June) (1999): 3.

———. "Contract Victory at Nicaraguan Maquila," (September-October) (1998) 5.

———. "Nicaragua Maquila Workers Win Union," (March-April) (1998): 1–2.

———. "Hired Thugs Disrupt Union Election," (September-October) (1997): 8.

———. "Sweatshop Task Force Fuels Controversy," (May-June) (1997): 1–2.

———. "Minnesota GAP Effort Focuses on Students," (January-February) (1996): 2.

Zamora, Rubén. "The Popular Movement." In *A Decade of War: El Salvador Confronts the Future*, Anjali Sundaram and George Gelber (eds.). New York: Monthly Review Press, 182–95, 1991.

Zeas, Moises Castillo. "Gringos Intervienen en Zona Franca," *El Nuevo Diario* (September 15, 2000).

———. "700 Corridos en la Chentex," *El Nuevo Diario* (September 5, 2000).

———. "Puede Haber Boicot en EU a la Maquila Nica," *El Nuevo Diario* (August 3, 2000): 8.

Government Reports and Publications (U.S. and Central America)

AFL-CIO and UNITE. "Comments Regarding Eligibility Criteria for Beneficiaries of the United States-Caribbean Basin Trade Partnership Act, Title II of the Trade and Development Act of 2000." Report Submitted July 17, 2000.

Dorman, Peter. "Worker Rights and U.S. Trade Policy: An Evaluation of Worker Rights Conditionality Under the Generalized System of Preferences." Washington, DC: Department of Labor, 1989.

Orantes, Ricardo Mendoza (ed.). *Código de Trabajo* (Salvadoran Labor Code). San Salvador: Editorial Jurídica Salvadoreña, 1999.

República de Honduras. *Código de Trabajo* (Honduran Labor Code). Tegucigalpa: Editorial Guaymuras, 1999.

República de Nicaragua. *Código de Trabajo* (Nicaraguan Labor Code) (4th ed.). Managua: Editorial Jurídica, 2000.

U.S. Department of Labor. *The Apparel Industry and Codes of Conduct: A Solution to the International Child Labor Problem?* Washington, DC: Department of Labor, 1996.

U.S. Embassy (Economic/Commercial Section). *Country Commercial Guide For Nicaragua.* Managua, Nicaragua: U.S. State Department, 2000.

U.S./LEAP. "Worker Rights and the Generalized System of Preferences (Guatemala)," Petition Filed with the Office of the USTR. June 15, 1999.

U.S. State Department. *Country Reports on Human Rights Practices For 1998: El Salvador.* Released by the Bureau of Democracy, Human Rights, and Labor. February 26, 1999.

U.S. State Department. *Country Reports on Human Rights Practices For 1999: Honduras.* Released by the Bureau of Democracy, Human Rights, and Labor. February 25, 2000.

U.S. State Department. *Country Reports on Human Rights Practices For 1999: Nicaragua.* Released by the Bureau of Democracy, Human Rights, and Labor. February 25, 2000.

Unpublished Manuscripts, Letters, Papers

Appelbaum, Rich. "Assessing the Impact of the Phasing Out of the Agreement on Textiles and Clothing on Apparel Exports in the Least Developed and Developing Countries," November (on file with author), 2003.

Armbruster, Ralph. "Globalization and Cross-Border Labor Organizing in the Garment and Automobile Industries." PhD Dissertation, University of California Riverside, 1998.

Bilbao, Jon Ander (S. J.). "La Fabrica y El Sindicato SITRAKIMIH." Unpublished Paper, 1999.

Bishop, Edward. "The Guatemalan Labor Movement, 1944–1959," PhD Dissertation. University of Wisconsin, 1959.

Brown, Sherrod (Congressional Representative-New York). "Dear Colleague Letter To President Clinton." July 21 (Signed by 64 House Members), 2000.

Bush, Archer. "Organized Labor in Guatemala, 1944-1949," Master's Thesis, Colgate University, 1950.

Hickey, Robert. "Preserving the Pattern: PACE's Five-Year Comprehensive Campaign at Crown Petroleum," (on file with author).

Howard, Andrew. "Labor Internationalism As A Strategy of Class Struggle," Paper Presented at the Annual American Sociological Association Conference. Los Angeles, California, 1994.

Independent Monitoring Team (Equipo Monitoreo Independient [EMI]—Honduras). "Ponencia Sobre Experiencias y Reflexiones del Euipo de Monitoreo Independiente en la Empresa Kimi de Honduras." Paper Delivered at Primer Encuentro Internacional Sobre Monitoreo Independiente en las Maquilas. San Salvador, El Salvador. January 12–15, 1998.

———. "Firma de Convenio: Acuerdo Para el Monitoreo Independiente en la Empresa Kimi de Honduras," (this document can be found in EMI, "Ponencia Sobre Experiencias y Reflexiones del Euipo de Monitoreo Independiente en la Empresa Kimi de Honduras." Paper Delivered at Primer Encuentro Internacional Sobre Monitoreo Independiente en las Maquilas. San Salvador, El Salvador, 1997.

International Labor Rights Fund (ILRF). "Opinion Presented by Arturo Alcade Justiniani Regarding the Case of Kukdong International," (www.laborrights.org/projects/sweatshops/kukdong) (2001).

Johns, Rebecca. "International Solidarity: Space and Class in the U.S. Labor Movement." PhD Dissertation. Rutgers University, 1994.

Keck, Margaret. Remarks Made During "The Empire Strikes Back" Panel, Latin American Studies Association, XXII International Conference. Miami, Florida. March 16-18, 2000.

National Workers Front (FNT—Nicaragua). No Date. "El Frente Nacional de los Trabajadores: Origen, Concepción, y Estrategia de Municipalización." Unpublished Paper.

O'Rourke, Dara. 2000. "Monitoring the Monitors: A Critique of Price-WaterhouseCoopers Labor Monitoring," (http://web.mit.edu/dorourke).

Sirkin, Alan. PVH Vice-Chairperson. Letter To Author. December 22, 1998.

Sweatshop Watch. "Globalization and Free Trade's Looming Threat to the World's Garment Workers," October (on file with author), 2003.

Interviews

Aguilar, Efraín. CUTH Secretary of Organization. San Pedro Sula, Honduras. September 14, 1999.

Aguillón, Sara. SITRAKIMIH Secretary-General. La Lima, Honduras. September 28–29, 1999.

Alfaro, Juan Francisco. CUSG Secretary-General. Guatemala City, Guatemala. August 10, 1999.

———. Guatemala City, Guatemala. February 5, 1997.

Axthelm, Joan. U.S./LEAP Staff Representative. July 20, 2000.

Barrantes, Roger. CST Representative. Managua, Nicaragua. Talk Before Witness For Peace Delegation. July 30, 2000.

Bennett, Tom. J.C. Penney Representative. Phone Interview. September 12, 2000.

Bilbao, John Ander (S.J.). Researcher, ERIC. El Progreso, Honduras. September 21, 1999.

Blanco, Felix. CTS Secretary-General. San Salvador, El Salvador. August 23, 1999.

Candido, Otilio. CTS Director of Organizing. San Salvador, El Salvador. September 7, 1999.

Casertano, Teresa. Inter-American Textile and Garment Workers Federation (FITTIV) Representative. Guatemala City, Guatemala. January 18, 1997.

———. Guatemala City, Guatemala. September 25, 1996.

CENDIH (Nicaragua Center for Human Rights) Representatives. Witness for Peace Group Delegation Interview. Managua, Nicaragua. July 24, 2000.

Chentex Worker. Managua, Nicaragua. August 1, 2000.

Chentex Workers and Union Members. Witness for Peace Group Delegation Interview. Managua, Nicaragua. August 1, 2000.

Cid, Nelly del. Researcher with the Equipo de Reflexión, Investigación, y Comunicación de los Jesuitas en Honduras (ERIC). El Progreso, Honduras. September 21, 1999.

Cisneros, David. CTH-FESITRANH Assistant General-Secretary. San Pedro Sula, Honduras. September 23, 1999.

Coats, Stephen. U.S./LEAP Executive Director. Phone Interview. September 12, 2000.

———. U.S./GLEP Executive Director. Phone Interview. April 10, 1994.

Coj, Julio. UNSITRAGUA Secretary of International Relations. Guatemala City, Guatemala. July 27, 1999.
————. Guatemala City, Guatemala. February 5, 1997.
CTN-A (Nicaraguan Workers Center-Autonomous) Representatives. Witness for Peace Group Delegation Interview. Managua, Nicaragua. July 31, 2000.
Cushing, John. U.S. Embassy Labor Attaché. Guatemala City, Guatemala. January 29, 1997.
Dejas, Alejandro. FITH Organizer. San Pedro Sula, Honduras. September 18, 1999.
Democratic Workers Central (CTD/COMUTRAS) Representatives. San Salvador, El Salvador. September 6, 1999.
Doumitt, Rhett. U.S./GLEP Representative. Guatemala City, Guatemala. September, 1996.
Dueñas, Rigoberto. CGTG Assistant Secretary-General. Guatemala City: Guatemala. August 9, 1999.
————. Guatemala City, Guatemala. January 30, 1997.
EMI. Group Interview with EMI Group Members. San Pedro Sula, Honduras, 1999.
Feigen, Ed. AFL-CIO Representative. Phone Interview. April, 1994.
FENASTRAS Representatives. San Salvador, El Salvador. August 30, 1999.
Fernández, Marío. U.S. Labor Embassy Attaché. Witness For Peace Group Delegation Interview. Managua, Nicaragua. August 2, 2000.
Fieldman, Bruce. FITTIV Representative. San Pedro Sula, Honduras. September, 1999.
————. UNITE International Representative. Phone Interview. March, 1997.
Fuentes, Homero. COVERCO General Coordinator. Guatemala City, Guatemala. August 13, 1999.
García, Daniel. STIT Director of Organizing. San Salvador, El Salvador. August 25, 1999.
García, Gilberto. CENTRA Director. San Salvador, El Salvador. August 24, 1999.
Gates, Leslie. CFO Representative. Phone Interview. April 5, 1994.
González, Zoila. 2nd Deputy Minister of Labor. Guatemala City, Guatemala. February 5, 1997.
Gutiérrez, Roger. FEASIES Secretary-General. San Salvador, El Salvador. August 25, 1999.
Hermanson, Jeff. UNITE Director of Organizing. Phone Interview. August 15, 1997.
Hernández, Juan. STIYASSC Secretary-General. San Salvador, El Salvador. September 9, 1999.
Honduran Apparel Manufacturers Association Representative. San Pedro Sula, Honduras. September 17, 1999.
Howard, Alan. Assistant To The President of UNITE. Phone Interview. August 16, 2000.
Kernaghan, Charlie. NLC Executive Director. San Salvador, El Salvador. August 22, 1999.
Kimi and Yoo Yang Workers. La Lima, Honduras. September 23, 1999.
López, Marlene. Lawyer, Movimiento de Mujeres, Mélida Anaya Montes (MAM). San Salvador, El Salvador. August 20, 1999.
López, Rosalinda Galacia. INEXPORT Union Member. Guatemala City, Guatemala. January 30, 1997.
Maldonado, Hugo. Director, CODEH. San Pedro Sula, Honduras. September 16, 1999.
Mancílla, Felix. Personnel Director. Mandarin International. San Salvador, El Salvador. September 10, 1999.
Mandarin International Workers. San Salvador, El Salvador. Group Interview. September 2, 1999.
Manzanares, Gladys. General-Secretary, CST Chentex Workers Union. Managua, Nicaragua. August 1, 2000.
————. Witness For Peace Group Delegation Interview. Managua, Nicaragua. August 1, 2000.
Maquila Worker. Managua: Nicaragua. August 1, 2000.
Maquila Worker. San Salvador, El Salvador. August 28, 1999.
Maquila Worker. Guatemala City, Guatemala. January 30, 1997.
Mejía, Marie. FITTIV Representative. Guatemala City, Guatemala. July 27, 1999.
Mi Kwang Union Members. Guatemala City, Guatemala. February 4, 1997.
MJ Modas Union Members. Guatemala City, Guatemala. February 4, 1997.
Molina, Norma. GMIES Representative. San Salvador, El Salvador. August 24, 1997.
Muñoz, Sergio. National Labor Committee (NLC) Representative. San Salvador, El Salvador. August 30, 1999.
Ortega, Pedro. General-Secretary, CST Textile Workers Federation. Witness for Peace Group Delegation Interview. Managua, Nicaragua. August 1, 2000.
Padilla, Bryon. STECAMOSA Secretary of Organization. Guatemala City, Guatemala. August 4, 1999.
————. STECAMOSA Secretary of Organization. Guatemala City, Guatemala. July 28, 1999.

Paredes, Maritza. Director, CODEMUH. San Pedro Sula, Honduras. September 28, 1999.

Parker, David. Economist, U.S. Department of Labor. Phone Interview. April 2, 1997.

Perillo, Bob. U.S./LEAP Representative. Guatemala City, Guatemala. July, 1999.

Robles, Rodolfo. Former General-Secretary, Coca-Cola Workers' Union. Guatemala City, Guatemala. January, 1997.

Rodriguez, Marina. FITTIV Representative. San Pedro Sula, Honduras. September 23, 1999.

Salguero, Flor de María. Organizer, Mujeres en Solidaridad. Guatemala City, Guatemala. January 30, 1997.

Salinas, Israel. CUTH General-Secretary. San Pedro Sula, Honduras. September 23, 1999.

SETMI Director of Organizing. San Salvador, El Salvador. August 28, 1999.

SETMI Members and Union Leaders. San Salvador, El Salvador. Group Interview. August 28, 1999.

SITRAKIMIH Union Members. La Lima, Honduras. September 25, 1999.

Smith, Dennis. Coordinator, CEDEPCA (Centro Evangélico de Estudios Pastorales en América Central). Guatemala City, Guatemala. August 4, 1999.

STECAMOSA Union Members. Guatemala City, Guatemala. August 5, 1999.

STECAMOSA Union Members. Guatemala City, Guatemala. July 28-30, 1999.

STECAMOSA Union Members. Guatemala City, Guatemala. September 26, 1996.

UNSITRAGUA Union Members. Guatemala City, Guatemala. February 4, 1997.

U.S. Embassy Officials (Nicaragua). Witness for Peace Group Delegation Interview. Managua, Nicaragua. August 2, 2000.

Journals, Newspapers, and Periodicals

Against The Current
America@Work
Campaign for Labor Rights Update
Dollars and Sense
El Diario de Hoy (El Salvador)
El Nuevo Diario (Nicaragua)
Envío
Extra!
La Prensa (Honduras)
La Prensa (Nicaragua)
La Prensa Gráfica (El Salvador)
La Tribuna (Honduras)
Labor Notes
Labor Research Review
Los Angeles Times
Maquila Network Update (Canada)
Mexican Labor News and Analysis
Monthly Review
Multinational Monitor
The Nation
New Labor Forum
New York Times
Periódico (Guatemala)
Prensa Libre (Guatemala)
Progressive
Report on the Americas
Report on Guatemala
Siglo Veintiuno (Guatemala)
Sweatshop Watch
U.S./GLEP Update
Witness for Peace Newsletter
Working USA
Z Magazine

Index

Page numbers in italics indicate listing in Figures or Tables.